ON THE EDGE OF
THE ABYSS

A Polish Rabbi Speaks to His Community
on the Eve of the Shoah

Essays by:
Rabbi Kalman Chameides

Annotation, editing, and translations by:
Leon Chameides, M.D.

Designed by Dauphin Design, Wethersfield, CT

Manufactured in the United States of America

ISBN 978-0-615-78546-2

Dedicated to my dear wife, Jean,
to our children, Daniel Stark,
Deborah Tova and her husband Rabbi David Small,
David Alon and his wife Aliza Rachel,
and to our grandchildren, Gabrielle Trudi,
Sharone Michal, Ilan Kalman, Nava Hanna, Noam Akiva,
Maia Hana, and Tamar Gail

— LEON CHAMEIDES

CONTENTS

Preface   ix

The Jews of Silesia and Katowice   1

Rabbi Kalman Chameides –
Katowice's Last Jewish Spiritual Leader   9

Urzędowa Gazeta – The Community Newspaper   25

I.   On the Edge of the Abyss   27
     A Seder in Bnei Brak   33
     Thoughts for the Ninth of Av 5693   39
     The Year 5693-5694   41
     The Blessing: Observation at a Cemetery   46
     True Heroism   50
     For the Defense of the Country   53
     5694-5695   57
     Haman's Arguments   65
     Jewish Children as Martyrs   70

II. Human Relationships: Between 'Man and Man'   77
     Jewish Ethical Behavior   80
     Modesty   86
     Gratitude   89
     Joy   90
     Jealousy   93
     The Individual and Society   95
     The Child   97
     "And God Said 'Let there be Light'
     and There was Light"   100
     Unity   102
     חקת – And Aaron Died there on Top of the Mountain   104
     The Life and Death of Moses   107
     שופטים – A Hassidic Interpretation   114
     Human Nature   116
     The Discussion   120
     Who Will Heal You?   122

Count the Days Between Pesach and Shevuoth   124
Denunciation   126
On the Margins of the Day: The School and the Home 130
Where is our Community Center?   132
Committee-O-Mania   134
Maxims of Wisdom   137

III. **Religious Relationships: Between 'Man and God'**   141
Art   143
The Call of the Prophets   145
פנחס   151
The Three Attributes of God   153
The Book of Koheleth   158
To Live Means to Act   166
The Power of Repentance   170
Faith and Action   174

IV. **National Relationships: Between the Jewish People** 177
and the Nations
"You Shall Dwell in Booths"   180
"And a new King Arose in Egypt who did not
Know Joseph"   182
Pirkei Avoth   185
Jewish Attitudes Towards other Faiths   188
Religion and Nationhood   192
The Tents of Jacob   197

V. **Communal Relationships: Between**   202
the Jewish People and Poland
Anniversary of the Resurrection of the Polish State   206
An Echo of Mourning   212
Holiday of the Sea   219
National Holiday   223
Ritual Slaughter   230

VI. **'By the Sweat of His Brow'**   233
Handwork in Judaism   236
The Holiday of Pesah   240
David's Harp   242

The Interest-Free Loan Society 246
On the Margins of the Day: Operation CKB 248

VII. 'Remember the Days of Old' 249
  5693 252
  ויחי 255
  על מה עבדה הארץ 257
  Hero and Martyr 262
  ויחי 269
  The Babylonian Exile 272
  After the Return from Babylonian Exile 280
  Ezra 286
  Nehemiah 289
  Rabbi Moshe ben Maimon on His 800th Birthday 295
  ויקח קרח – And Korah Took 302
  On the Margin's of the Day: Rabbi Kook's Death 304
  Four Coins 306
  The Festival of Rejoicing 310
  The Flaming Message of the Hanukkah Lights 312

VIII. 'A New Light Shall Illuminate Zion' 315
  פכים קטנים – Small Vessels 319
  The Broken Tablets 323
  Theodore Herzl 328
  Herzl's Dream 331
  Chaim Nachman Bialik 337
  Herzl and Bialik 345

PREFACE

While gathering material for the Katowice *Yizkor* book,[1] Ms. Cila Katriel from Tel Aviv found 114 of 118 issues of the newspaper published by the Jewish community of Katowice between 1932 and 1937 in the Biblioteka Śląska (Silesian Library) in Katowice and was kind enough to give me a copy of the microfilm. I have since been able to locate four other issues.

The newspaper is a rich source of information about the organization of community life in those precarious years. What particularly thrilled me was that my father, Rabbi Kalman Chameides, was its editor and that it included many essays written by him. Since I was just a little over seven years old when I last saw my father, these essays have given me my only opportunity to try to understand his thought process, philosophy, and religious views. I was especially interested in his comments on the turbulent events of his day. There are many *shoah* memoirs and some writings by politicians from before the *shoah*, but no literature that informs us how community Rabbis viewed the events. Did they recognize the precariousness of the community and anticipate the tragedy to follow? How did they prepare their community to meet the oncoming storm? The essays give us a glimpse into the mind of a remarkable individual, and provide us a flavor of the times.

The Talmud states: "He who translates a verse verbatim is a liar but he who alters it is a villain and a heretic."[2] The original German and Polish in which these essays were written are majestic, soaring, and flowery. English is a rich language but, especially in modern times, a more direct language in which words are used more sparingly. In translating these essays I have tried to be true to the original and recreate some of their mood and rhythm.

Rabbi Dr. Jacob Cohn wrote a history of the community for

---

[1] Yosef Chrust and Yosef Frankel (eds), *Katowitz Perihatah ushkiata shel hakehilah-hayehudit. Sefer Zikaron*, (Tel Aviv 1996).

[2] Babylonian Talmud Kiddushin, 49a.

the dedication of the Katowice Synagogue in 1900.[3] He started it in the traditional Jewish manner with a quotation from the Bible, a phrase from Job: "though your beginning was small; in the end you will grow very great." It was meant as a summary of his hopes for the community. But strange as it seems, he made an error. For the sentence he quoted was not Job 8:9 (his reference), but Job 8:7. Job 8:9 reads: "We are of yesterday and know nothing; our days on earth are like a shadow." Rabbi Cohn proved to be not only a Rabbi and a historian, but, unwittingly, also a prophet.

I would like to express my appreciation to my brother, Zwi Barnea, for his encouragement, advice, and generosity in sharing his vast knowledge of languages and their nuances. I am also grateful to Professor Berel Lang, Rabbi Dr. David Dalin, and the late Rabbi Abraham Karp for reviewing the manuscript and making helpful suggestions for its improvement.

Finally, I would like to thank my dear wife, Jean, for her understanding, love, and patience and to God for allowing me "to reach this day" and for giving me the opportunity to read my father's words and be challenged by his ideas, many of which are as relevant today as they were more than 70 years ago when they were written.

---

[3]   Jacob Cohn, *Geschichte der Synagogen-Gemeinde Kattowitz O.S.* (Kattowitz, 1900).

THE JEWS OF
SILESIA AND KATOWICE

Silesia

Slavs and Germans have inhabited Silesia, currently the southwestern section of Poland. In 1163, the area was divided into Lower Silesia in the North and Upper Silesia in the South, each ruled by a Polish Piast prince. The Piast rulers encouraged German immigration to increase agricultural productivity and develop the area's mining and textile industries. Silesia then became part of Bohemia, and in 1526 when the Austrian archduke Ferdinand acceded to the Bohemian throne, part of the Habsburg Empire. Frederick the Great of Prussia conquered most of Silesia in 1742 during the War of Austrian Succession (1740-1748). A small portion, however, remained part of Austria and was subsequently annexed to Moravia.

The mining of lead, zinc, iron, and coal made Silesia into one of the chief industrial and manufacturing regions in Europe during the industrial revolution in the latter part of the 19th century. Coal produced the steam that powered the machines that created the goods, as well as the ships and railroads that moved the finished products. At the end of World War I, the Allies planned to reorganize Europe in accord with President Wilson's 14 points. The plan included the birth, or rebirth, of independent nations, one of which was Poland. At the Paris Peace Conference (January 1919), Poland demanded that Upper Silesia be included in its new territory. Because of conflicting claims with Germany, it was decided to hold a plebiscite under the supervision of a French, British, and Italian inter-allied commission. An "Abstimmungskampf" or propaganda war, which often erupted into physical violence by both sides, preceded the plebiscite. Germany won the plebiscite (59.7% to Poland's 40.3%) on March 20, 1921, but several violent uprisings by the Poles resulted in a decision to divide Upper Silesia. Poland acquired most of the coal and steel producing areas.[4] Lower Silesia

---

[4] Sigmund Karski, "Der Abstimmungskampf in Oberschlesien 1920-1921" in *Oberschlesisches Jahrbuch 1996* (Gebr Mann Verlag, Berlin) 137-162.

Interwar map of Poland showing division of Silesia between Germany (Schlesien) and Poland (Śląsk)."

remained part of Germany until the Allied victory in World War II, when all of Silesia became part of Poland.

The earliest documented evidence of Jewish settlement in Silesia is from the 11th and 12th centuries when Jews fled from the Crusades and settled in Breslau (Wrocław) in Lower Silesia, and in a number of villages in Upper Silesia.[5] Renewed persecutions in Western Europe during the Great Plague (1349), forced many Jews to flee to Silesia where conditions were more favorable. However, persecutions stimulated by economic competition and fanned by the wondering preacher Johannes von Capestrano, known as "the whip

[5]   N. Bałaban, *Kiedy i skąd przybyli Żydzi do Polski* (Warsaw, 1931), 10.

of the Hebrews," followed Jews into Silesia. These culminated in a royal decree issued in 1582 by Rudolph II, expelling them from Upper Silesia. By 1600 only 120 Jews remained, mainly in Zülz, which received special permission because of the Jews' vital role in the community's economic life.[6] The Thirty Years' War (1618-1648) devastated Silesia, and Jews were then allowed to return in order to rebuild it. The Chmielnicki massacres (1648) forced many Jews to flee Poland and resulted in a number of new Jewish communities in Silesia, including Myslowitz (1628) and Oppeln (1648). By the time Prussia annexed Silesia (1742), 1000 Jewish families resided in four communities, Glogau and Zülz in Upper Silesia, Silesian Landesjudenschaft,[7] and Breslau in Lower Silesia. Their number increased slowly, and during the inter-war period (1918-1939), Jews constituted about 1.5% of the total population of Upper Silesia. Most Jews in Upper Silesia identified with the German language and culture, and lobbied to remain part of Germany during the "Abstimmungskampf" preceding the plebiscite of 1921. When, in 1923, it was decided to divide Upper Silesia, many Jews moved to the German portion of Upper Silesia or to other parts of Germany, while Jews from eastern Poland, especially Galicia, took their place.

Katowice

Katowice, now the capital of Polish Upper Silesia, developed from a conglomeration of villages, and received a city charter in 1865. Jews had settled in the vicinity of what would become Katowice at the end of the 18th century, but the first recorded Jews were the family of a wholesale iron merchant, Hirschel Froehlich in 1825.[8] As the Jewish population increased, they became active in the political process that culminated in the granting of a municipal charter, and Jews held a significant number of seats in the early city councils. As Upper Silesia, with its abundant coalmines, grew in importance, Katowice became its administrative and economic

[6] I. Rabin, I "Vom Rechtskampf der Juden in Schlesien 1582-1712" in *Wissenschaftliche Beilage zu den Jahresberichten des Jüdisch-Theologischen Seminars fur das Jahr 1926* (Breslau, 1927).
[7] Organization of countryside Jews.
[8] Jacob Cohn, 1.

center and an important rail junction between east and west.

Its strategic location, excellent railroad accessibility, and abundant hotel space, made Katowice a site for a number of important international Jewish conferences. In 1884, Leo Pinsker founded the Chovvei Zion movement, forerunner of the Zionist Organization. The Agudath Yisrael organization and political party was established there in 1912. In March 1933, at a fateful meeting of the World Council of Zionist Revisionists, Zeev Jabotinsky took his faction out of the World Zionist Organization. As an important railroad junction, Katowice was also the transit point for thousands of Jewish refugees who, beginning in the 1880s, streamed from Russia to Western Europe. Many then went on to the United States. The Jewish community of Katowice organized a committee, which met each train to make sure that the destitute and desperate Jewish migrants had enough food and other basic necessities.

Organization of the Jewish Community
Despite the fact that Katowice became part of Poland in 1923, the community's legal status continued to be defined by the Prussian Law of July 23, 1847, which is often cited in the community by-laws[9] as a basis for its legitimacy. That Law established the Synagogengemeinde (Synagogue Community) as a legal entity and defined both its obligations and its power. Its obligations included the establishment, at the community's expense (Article 58), of institutions to provide social and religious needs, including the care of the poor and sick (Article 59), Jewish schools and religious education for the young (Articles 60-67), and a cemetery (Article 58). At first, a Jew could only leave the community by being baptized and joining another recognized community, but a law of July 28, 1876 made it legal to leave one community without necessarily joining another. To cover expenses, the community was authorized to levy and collect taxes, a function enforced, if necessary, by the civil authorities. The Jews of Katowice petitioned

---

[9] The community's first by-laws were adopted in 1866 and revised in 1881. A further revision was adopted on June 24, 1913. The references to the article # refer to the final revision of February 19, 1930.

to be recognized as a Synagogegemeinde in 1862. Permision was granted in 1865, even before the city received its municipal charter.

An Assembly of Representatives, whose 21 male members were elected by proportional representation of the electorate, and an Administration, which consisted of nine members elected by the Assembly of Representatives, governed the Jewish community. The term of office of each body was five years. The community by-laws include provisions for making the elections secret and fair. Whereas the right to vote was given to all adults residing in the district who were financially independent and had fulfilled all their financial obligations for the two years preceding the election, the right to be elected was limited to males.

The Jewish Community Organization functioned under the auspices of the State government. The Governor of the Province (Wojewoda) appointed an Election Commissioner who, in his capacity as Chairman of the Elections Committee, supervised the elections to the Assembly of Representatives (Article 26 #1), and to the Administration (Article 71 #8). All challenges to the balloting process were submitted to the State for resolution (Article 38). State Authorities had to approve the elected members of the Administration before they were installed into office (Article 73 #1). That this was not only a formality, is demonstrated by the elections of May 1932, when the Wojewoda (Provincial Governor) refused to approve the Community Administration chosen by the Representatives. The incumbent Administration was charged to continue alongside the newly elected Assembly of Representatives. On August 16, 1933, the Administration informed the Wojewoda of its resignation. The Wojewoda accepted the resignation, appointed a new Administration headed by Bruno Altmann, dissolved the Assembly of Representatives, and appointed a new one headed by Dr. Mayer, a lawyer. The basis of this dispute was probably due to friction within the community between the former German Jews, who continued to hold power, and the newly arrived Jews from eastern Poland, especially Galicia. The Governor was clearly interested in having the leadership identify with Polish culture and aspirations, and did not want it dominated by "Germanophiles."

The community maintained a wide range of social and educational institutions.[10] Every member of the community was entitled to burial in the community's cemetery (established in 1868). This was in contrast to other communities, where burial was at times turned into a bargaining session. A Central Mutual Welfare Office, which coordinated all charity institutions, such as the public kitchen, the women's organization, associations for assistance to the sick, support for the poor, help for transient Jews, and the granting of interest-free loans, was established in 1929. In the 1930s, about 25% of the community's budget was allocated for social welfare, which included medical care for the indigent, direct subsidies of money and food, clothing for children, and hot meals. In addition, the community maintained a synagogue, a *mikva* (ritual bath), hired religious functionaries, including the Rabbis, to minister to the needs of its members, and supported a variety of supplementary schools for children.

The Jewish community of Katowice was justifiably proud of the fact that it had initiated a graduated income tax in 1912. Seventy-five per cent of the budget was covered by this tax. In contrast, 50% of the budget in other communities was derived from the sale of kosher meat, thus raising its price. The Katowice community felt that this placed a disproportionately large burden on the poorest members, and that a graduated income tax, paid by all members who resided or derived their income within the community, was a fairer system. The administrative detail of this tax can be seen from the following regulation: "In families with mixed marriages, the Jewish partner has the right to deduct that part of the income that the non-Jewish partner pays to the Church. If however, the couple do not file State taxes jointly, then the Jewish partner must pay the full tax" (Article 161 #3).

Until 1922, the community of Katowice was an almost homogenous German Jewish community with one Synagogue. When Katowice was transferred to Poland, many Jews left and were replaced by newcomers from eastern Poland. This movement

---

[10]   Urzędowa Gazeta Gminy Izraelickiej w Katowicach (UGGIK) #3, March 1932.

accelerated with the global economic catastrophe of 1929. Impoverished Jews came to Katowice, seeking the slightly better economic opportunities provided by Upper Silesia, with its rich natural resources. The Jewish population of Katowice varied between 3.4% and 6.6% of the total population and, just prior to the World War II, the community numbered a little over 9,000. Inevitable friction developed between the diminishing percentage of German Jews who continued to hold power and leadership roles, and the newly arrived Polish Jews. This was aggravated by an increasing political and religious factionalism among Polish Jews. Yiddish and Polish gradually replaced German as the spoken daily language. The new arrivals were not satisfied with the formality of services in the Synagogue with its German *nusach* [prayer tradition]. They established smaller prayer houses including a number belonging to Hasidic sects. Most prominent among the latter were the Radomsky Hasidim. At the same time, Jews coming from the tight societies of the small towns *(Shtetl)* into the big, increasingly cosmopolitan cities like Katowice, assimilated, and some even converted to Christianity.

In addition to internal friction, the Jewish community of Katowice also had to deal with growing anti-Semitism. Hitler's ascent to power Germany in 1933, the loss of civil liberties, and the pauperization of German Jews caused thousands of German Jewish refugees to flee to nearby countries. The Jewish community of Katowice, already burdened with its own problems, found itself host to many of these desperate refugees. Anti-Semitic incidents continued to increase in Poland itself, and accelerated after the death, in 1935, of Marshall Jósef Piłsudski, popular war hero and semi-dictatorial leader of Poland. With government approval, non-Jews boycotted Jewish merchants and on December 9, 1935, a bomb was thrown into the Katowice Synagogue. Anti-Jewish agitation became so pronounced that a delegation representing the Jewish community and the Silesian Union of Rabbis petitioned the Governor to intervene on their behalf.

Religious Life

The first synagogue in Katowice was dedicated on September 4, 1862 but shortly after it was built, the rapid increase in the Jewish population outstripped its capacity. A much larger and more ornate synagogue (Figures 1 and 2) was dedicated in September 1900. It dominated the Katowice skyline, was situated in the finest section of the city, and could accommodate 1,184 worshippers. It served the community until September 1, 1939, when the Germans entered Katowice.

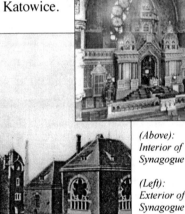

(Above): Interior of Synagogue

(Left): Exterior of Katowice Synagogue dedicated in September 1900.

In the course of its history, the Jewish community was served by a number of distinguished Rabbis: Dr. Jacob Cohn (1872-1910); Rabbi Philip De Haas (1912-1920); Rabbi Louis Lewin (1920-1925); Rabbi Jechezkiel Lewin (1925-1928); and Rabbis Kalman Chameides and Mordechai Vogelmann (1928-1939). Three of the Rabbis (De Haas, L. Lewin, and Chameides) were ordained at the Jewish Theological Seminary of Breslau (Wrocław).

Shortly after the outbreak of WW II, Germany annexed Silesia. On September 4, 1939, the invading Germans packed the synagogue with dynamite and destroyed it. The Jewish population was forcibly transferred to nearby towns such as Sosnowiec. Thus Katowice, or Kattowitz as it was renamed, became "Judenrein" within months of the outbreak of the war.

RABBI KALMAN CHAMEIDES
KATOWICE'S LAST JEWISH SPIRITUAL LEADER

Rabbi Kalman Chameides was one of two Rabbis who served the Jewish community of Katowice from September 1, 1928 until the outbreak of WW II in September 1939. He was entrusted with this responsible position immediately after his rabbinical ordination, when he was only 26 years of age. Unfortunately, most of his contemporaries and his entire family, except for his two sons, were victims of the Shoah, so that the only information we have about him has been gleaned from a search of the "paper trail" that he left behind.

Early Life and Education
Kalman Chameides was born on April 5, 1902 to Miriam (Luft) and Szulim Chameides in Szczerzec, now known as Shcherits (approximately 30 km south of Lviv), a town that was overwhelmingly Jewish. In 1900, there were 1,324 Jews out of a total population of 1,730.[11] He was one of five living children and received his early religious education from his father, who was the town's ritual slaughterer *(shochet)*, and from local Rabbis. The outbreak of WW I and the turmoil, poverty, and destruction that occurred in its wake, forced him to leave school at the end of the 5th grade.[12]

With the help of relatives, he moved to Vienna in 1920 and "under the most trying living conditions," he studied for the matriculation examination, which he passed in 1923. During this time, he attended the Hebrew Pedagogium, a seminary for the training of Hebrew teachers, under the direction of Rabbi Hirsch Zvi Perez Chajes, Chief Rabbi of Vienna. Chajes had a magnetic personality, was a great orator, a fervent Zionist, and tended towards liberal orthodox religious views. He appears to have influenced the young Chameides and acted as his mentor. As soon as he passed the

[11] *Pinkas Hakehiloth. Polin.* Volume 2: East Galicia (Yad Vashem, Jerusalem 1979) 520.
[12] Kalman Chameides, "Curriculum Vitae. Wrocław, August 6, 1928" in Archiwum Państwowego w Katowicach Wydział Administracyjny, 1992, 278-279.

matriculation, Kalman Chameides was admitted to the Beit Midrash LeRabanim (Israelitisch-Theologische Lehranstalt)[13] and the Philosophy Department of the University of Vienna,[14] both Chajes' alma maters. The Beit Midrash LeRabanim was founded in Vienna in 1893 and was directed by Adolph (Arye) Schwartz, a Talmudic scholar ordained by the Jüdisch – Theologisches Lehranstalt in Breslau. Chameides' enrollment at the Israelitisch-Theologische Lehranstalt represented an intellectual and religious departure from his past. Whereas he remained punctilious in his practice of Jewish laws and traditions, as evidenced by his careful attention to the details of the Laws of Passover,[15] and the involved, detailed question that he posed to a Talmudic authority,[16] he parted ways from many of his Orthodox colleagues in his favorable attitude towards western scholarship, his strong support of Zionism and its heroes, his support of spoken Hebrew, and his acceptance of the historical interpretation of Biblical authorship (e.g., his acceptance of a second Isaiah and the authorship of Samuel and Kings during the Babylonian exile).

After two years of study in Vienna and with the help of Rabbi Chajes, he was awarded a one-year Hamelitz scholarship to study Hebrew Language and Literature at the newly opened Hebrew University in Jerusalem.

In 1926, Kalman Chameides returned to Europe and enrolled at the Beit Midrash Lerabanim (Jüdisch-Theologisches Seminar) in Breslau and the University of Breslau, where he studied ancient philology. Zechariah Frankel had established the Beit Midrash Lerabanim (Jüdisch-Theologisches Seminar) in 1854 as a Rabbinical School, whose educational methodology was modeled on the University, rather than the traditional Yeshiva. The school emphasized published research and modern tools of scholarship, and placed a high value on secular education. The school boasted a superb library and published a monthly scholarly journal (Monatschrift für Geschichte

---

13 Reuven Mas, *Sefer hazikaron lebet midrash lerabanim bevina*. *Divrei Zichronot Vedivrei Mada* (Jerusalem, 1946).

14 Application for Admission supplied by the University of Vienna.

15 Kalman Chameides, "The Laws of Passover" in UGGIK #28, March 1933, 3.

16 Arieh Zwi Fromer, *Sheeloth Utshuvoth Eretz Zwi* (Lublin, 1939) #81, 180.

und Wissenschaft des Judentums). The Seminary emphasized orthodox *practice* of Judaism, but also promoted the concept that social and historical forces influenced the development of the oral law. In its philosophy and educational methodology, it was the forerunner of the Conservative movement of Judaism, and the Jewish Theological Seminary in New York. Rabbi Kalman Chameides was ordained on Sunday, January 29, 1929 and received the prestigious Rosin-Preis prize for his studies on the Midrash and Philo.[17]

Rabbi in Katowice

Rabbi Dr. Jecheskel Lewin was the Rabbi of the Jewish community of Katowice from 1924 to 1928, when he accepted a position as Rabbi of the progressive synagogue in Lwów.[18] The Katowice Community Administration decided that the rapidly growing population necessitated the services of two Rabbis,[19] a situation that apparently had prevailed during World War I. Rabbi Kalman Chameides was appointed on September 1, 1928 and Rabbi Mordechai Vogelmann on November 15, 1928.[20] Former members of the community recall that there was concern that Rabbi Chameides did not speak fluent Polish, and that part of his agreement stipulated that he learn Polish within two years.[21] He kept his promise, delivered a sermon in Polish within the two year period and, judging from the essays in the local community newspaper, he mastered that language as he had previously mastered Yiddish (his mother tongue), German, and Hebrew.

It should be noted that September 1, 1928, the day that Rabbi Chameides began his service to the community was the first day of the Jewish New Year. His predecessor, Rabbi J. Lewin, apparently took the position in Lwów just before the High Holy Days, and gave

---

[17] *Bericht des Jüdisch-Theologisches Seminars für das Jahr 1928* (Breslau, 1929), 4.

[18] Kurt I. Lewin, *A Journey Through Illusions* (Fithian Press, Santa Barbara, 1994), 12.

[19] Letter from the Jewish Community to the Silesian government dated September 5, 1928 in Archiwum Państwowego w Katowicach Wydział Administracyjny, 1992, 276.

[20] Letter from the Police Department to the Security Division of the Silesian Government dated October 26, 1937, in Archiwum Państwowego w Katowicach Dyrekcja Policji w Katowicach, 180, 19.

[21] Aharon Eshel-Kaufman, "An Exciting Small Community" in Yosef Chrust and Yosef Frankel, 1996, 37.

the community little notice. The community leaders turned to the Jewish Theological Seminary in Breslau for help in filling the position for the High Holy Days. Among their requirements was that the candidate be an excellent orator with a superior command of German. The 26-year-old Rabbi Chameides, who was sent by the Seminary, must have made a deep impression, since he was immediately offered the position on a permanent basis. While in Katowice for the Holy Days, he stayed at the home of Bruno Altmann, Head of the Administration, on Rynek 11 (now Warszawska 1).

Bruno Altmann was one of 10 children of Leopold and Charlotte (Timmendorfer) Altmann who came to Katowice shortly after their marriage in the 1860s. Leopold Altmann had been a community leader, a member of the Assembly of Representatives (1872 to at least 1900),[22] and President of the Chevra Kadisha (1898 to at least 1900).[23] He had founded and managed a successful hardware and ironware store on Rynek 11 (now Warszawska 1). Only two of Leopold and Charlotte's children remained in Katowice after it became part of Poland and one of them, Bruno, became the head of the Community Administration (1919-1939). Bruno was effective in maintaining a spirit of cooperation and understanding between the established German Jews of the city and the newly arrived Polish Jews, and had an excellent relationship with the State authorities. Bruno Altmann was married to Jettchen Königshöfer from Fürth, Germany and when she tragically died in childbirth (1912), he married her sister, Hanna. The family ties were strengthened when Bruno's sister, Martha, married Isaak Königshöfer, brother of Jettchen and Hanna. It is not clear whether it was fate or human intervention that caused Gertrude (Trude) Königshöfer, daughter of Martha and Isaak, to visit her uncle and aunt for the holidays in 1929. Whichever it was, the wedding of Rabbi Kalman Chameides and Trude Königshöfer was celebrated at the Altmann home on September 24, 1929.

During his 11 years of service, Rabbi Chameides became a beloved advisor, confidant, and religious authority to the members

22 Jacob Cohn, 18.
23 Jacob Cohn, 42.

Gertrude Königshöfer and Rabbi Kalman Chameides on their engagement (above) and their wedding day (left).

of the Katowice Jewish community. He was known as a fine orator in four languages (German, Polish, Yiddish, and Hebrew). It was common for him to start a sermon in Polish, continue it in German, and finish in Yiddish in order to reach the entire community. The following is a contemporary description of him: "Rabbi Kalman Chameides is an impressive presence. He does not give up the 'spiritual' in his everyday behavior, bearing, or speech; his speech is refined and his tone, lofty. An excellent orator, he knows how to mold the rules of the various languages. He speaks German with conviction and Polish with feeling. He knows his heterogeneous community quite accurately, and wields a strong influence on them. We dare not judge his Jewish scholarship, which, by reputation, is quite distinguished. He is Orthodox with a strong Zionist ideology."[24]

In addition to his rabbinical duties, which he shared with Rabbi Vogelmann, Rabbi Chameides was the "Av Beth Din" or head of the Jewish court system, which adjudicated disputes between Jews according to Jewish law, an army chaplain (1937), and a local educational leader. He served as an expert witness in the successful slander suit against Chowański, editor of Błyskawice, an anti-Semitic newspaper.[25, 26]

[24] "Aus Polnisch-Schlesien. Unserer Rabbiner" in *Jüdische Wochenpost mit Wirtschaftsblatt* 3 (1936) #1, 2.

[25] UGGIK #56, May 1934, 2.

[26] Marcin Wodziński, "Walking in the Steel Boots of Faith...Anti-Semitic Journalism in the Voivodship of Silesia 1922-1939" in *Jews in Silesia* (Ksiegarnia Akademicka Cracow 2001).

Despite his relative youth, his influence reached beyond the town borders. He was elected President of the Association of Silesian Rabbis in 1934,[27] and, in 1936, took an active role in the Jewish defense against a proposal in the Sejm (Parliament) to ban Jewish ritual slaughter.[28] When the nearby community of Będzin could not agree on a successor to their deceased Rabbi, they called on Rabbi Chameides to replace him temporarily.[29] He traveled there three times a week from 1937 to 1939.

Educator for Adults and Children

Rabbi Chameides was very involved in educating children and adults. He provided religious instruction to Jewish children in the public schools. The community newspaper has many notices of his lectures to the Jewish social organizations in Katowice. He spoke frequently at the Bnei Brith Lodge, took an active part in the Hebrew Club, and was an active participant in the religious Zionist organization.

The community maintained a supplementary educational system and Rabbi Chameides headed the Talmud Torah, a five-year school for religious instruction founded in 1927/28. He broadened and reorganized its curriculum, and introduced many pedagogic innovations. He was the major force behind the establishment of a girls' school, Beis Yaakov, in Katowice[30] in 1930, and brought Ms. Chava Taube, a graduate of the Beis Yaakov Teachers' Seminary in Będzin to head it. The first class included eight girls and met in the Chameides home. The course of study was five years, and by 1939, the school had 250 students. In 1935, he initiated the establishment of a Coeducational Hebrew School with Hebrew as the language of instruction.[31] This school emphasized Jewish nationalism, Zionism, and Hebrew language in a religious atmosphere in an attempt to

---

[27] UGGIK #53, April 1934, 8.

[28] UGGIK #98, February 1936, 2.

[29] A. S. Stein, (Ed) *Pinkas Bendin* (Association of Former Residents of Bedzin Tel Aviv 1959) 63, 161.

[30] Formal religious education for girls was instituted in 1917 when Sarah Schenirer established the first Beis Yaacov school. The schools were affiliated with the Aguda movement.

[31] Yaacov Teitelbaum, "The Jewish Community in Katowice" in Yosef Chrust and Yosef Frankel, 78.

synthesize Modern Hebrew culture with traditional Judaism.[32]
Rabbi and Mrs. Chameides, Rosa Altmann, and Margret
Beinhof established an adult educational program in 1935. Its goal
was to prepare women for the modern world, with an assumption
that many would leave Poland. To this end, the curriculum included
instruction in English and spoken Hebrew. In 1936, 250 women
attended the program on a regular basis.

The War Years

Days before the outbreak of the war, Rabbi Chameides, together with
his wife and two sons, Herbert (born in 1932) and Leon (born in 1935)
fled to his birthplace, Szczerzec located in Eastern Galicia and
therefore, under Russian control.[33] Since under Soviet rules, communal
occupations were considered to be "parasitic," Rabbi Chameides was
employed in nearby Lwów in a store selling jams. During this time,
several post cards sent to family in England reveal a desperate attempt
to obtain exit visas. In 1940 he wrote: "You must not remain silent.
Trude must once again regain her health. I mean this literally and do
not exaggerate. Help us!" On another occasion, his wife wrote: "So
far, thank God, we have not yet gone hungry," and Rabbi Chameides
added, "hopefully we will see each other again."

The Germans attacked the Soviet Union on June 22, 1941 and
entered Lwów on July 1. In August, the German authorities
established a Judenrat (officially known as Jüdische Gemeinde der
Stadt Lemberg), with Dr. Yoseph Parnas as its first Chairman. Rabbi
Chameides was appointed to its Religious Affairs Department, which
was responsible for religious matters within the community. The other
members of this department were Rabbi Moshe Elhanan Alter, Rabbi
Israel Leib Wolfsberg, Rabbi Nathan Nute Leiter, Rabbi Shmulke
Rappaport, Rabbi Moshe Ehrenpreiss, Rabbi Hersh Rosenfeld, Rabbi
Anschel Schreiber, and Rabbi Dawid Kahane.[34] Only the latter

---

[32] UGGIK #105, June 1936, 2.
[33] A secret addendum to the German Soviet Non-Aggression Treaty of August 23, 1939,
provided for the division of Poland between the two countries.
[34] David Kahane, *Lvov Ghetto Diary* (The University of Massachusetts Press, Amherst
1990), 23-24.

survived the war. In addition to their religious duties, these Rabbis tried to influence the leadership of the Judenrat. For example, in March 1942, the Germans announced plans for a "resettlement" and asked the Judenrat to prepare lists and participate in the roundup of Jews. After two days of discussions by the Religious Affairs Department, a decision was reached to send a delegation consisting of Rabbis Yisrael Leib Wolfsberg, Moshe Elchanan Alter, Kalman Chameides, and Dawid Kahane[35] to Dr. Landesberg, Head of the Judenrat, and warn him that such participation was not in accord with Jewish Law. "We explained that in times of trial such as these we were duty bound to draw attention of the leader of such a large Jewish community to the enormous responsibility associated with complying with the German orders. According to Jewish law and morality, he was to seek other ways. When our enemies come to us saying: 'Bring one of you so that we may kill him. If not we will kill you all' – it is better that all die and not one Jew be delivered to the enemy. This is what the Halakah rules."[36]

In the summer of 1942, the administration of Jewish affairs in Lwów was transferred to the SS. A massive, systematic, and well-planned *Aktion* lasted form August 10 until August 29, and resulted in the deaths of 50,000 – 60,000 Jews. The victims included hospitalized patients, infants in delivery suites, and children in orphanages. Prior to this, killing of Jews in Lwów had been sporadic and random, and the mood remained optimistic that the free labor the Jews provided would somehow allow most to survive.[37] However, the cruelty and organized murder during the August *Aktion* destroyed any illusion that any Jew would survive. That this almost became a reality is borne out by the statistics. In October 1941, there were 119,000 Jews in the Lwów ghetto; by November 1942, there were only 29,000,[38,39] and by the time the Soviet army

[35] Philip Friedman, *Roads To Extinction. The Destruction of the Jews of Lwów.* (The Jewish Publication Society, NY 1980), 269.

[36] David Kahane, 43-44; 156-157.

[37] Filip Friedman, *Zagłada Żydów Lwowskich*, (Wydawnictwa Centralnej Żydowskiej Komisji Historycznej przy Centralnym Komitecie Żydow Polskich #4, Lódz, 1945), 15.

[38] Philip Friedman, Roads To Extinction, 288.

[39] Filip Friedman, 23.

liberated Lwów on July 27, 1944, only 823 Jews remained alive.[40] On August 14, 1942, Rabbis Dawid Kahane and Kalman Chameides, as representatives of the Religious Affairs Department, met with Metropolitan Andrei Sheptyts'kyi, a meeting arranged through a Ukrainian priest, Dr. Gabriel Kostelnik.[41] The main purpose of the meeting was to request the Church to hide several hundred Torah scrolls, which had been collected at the Jewish community building at 12 Bernstein Street. They also resolved to ask the Metropolitan for shelter for the duration of the *Aktion*. Shelter for the Rabbis' children was raised during the meeting. The Metropolitan offered to shelter both Rabbis and their daughters, but was concerned about hiding boys since they could easily be identified as Jews. After consulting with his brother, Ihumen Klementyi, head of the Studite Order monasteries, he agreed to shelter the Rabbis' sons.

Andrei Sheptyts'kyi (1865-1944) attained the highest ecclesiastical post in the Greek Catholic, also known as the Uniate, or Ukrainian Catholic Church, which was established at Brest in 1596 as a union between the Orthodox and Roman churches. He occupied the position of Metropolitan-Archbishop of Lviv and Halych with jurisdiction over the province of Galicia in western Ukraine, for more than four decades (1901-1944).[42] In the pre-war years, Metropolitan Sheptyts'kyi maintained warm relations with the Jewish community, contributed to the welfare of Jewish poor, and showed evidence of a knowing both spoken and written Hebrew.[43, 44] In the first days after the German attack on the Soviet Union on June 22, 1941, Rabbi Jecheskel Lewin, Rabbi Chameides' predecessor in Katowice and a long-time friend of the Archbishop, asked for his help in stemming a campaign of terror and murder unleashed by Ukrainian nationalists against the Jewish community. The Metropolitan urged Rabbi Lewin

[40] Filip Friedman, 25.
[41] David Kahane, 57-58.
[42] Paul R. Magocsi, *Morality and Reality. The Life and Times of Andrei Sheptyts'kyi* (University of Alberta, 1989).
[43] Shimon Redlich, "Sheptyts'kyi and the Jews During World War II" in Paul Magocsi, 45-162.
[44] Philip Friedman, "Hurban Yehudei Lvov" in *Enziklopedia shel Galuyot* (Jerusalem, 1955), 670.

to remain in his residence, but he insisted on going home. On his way home, Rabbi Lewin attacked, brutally beaten, and taken to the Brygidki prison, where he was killed.[45]

Under the Metropolitan's leadership and with cooperation of the church hierarchy, especially his brother Ihumen Klementyi, about 100-200 Jews were saved.[46] Yad Vashem honored Klementyi Sheptyts'kyi in 1995 as a Righteous Among the Nations. The Metropolitan has not been similarly honored. The Commission for the Righteous of Yad Vashem acknowledged his role in saving individual Jews but felt that he did not satisfy the higher requirements of a leader of the Church.[47] The Metropolitan's actions in saving Jews has been recognized by an act of the Canadian Parliament on May 21, 2012 and by the ADL, which awarded his memory the Jan Karski Courage to Care Award on October 31, 2013.

In September 1942, Rabbi Chameides made two successful, but highly dangerous, journeys to Szczerzec traveling each time in a truck transporting workers, and brought his two sons to the Metropolitan's residence at St. Jur in Lwów. Subsequently, his wife, Gertrude, joined him in the Lwów ghetto.

The ghetto was closed, and the Judenrat was liquidated on September 7, 1942. Only those with a work assignment were still permitted to live. Rabbi Chameides' name appears on a list of "unentgeltlichen Arbeitnehmer für Oktober 1942" (uncompensated workers for October, 1942) under the heading "Friedhofsabteilung Gruppe R (Cemetery Division group R).[48] He was apparently assigned to work as a gravedigger in the Lwów cemetery.

Final Letter

In this atmosphere of hunger, terror, and murder, with the borders of his world narrowing and closing in on him, with his two sons in a Christian monastery, Rabbi Chameides wrote a remarkable letter

[45] Kurt I. Lewin *Journeys Through Illusions* (Fithian Press, Santa Barbara, CA 1994), 36.

[46] Philip Friedman, "Ukrainian-Jewish Relations" in *YIVO Annual of Jewish Social Science* (YIVO Institute for Jewish Research, New York 1959), 259-296.

[47] Letter dated April 29, 1996 from Dr. Mordecai Paldiel, Director, Department for the Righteous, Yad Vashem, Jerusalem.

[48] United States Holocaust Memorial Museum, Washington DC

full of despair, hope, compassion, and love (Figures 1 and 2) which was discovered in the private files of Metropolitan Sheptyts'kyi.[49]

[49] I am most grateful to Bishop Michael Hrynchyshyn of Paris, France who made a copy available to me.

Lemberg, October 26, 1942
"And the righteous lives by his faith"
Hab.

Excellency!

In view of the treacherous circumstances, I have not had an opportunity until today to express to you, Excellency, my deepest gratitude for the warm, brotherly reception that I received from you at a time of affliction. From the depths of my sad soul I prayed for God's blessings for you, Excellency, and for your household, while my elder friend and I were allowed to rest in your presence over a few days from the vicissitudes of the cruelest of all persecutions.

Unfortunately, we left too soon! My fellow-sufferer is no longer here. But I too have suffered through months of difficult struggles and bitter experiences. Only my faith in God has sustained me! Only hope in the speedy revelation of His grace has been my guiding star during these weeks, overshadowed by death!

If my dear colleague, Dr. Kohane and I - as stated in a personal oral explanation by Dr. Kohane to his eminence Father...- have now decided to place ourselves under the protection of the Church and to ask for your sympathy and aid, it is not only because of an inborn instinct for self-preservation common to all of us, but also from a firm faith and hope that in the future we might have an opportunity to work for the welfare of humanity and for a world united in faith in the spirit of that immortal doctrine which reconciles and liberates all people - love of one's fellow man. We want to participate in the establishment of a large sublime dome of love under which all people of goodwill will find a place.

Who can sympathize as deeply as we with the tale of woe of the great divine sufferer? Who, better than we, can capture the light shining from his face engraved by pain? Like he, we cry daily and hourly: "eli, eli, lama schebaktani!" His comforting image, encircled with a halo of divine martyrdom stands out among the images of countless martyrs of our sorely tried nation hovering before our eyes, when we have had to bear the crown of thorns on our bowed heads - the derision of a world seething with hatred!

Excellency! Haste is essential! You can still snatch us away from the abyss whose jaws are about to swallow us!

May you soon help us to outlast this time of world conflagration, so that we, as God's faithful servants and executors of his will on earth, may be allowed to greet the approaching dawn of a refined humanity in community with all the faithful!-

K. Chameides

The letter was written on October 26, 1942 so it undoubtedly had to be smuggled out, since the ghetto was closed on September 7. Only the author's, not the recipient's name, is mentioned, probably out of fear that it might get into the wrong hands. For the same reason, the author misspells Rabbi Kahane's name as

"Kohane," and leaves a blank for the intermediary priest's name. The letter is beautifully handwritten in an elegant German. Each word was obviously very carefully chosen for maximum meaning to its recipient, and to emphasize the common bond of humanity and brotherhood of the writer and recipient, despite their different theological world views. Some words are chosen to evoke a clear emotional response in a prince of the Church. For example, in the fourth paragraph the word "Leidensgeschichte" (history of suffering) is used in Christian theological terminology for Christ's Passion. In the third paragraph, the word "Dome" (dome) can also refer to a Cathedral. In the fourth paragraph, the phrase "Dornenkrone auf unserem gebeugten Haupte" (a crown of thorns on our bent heads) would evoke a familiar image and a sympathetic understanding in a Christian theologian. For the same reason, the author uses the Aramaic phrase "eli, eli, lama schebaktani" which, according to the Gospels of Mark[50] and Matthew[51] were Jesus' last words, rather than the Hebrew version from Psalms 22 ("Eli, eli lama azavtani").

The first paragraph is an expression of gratitude to the Metropolitan for hiding the writer's children but also for his warmth and understanding. The "alterer Freund" (older friend) must refer to Rabbi Dawid Kahane despite the fact that they were contemporaries, since the two went to see the Metropolitan together. The temporary feeling of peace that he describes finding in the Metropolitan's presence is reminiscent of Rabbi Kahane's description of that same visit: "The walls of the Jura Mountain palace left an odd impression on me. It seemed as if I had been suddenly lifted from a raging sea whose mighty gales threatened to overwhelm everything in their range, onto a quiet and peaceful island where every tree, every blade of grass, every flower seemed to ask in astonishment: 'Is it really true that a terrible storm rages out on the sea?' The stillness prevailing among these walls was so soft we could hear clearly the beating of our hearts. After a wild, nervous tumult of the ghetto, I really thought we were walking on a different planet."[52]

---

[50] The Gospel According to St. Mark 15:34.
[51] The Gospel According to St. Matthew 47:46.
[52] David Kahane, 58.

The second paragraph is a reference to the terrible days of the *Aktions* during the months of August and September. It is not clear whom he refers to as his "Leidensgenosse" (fellow sufferer). His wife was still alive. Rabbi Kahane was already in hiding, but it is possible that he might not have known this.

In the third and fourth paragraphs, Rabbi Chameides feels a need to explain why he wanted to seek refuge in the Church, which, for unknown reasons, he never carried out. It is an expression of hope in a hopeless world; a conviction that those who suffered so much developed unique insights and perspectives to help perfect the world in the future. It is not clear why he indented the fourth paragraph. He ends this paragraph on a note of reality, by indicating the special place that Jews martyred for the sanctification of God, including Jesus, have had in Jewish history. He reclaims Jesus for Jewish history, since, had Jesus lived during this time, he too, would have been subject to the same persecutions as his fellow Jews.

The final two paragraphs are a plea for help. In November 1942, Metropolitan Sheptyts'kyi published a pastoral letter, "Thou Shalt Not Kill," in the *Lwiwski Arkhieparkhialni Widomosti,* the organ of the Galician Uniate Church. In this pastoral letter, read in all Churches of his denomination, he stressed the importance of this commandment, and threatened all offenders with excommunication.[53] He wrote the pastoral letter "in order to fulfill our duty to the Almighty as shepherds of souls and preachers of the Gospel, to warn our faithful, with heaven and earth as our witnesses, against the evil deeds which have recently spread among us so frightfully, and call for penitence on the part of persons who committed the sin of murder."[54] The letter does not specifically mention Jews, but censorship would have prevented him from doing so. It is not known whether the timing or publication of this pastoral letter was influenced in any way by the October 26 letter from Rabbi Chameides.

---

[53] Philip Friedman, *Ukrainian-Jewish Relations* (YIVO Annual of Jewish Social Science), 291.
[54] David Kahane, 159.

The quote at the beginning of the letter is from Habakkuk 2:4 ("And the righteous lives by his faith"). In view of the last two paragraphs of the letter, the quote may at first reading be viewed as a challenge to the faith of the recipient. In other words, a truly righteous person is challenged to put his expressions of faith into action. However, considering the care with which the writer selected every word, it is important to examine the context in which the sentence appears. It will then be understood that this is both an expression of the writer's despair, as well as his faith in the eventual victory of good over evil.

Habakkuk prophesied about Nebuhadnezzar's invasion of Israel, the suffering that would result, and the eventual downfall of the aggressor at the hands of Persia and Medea. The prophet complains to God about the seeming lack of justice; that the wicked seem to prosper while the righteous (Israel) suffer. He is advised to wait with patience for the eventual victory of good over evil. Habakkuk's description of events, so similar to those of the German occupation, must have given the writer a measure of comfort, and allowed him to use it as an expression of spiritual defiance. The righteous (the Jews) must have patience for in the end they will survive as a people.

Approximately 10 years before this letter was written, Rabbi Chameides wrote an article in which he enumerated attempts to summarize the entire Jewish religion in as succinct a manner as possible: "Finally, Habakkuk condensed them into one rule, 'the righteous lives by his faith (in God)'. Thus is established that faith in God and trust in Him is the last link in the chain of regulations and maxims with which our sages strove to express the essence of our religion. One word: 'Emunah', which in Hebrew means faith, trust, loyalty, and constancy, revealed itself in the final analysis, as the most appropriate and exact description of the Jewish entity."[55]

On November 18, a new registration of Jews took place in the ghetto and those working in military factories received the letter W

---

[55] Kalman Chameides, "About Jewish Ethics" in UGGIK #5, March 1932, 5.

(Wermacht), and those working in defense industry received the letter R (Ruestungsindustrie).[56] Rabbi Chameides acquired a work certificate from the Rohstoff Company.[57]

The last information available on Rabbi Chameides is contained in a penciled note that his wife, Gertrude, wrote and managed to have hidden for her sons. It reads: "My husband died on the 18th of Teveth or 25th of December at 11 o'clock in the evening from typhus. My parents-in-law died on the 4th day of Chanukah [December 4]. Kalman is buried next to Rabbi Laib Breude and Dayan Ehrenpreiss. At his head and feet is buried a bottle which contains his name, Kalman Ch." Gertrude Chameides died under unknown circumstances between the end of December 1942 and the liquidation of the Lwów ghetto in June 1943.[58] At the time of their deaths, he was 40 and his wife was 38 years of age.

[56] Filip Friedman, *Zagłada*, 21.
[57] David Kahane, 84.
[58] Eliyahu Jones, *Żydzi Lwowa w Okresie Okupacji* 1939-1945 (Łódz, 1999), 234.

URZĘDOWA GAZETA GMINY IZRAELICKIEJ
THE COMMUNITY NEWSPAPER

The semimonthly Urzędowa Gazeta Gminy Izraelickiej w Katowicach (Official Newspaper of the Jewish Community of Katowice) was initiated and edited by Rabbi Chameides[59] as a forum of communication between the administrative and religious leadership and members of the community. Its first issue appeared in January 1932, and 118 issues were published through December 1936. It is not clear whether the newspaper was published after that. A single copy, from September 1938, has been found, but bears a different name, "Wiadomości Gminne. Organ Gminy Żydowskiej w Katowicach" (Community News. Organ of the Jewish Community in Katowice). It does bear the number 152, so it appears to be a continuation of the same paper under a different name. In the early issues, all administrative articles were written in both Polish and German, but, as Polish-German hostility increased, and the community's demographic makeup shifted, the number of articles in German decreased, and they were relegated to the back pages.

Front page of first issue, January 1932.

59 UGGIK #1, January 1932, 6.

The newspaper is a rich source of information about the organization of community life in those precarious years on the threshold of World War II. Rabbi Chameides wrote many articles, about half in German and half in Polish. Most were probably based on sermons delivered in the synagogue. In fact, the essays have the staccato rhythm of an oration. Emphasis for the listener is underlined by the use of short repetitive phrases. These are not academic papers; they were written for intelligent laymen with a variety of backgrounds about Jewish religious practices and beliefs. They constitute a body of work that gives insight into Rabbi Chameides' religious philosophy, and how he viewed the world of the 1930s, especially the ever-worsening Jewish condition. Each essay is carefully crafted. The language is soaring, at times almost poetic, and the ideas are always well grounded on Jewish classical texts. His essays deal mainly with behavior, ethical conduct, national and Jewish existential issues, the gathering storm of anti-Semitism, and words of encouragement and hope. Each of these issues is carefully woven into a tapestry of Jewish tradition and sources. He tends to use the Aggadic literature, consisting of stories and parables, more than strictly legal sources. His broad education is evident from his use of quotes from Polish poets, German authors, English writers, and quotations in Hebrew, Aramaic, Latin, English, and French.

The following are translations of Rabbi Chameides' essays that appeared in the Urzędowa Gazeta between January 1932 and December 1936. They are divided them into eight sections, roughly according to topic, and within each section, are arranged chronologically.

I

ON THE EDGE OF THE ABYSS

The essays in this section show that Rabbi Chameides clearly understood the temper of the times, and the mortal danger that awaited the Jews. Nineteen-thirty-three marked the true beginning of the Shoah. Hitler was appointed as Reich Chancellor (Prime Minister) of Germany on January 30. The first concentration camp, Dachau, was established on March 23, and was followed by the establishment of concentration camps in Esterwegen and Sachsenhausen. On April 1, the Nazis proclaimed a general boycott of all Jewish owned businesses. Stars of David were painted on Jewish shops, and Jews were beaten and terrorized. Jews were dismissed from the civil service, and denied admission to the bar on April 7 and from all universities soon thereafter. The Gestapo was formed on April 26 and books written by Jews were burned on May 10 in front of the Berlin Opera House and opposite the entrance to the University of Berlin. As a result of these increasingly harsh measures, thousands of Jews left Germany for Palestine, the United States, and any other country that would allow them to enter. The tragedy was that so few countries opened their borders. Most Jews found the bureaucratic gates tightly locked. The brief but poignant observations in "Thoughts for the Ninth of Av 5693 [1933]" are an apt reaction to that year's events.

In April, the following editorial appeared in the newspaper of the Katowice Jewish community.[60] "The festival of Pesach, a festival commemorating the deliverance of the Jews and the granting of their freedom, is being celebrated this year in all Jewish homes in the world under the cloud of both sad and frightening events in Germany."

"The Biblical sentence, 'And there arose on the throne of Egypt a new Pharaoh who did not know Joseph', has never been so realistic and truthful as in our time. Thousands of Jewish families, who for many years and in the majority of cases for many generations have lived in Germany and have been loyal to their fatherland, became sacrifices of this change in government. An innumerable number of these families have been forced to emigrate,

---

[60] UGGIK #30, April 1933, 1.

leaving behind everything that they have been able to accumulate over many years of their hard work and saving."

"The largest numbers of these unfortunate, good émigrés, especially those who are coming to Poland, direct their first steps to Katowice as the most important town after the border. These uprooted families are searching for refuge and help here. The Community Administration is trying to do everything in its power to ease the lot of these families in their hour of misfortune. Unfortunately, the material means, which the Administration has at its disposal for this purpose, are not sufficient."

"Government agencies are helping us by supplying free railway tickets to those who are lucky enough to be able to go elsewhere. Unfortunately, we have been unable to receive additional funds from these agencies, and therefore the community must bear the remainder of the cost."

The Jewish community of Katowice did not escape the official anti-Semitic propaganda and acts of hostility. Jewish businesses were boycotted and firebombed. There was an attempt to bomb the Synagogue and Polish artisan guilds passed "Aryan Regulations," which resulted in the expulsion of Jewish artisans. By 1937, there were anti-Jewish pogroms in the streets. In a letter, Rabbi Chameides described Poland as "a country that devours its inhabitants...Life is becoming more difficult each day. I must now avoid leaving my home in the evening for fear of the night and the mischief makers who gather in the streets."

The last paragraph of the essay, "A Seder in Bnei Brak," must be read in this historical context. It is the first mention by the Rabbi of possible Jewish martyrdom: "A threatening reality has overtaken us and is demanding the greatest sacrifices from us. Accordingly, let each of us understand the first verse of our daily prayer "Shema," "Love your eternal God with all your heart, with all your soul, and with all your might." With all your soul – even if you have to pay for loving the God of your ancestors with your life. But Jewish martyrology must not weaken our resolve for self-preservation. For after this dark night, the dawn of freedom will shine at last, and the words of our prophet will be fulfilled."

This essay is also interesting in that in it, Rabbi Eliezer bemoans his alienation from his father as the most painful episode of his life. In reality, a much more prominent and painful episode must have been his banishment from the Academy by his colleagues (Bava Metzia 59b). One wonders whether Rabbi Chameides chose the filial alienation as the more painful episode because of his own break with the tradition of his father. One can't help but wonder whether he had himself in mind when he wrote: "...a deep hurt torments me. My heart is sick. When, after years of separation, I embraced my father once again, he was a decrepit old man. I was never able to find a way to his heart. Years of discord and separation, which cast a shadow over my life to this day, stood between us. Wounds opened in youth, never seem to heal. Ruts created by suffering and anguish in the dawn of our lives are not so easily smoothed over later in life. An absence of love and understanding from parents leaves an indelible imprint on the rest of our lives."

There is an ominous feeling of despair in "The Blessing." "At no time in history has mankind, and especially our sorely tired people, yearned for a blessing of good fortune and a cheering, illuminating ray of sunshine as in our cloudy, present time. Our souls are weighed down by an oppressive, paralyzing feeling that the source of all blessings has dried up for us; that the gates of hope have been barricaded; that the most difficult of all eras of our tragic-heroic history is about to dawn for us."

Rabbi Chameides never tired of pointing out to the Christian community that their behavior was contrary to the most fundamental principles of their religion. In "True Heroism," he wrote, "When the shadows grow longer and the night approaches, we Jews light the small Chanukah candles. As the world sinks into chaos and disorder, we – the last Priests of the Temple of love of ones fellow man – want to renew the flame in our candles; to once more give the world a gift of a gospel, since the old one has been forgotten. Gospels of love, of compassion, of pity...Since you have broken the old tablets we want to chisel new ones for you. New tablets with the old commandments: Do not murder, do not hate..."

Rabbi Chameides was elected President of the Association of Silesian Rabbis In 1934. "For the Defense of the Country," was one of his addresses in which he urges the Silesian Jewish community to support Poland's effort in building an effective air force and anti-gas defense system.

1934/35 (5694-5695) brought increased misfortune into Jewish life. The economic depression continued and had a devastating effect on the lives of individual Jews as well as on communal life. In addition, torrential rains caused many rivers in Poland to overflow their banks, causing massive flooding and washing away the hopes and meager possessions of many. Anti-Jewish hatred gathered momentum in Germany, and spilled its venom across the border into Poland. Physical assaults on Jews in Germany became a regular occurrence, and there was an organized campaign to expel them from villages. On May 1, the Nazi propaganda newspaper, Der Sturmer, revived the medieval blood libel, and accused Jews of using Christian blood in baking matzot for Passover. Nazi broadcasts to the Arab world proved successful when, on August 3, anti-Jewish riots erupted in the Algerian city of Constantine. By the end of 1934, more than 50,000 Jews had left Germany. The Nuremberg Laws, which legally sanctioned the exclusion of Jews from German life, were enacted on September 15, 1935. As a result of Arab riots in Palestine, the British Government limited the number of Jews who could enter although certificates could be obtained with payment of 1000 pounds sterling, which few could afford.

In "Haman's Arguments," Rabbi Chameides contrasts the "simple" anti-Semitism of Haman, with that of the 1930s. Especially prophetic, in view of what was to transpire five years later, is his view that the anti-Semites "want to defame and degrade us. First, they proclaim a sentence of death for our spirit in order then, with a clear conscience, to bury our physical existence."

The remarkable essay, "Jewish Children as Martyrs," was a speech given in the cemetery on 9 Av, the saddest day in the Jewish calendar, which commemorates many tragedies in Jewish history, including the destruction of the two Temples. The subject, Jewish

Children as Martyrs, is most unusual. In 1935, the 9th of Av corresponded to August 8. One can assume that it was probably prepared during the month of July. Rabbi Chameides' second son was born on June 24, 1935. The essay written shortly after the birth of his first son, in 1932, deals with the child in Jewish culture, and is most optimistic. The mood is very different here, corresponding with the deterioration of the Jewish condition. In the first few paragraphs of this essay, when he speaks about the fact that children are the result of decisions made by adults, one can almost hear a refrain – "what have I done? How could I have brought a child into this kind of world? What miserable future is awaiting him?" The last paragraphs are prophetic of what would be in store only four years hence.

A SEDER IN BNEI BRAK[61]

"Rabbi Eliezer, Rabbi Yehoshua, Rabbi Elazar ben Azaria, Rabbi Akiba, and Rabbi Tarfon sat after a Seder feast in Bnei Brak, and spoke about the Exodus from Egypt the entire night, until their students came and announced: 'The time has come to say the morning Shema prayer.'"[62]

These sages discussed the Israelite Exodus from Egypt the entire night, until the arrival of dawn. What exactly was the content of such long discussions and conversations? Centuries have passed since that night. No one can remove the veil that obscures the content of those discussions. But, using our imagination, let us try to reconstruct it on the basis of information contained in both Talmuds. "Everyone must consider as if he himself participated in the Exodus from Egypt," the author of the Hagada tells us. We must not treat the Exodus as a bygone event, as the past, as ancient history, as being unconnected to the present. When we recall those ancient times, they subconsciously awaken concerns about our own current troubles and anxieties; we feel the yoke of the burden that makes us stoop today. In light of the miraculous past, however, we must also become aware of the miracles and extraordinary events with which our lives are blessed. We are surely not exceeding the limits of veracity in asserting that the stories these sages told must have included personal experiences; that in addition to the Exodus from Egypt, their own lives must have been a topic of conversations. They must have told each other about the pain and disappointments they endured; of the high hopes that did not materialize or were smashed against the hard rocks of reality; of plans and dreams coming undone in the storm of life. Those teachers must have shared the pain and despondency that tore their souls. They must have revealed to each other, events that had depressed, worried, humiliated, and oppressed them for a long time.

[61] UGGIK #29, April 1933, 4. Original in Polish.
[62] The Passover Hagadah.

I

Rabbi Eliezer opened the conversation. "When I was a 22-year old youth, I fulfilled my father's wish and herded cattle. At that time, I didn't have the faintest idea about Jewish scholarship. Jewish thought was an inaccessible and foreign territory for me. I performed the ordinary work of a simple field hand and saw no need for higher Jewish education. Nature was my teacher. I was brought up in her bosom. I sought answers for all my questions in her eternal book. One day, as was usual for me, I followed the herd. A deep, serene, silence reigned all around me. Under a light breeze, nature closed its eyes and fell asleep. The sky was bright and transparent, and a stream of sunlight poured on the world. A deep yearning awakened within me in this divine, solemn solitude. A yearning to learn the answers to the great riddles of existence. A deep, hitherto unknown-to-me thirst for knowledge about the supernatural filled my heart. Pastoral life suddenly seemed to me without substance or purpose. I was overcome by an ever increasing desire to study at the famous schools in Jerusalem; a desire to quell my thirst for knowledge at the eternal springs gushing forth in the Holy City. Suddenly, I thought about my age – I was already 22, and still illiterate. Ashamed, and feeling helpless, I sat down on a stone and started to cry. In my heart, I reproached my father for neglecting my intellectual education and for abandoning me in spiritual darkness. At that moment, my father came. "Why are you crying?" "Father, I will no longer be able to perform your will and tend cattle because I cannot overcome my inner drive to study." Father was shocked. He called study sterile, fruitless, and my work, indispensable. The next evening, I ran away from my parents' home and wandered towards Jerusalem. Since then, through hunger and cold, I have worked on self-improvement. I passionately absorbed every word of my teachers. I became one of the best and most diligent of students. My father cursed me, and disowned me when he found out about my happiness. Years passed. Years of work; years of poverty; years of superhuman effort. All that work was not wasted. I won the recognition of scholars, and achieved fame and honor. Finally, after convincing my father that this was my calling and destiny, I was reconciled with him. And yet, a deep hurt torments me. My heart is sick. When, after years of separation, I embraced my father once again, he was a decrepit old man. I was never able to find a way into his heart. Years of discord and separation, which cast a shadow over my life to this day, stood between us. Wounds opened in youth never seem to heal. Ruts, created by suffering and anguish in the dawn of our lives, are not so easily smoothed over later in life. An absence of love and understanding from parents leaves an indelible imprint on the rest of our lives.

II

Rabbi Eliezer's friends listened to the sad story of his life with intense concentration. They understood and commiserated with him. A small light, penetrating the deepening darkness, twinkled as Rabbi Yehoshua spoke next. "The story of my life, dear friends, is entirely different. I was lucky enough to spend my youth in an environment that gave full support to my values and abilities. My parents nurtured my education and upbringing with unusual openness, care, and understanding concern. My mother took my cradle to school and placed it near the teacher's desk so that my soul would absorb the words of the holy text and from its very beginning dedicate itself to the lofty principles of our tradition. My parents' hopes and dreams were fulfilled. I dedicated myself to obtaining an education and I achieved an honored position in the field of scholarship. I am considered one of the outstanding contemporary scholars. But truthfully, am I happy and satisfied with my lot? I wish I were! I am poor and live in constant want. Oh, how true are the words of King Solomon: 'People scorn the words of the poor.' Once, when there was an election for president of our academy, my colleagues could not decide whether to entrust me with that position. 'Rabbi Yehoshua,' they said to each other, 'is indeed known for his vast knowledge, and his unusual perception. He is a person who has made great scholarly contributions, and possesses invaluable qualities of character. But how can we appoint him as our representative? He has no material means with which to enforce his authority and high standing in society, and thereby project an image of luster and spark. So I did not achieve my life's ambition. My blossoming talents faded with time and gradually died without bringing blessings and benefit to humanity. I became closed in, a numb scholar without direct influence on the improvement of public life. I am slowly dying, lonely and far from the arena of battle."

III

Rabbi Yehoshua became silent and his words were swallowed by the silence of the night. The famous Rabbi Akiba now began to speak. The particulars of his life were already well known. He expressed himself plainly, but precisely. His words were full of bitterness and suppressed indignation. "I served as a herdsman in the house of the wealthy Kalba-Sabua for 40 long years. I accidentally met his daughter and, on first sight, I felt that Providence destined her to become my wife. I begged her father for her hand but Kalba-Sabua haughtily scorned me and threw me out of his house. A wide gulf separated us. He – a wealthy and highly respected citizen. I – a poor shepherd. His daughter, however, returned my love and encouraged me to get an education since she did not wish to marry an illiterate man. I sat in the Beth Hamidrash for 24 years. My name sparkled in the sky of scholarship. Thousands of students flock around me and listen to my words of wisdom with inspiration and admiration. And yet, a dark, gloomy shadow is cast across my path. Because of my lowly origins, there are many who refuse to follow my opinions, or respect me. They reproach me because my parents were shepherds and call me 'Akiba with a shepherd's bag.' I labor day and night in vain. In vain do I dedicate my entire being, without rest, to the study of the Holy writings. They will never consider me worthy of a high position. They will always consider me an upstart. I don't have a noble coat of arms, an aristocratic ancestry, 'Yichus.'"

IV

All were silent in embarrassment. Rabbi Akiba's story made a deep impression on them. In his words, they heard a bitter accusation and a well-grounded reproach. The prejudice against his background and class origin was indeed a stumbling block on Rabbi Akiba's life journey and tipped the scales against him in realizing his full potential. Rabbi Tarfon interrupted the uncomfortable silence. His tale was almost superfluous because the tragedy of his life was well known and closely tied to the tragedy of the entire nation. Rabbi Tarfon had been a venerable priest. He was a priest not only by virtue of his ancestry but also because of his calling; a priest with a deep all-encompassing holiness and faithful to his position as the people's representative to God. He had been privileged to fulfill his priestly duties in the Temple in Jerusalem. Now the Temple lay in ruins. He had been a witness to the terror of the destruction of the Holy Sanctuary. With his own eyes, he witnessed the flames turn the altar, the holy place of his activities, into cinders. Since then, he has suffered an inconsolable grief. He has been orphaned, deserted. For, after all, what good is a priest without of an altar, without God's Sanctuary?

V

We should not be surprised that the last to speak was Rabbi Elazar ben Azariah, both because he was the youngest and because he had the least cause for complaint or regret. He was a descendant of Ezra, had always been surrounded by wealth and splendor and, in addition, he was generously endowed with talent by God. Material concerns never crossed the threshold of his home. As a result of circumstances, he was appointed head of the academy at the tender age of 18. On the surface, it would seem that his life was a series of uninterrupted successes and good fortune. But who can see the secrets of a person's heart? Let us listen to him. Let him tell us how he views his life. "When I accepted the highest position in Israel, I was in the spring of my life. I ruled that one should tell the story of the Exodus from Egypt at the Seder even at night. But no one would listen to me. I was unable to sway others or speak with authority to my brothers. My words remained lonely, without an echo. I was unable to prevail over the opinions of my subordinates. I was not up to the task given me by Providence. My voice was a voice crying in the wilderness." Great is the affliction of a commander abandoned by his troops...

Who of us cannot see his own reflection in the mirror of these stories? Rabbi Eliezer suffered from a lack of understanding by his parents. Rabbi Yehoshua considered himself a sacrificial lamb to his poverty. Rabbi Akiba felt himself afflicted and wronged as a result of prejudice against his class. Rabbi Eleazar ben Azaria fought in vain to gain the confidence of his colleagues. And there are many amongst us who, like Rabbi Tarfon of yore, has seen his sanctuary destroyed by his enemies; his source of livelihood turned into a pile of ruble. There are so many priests among us who have been deprived of their altar!

The Seder in Bnei Brak lasted the entire night and might have continued if the students had not interrupted their sad discussion by calling out: "Enough personal reminiscences, our distinguished teachers! Behold dawn is arising and announcing a new era for our nation! A new generation is awaiting your advice and consolation. The time has come to recite the Shema prayer."

The words of these students resonate with us today and call on us to persevere in this terrible catastrophe that has struck our people and to preserve our hope and courage. A time has come when we too must fulfill the important words of the Shema prayer. A threatening reality has overtaken us and is demanding the greatest sacrifices from us. Accordingly, let each of us understand the first verse of our daily prayer, "Shema." "Love your eternal God with all your heart, with all your soul, and with all your might." With all your soul – even if you have to pay for loving the God of your ancestors with your life. But Jewish martyrology must not weaken our resolve for self-preservation. For, after this dark night, the dawn of freedom will shine at last and the words of our prophet will be fulfilled:

העם ההלכים בחשך ראו אור גדול
ישבי בארץ צלמות אור נגה עליהם

The nation that walked in darkness will see a great light
A great light will shine on those who walk in the shadow of death

THOUGHTS FOR THE NINTH OF AV 5693[63]

The Eternal Target

"When the Roman army encamped before Jerusalem, the commander-in-chief wanted a sign, which would inform him what the outcome of the campaign would be. He shot an arrow in an easterly direction. The arrow changed its direction of flight in mid-air and flew towards Jerusalem. Next, the commander shot an arrow westward and it too headed towards Jerusalem. The commander tried shooting in all directions, but the arrows always had only one destination – Jerusalem. Thus, he was assured of victory" (Gittin 56a).

And so it has remained to this very day. In whatever direction an arrow is shot – east, west, north, or south, it eventually finds Jerusalem and the children of Jerusalem.

The Locked Temple

"When the Temple was in flames, the young priests, with keys to the Temple in hand, climbed to the roof of the All Holy and raised their beautiful voices: 'Master of the universe! Take back your keys since we have not been worthy to be managers of your house!' They then flung the keys heavenward. A fiery hand came down, and reclaimed the keys" (Ta'anit 29).

Ever since, many young priests have knocked on the doors of holy places and found them locked.

The Dispersion

"God has done his people a favor by scattering them. If they are oppressed in one place, they thrive in another" (Pesahim 87).

How difficult, O God it is to suffer your favors...

Cry Quietly...

"At night, Jerusalem cries and, in the mute silence of the night, the lament can be heard far away. Perhaps from somewhere, someone will come to her aid. Perhaps there is still compassion in some distant heart" (Sanhedrin 104).

Today, Jew, you must cry quietly so that no one hears you. Otherwise you will branded a traitor, and be called pushy...

How are you doin', Jew?
"One time, a Jew passed by the Roman Caesar and greeted him.
The Caesar called out: 'Who are you?'
'A Jew, your Majesty.'
'And you dare to greet me?'
Caesar gave an order to behead the Jew as punishment. And it was done.

Once a Jew went by the Roman Caesar and did not greet him!
The Caesar called out: 'Who are you?'
'A Jew, your Majesty.'
'And you dare not to greet me?'
Caesar gave an order to behead the Jew as punishment. And it was done" (Midrash).
Jewish head, how are you doin?....

The Savior
"On the day that the Temple was destroyed, the Messiah was born" (Midrash).
Must a Temple always be destroyed in order for a Messiah to be born?

The Rebbe
"Approximately one hundred years ago, in a small southern German town, the Rabbi ordered the community to gather on the eve of the 9th of Av in their most festive clothes in a brightly lit synagogue. He climbed to the lectern and vigorously protested against the sadness of the 9th of Av and against their longing for Palestine. He accused millions of his mourning brothers of treason against their fatherland and called out enthusiastically: 'Jerusalem is here! Germany is our Palestine!'."...(Hirsch Vol I)

Your reverence, you have unfortunately erred....

THE YEAR 5693-5694 [1932-1934][64]

שמר מה מלילה, שמר מה מליל
Watchman, what of the night
Watchman, what of the night? (Isaiah 21:11)

Our religious writers used to equate *golus* [exile] with the night. In this comparison there is in truth, no exaggeration, no free metaphor, no poetic license, especially if we recall the extremely dark *golus* events of this year, 5693, which is just ending. A future Jewish historiographer will document the events of the past year with a trembling hand. The Talmudic tradition, according to which God dictated the entire Torah to Moses, comes to mind. When Moses was writing the last chapters of the Five Books, which deal with his own death, tears came to his eyes. הקב"ה אומר ומשה כותב בדמע – God dictates and Moses writes with tears in his eyes" (Bava Batra 15a). God speaks, dictates history, directs, and administers us and, in view of our martyrology, we note each incident with tears. What then did this past year bring us?

Modern *Golus*

We have not experienced a golus in the true meaning of the word, namely homelessness and exile, for a long time. The words of the prophet, כלי גולה עשי לך – prepare yourself articles for wandering; prepare yourself to be a vagabond (Jeremiah 46:19), had lost their literal meaning for us. They had stopped chasing and pursuing us from country to country. Theoretically, and officially, we have been granted equal rights. And when thousands of our brothers perished on the battlefields of Europe during the world war [WW I], we thought that the spilled blood and memory of shared experiences and suffering would become a strong and lasting bond between us and the nations among whom we have lived for such a long time. Friendships sealed in the shadow of death, shared toils and troubles,

64 UGGIK #40, September 1933, 4-5. Original in Polish.

shared experiences of pain and suffering – aren't these the strongest bonds and best assurances for a future peaceful coexistence? We said to ourselves בדמיך חיי – the blood of innocent brothers will be transformed into a source of life. A "tree of life" will blossom on the battlefields irrigated with the blood of millions of people. Hatred will be transformed into love ומעז יצא מתוק – a shared misery will become the source for an everlasting brotherhood. That is what we thought. That is what we imagined. In some countries, there was brutal anti-Semitism, but, in general, persecution of Jews took on a subtler, more diplomatic, more calculated form and, especially in the West, it became almost exclusively an aristocratic disease.

Until 5693, when a new wave of hatred flooded the largest country in middle Europe. The era of individual freedom has disappeared. The short dream of emancipation has vanished. Those who trusted in the light of the sunrise of emancipation and had faith in its motto – Liberté, Egalité, and Fraternité for all, without regard to religion or national origin, suffered a bitter disappointment and now find themselves in a state of material and psychological despondency. They are comparable, to use the words of our prophet, to a hungry person who dreams that he is eating and satiating his hunger, only to awaken and be surprised that there is no food and that his hunger pangs have not been relieved. Or to one who is thirsty and dreams that he is drinking and quenching his thirst, only to awaken and find that he has nothing to drink, and that his thirst has not disappeared (Jeremiah 15:3). Discharged from employment, deprived of all legal rights, their dignity humiliated and disgraced, thousands of our brothers in Germany have had to flee their native country, to which they pledged their loyalty and dedicated their lives, and to wander like vagabonds seeking refuge in neighboring hospitable lands or in our new national home. Thousands of these once wealthy brothers wander about in strange countries looking for shelter, an embrace, and a piece of bread. [65] האמנים עלי תולע חבקו אשפתות – not long ago German Jews were the leaders of world Jewry, enriching the treasury of their nation with their material and spiritual

---

[65] "They, that were brought up in scarlet, embrace dunghills" (Lamentations 4:5).

wealth. Today, they stand on the edge of a precipice, holding a wanderer's staff. That is the *golus* of our times!

Victory of a Warped Idea

To the already numerous distinctions that divide Europe and the nations of the world into political, religious, national, and economic factions, yet another criterion, a firebrand of discord and hatred has been added, the idea of an Aryan race. The unfortunate racial idea developed and publicized by Gobineau[66] and the pseudo-intellectual Chamberlain,[67] has been resurrected by a strange confluence of conditions of our times, and has won a significant number of fanatic followers and passionate supporters, even in so called intellectual circles. According to this revived theory, considered by scholars of conscience as humbug, the value of a human being is not determined by his spiritualism, intelligence, character, ethical and intellectual standards, but by his race, his ancestry, his blood. Isn't this idolizing of blood, this distinguishing of races on the basis of external bodily features, the height of materialism and blasphemy? Isn't this opposed to the most elementary principle of our faith, as well as that of the Christian religion – that human beings are created in the image of God? But even from an intellectual point of view, this entire theory is laughable, since there is no race in the world that has maintained its racial purity, and there is no nation in whose veins foreign blood does not flow. In contrast to this murky racial theory, we refer with satisfaction to the wise view of the Mishna (Yadayim 4) which states that as a result of destruction caused by wars and migration of peoples during the reign of the Assyrian King Sanherib, the nations were mixed with each other and individual racial characteristics were obliterated.

[66] Arthur de Gobineau, 19th century French author of the "Essay on the Inequality of Human Races," which helped inspire German racism.

[67] Houston Stewart Chamberlain (1855-1927), a British born Germanophile, political philosopher, and son-in-law of Richard Wagner, whose advocacy of the racial and cultural superiority of the so-called Aryans in European culture, influenced German nationalism, especially the Nationalist Socialist movement of Hitler. According to this view of human anthropology, the races of humanity differed in quality. The north Europeans or Aryans ranked highest while Jews were so degenerate and low that they threatened Europe's culture and social fabric.

It is probably superfluous to prove that Judaism never acknowledged a racial theory, and considered purity of faith as the only criterion of human worthiness. As a rule, we have not willingly received members of other faiths into the bosom of Judaism since, as an always persecuted and oppressed minority, we did not want to entice others into our misery, and to harness foreigners to the chariot of our fate. Isn't it strange that even during the darkest hours of our history up to, and even including, our own days, there are converts to Judaism who, through their action, take on the entire burden of our existence? We have always considered it our duty to point out to a potential proselyte, the result of his action for his future life, by saying to anyone considering conversion to Judaism: "What induces you to change your faith? All Israel is oppressed, disgraced, and scorned." If, despite this, he answers that he wants to become a Jew, he is taught all the rules and regulations and, after immersing himself in a ritual bath and satisfying all the traditions, הרי הוא כישראל – he is henceforth considered as a fully worthy Jew from every point of view (Yevamot 47a). A proselyte could rise to the highest positions. Jethro was Moses' father-in-law. Ruth, the daughter-in-law of Moab, was the mother of the house of David. Shemaiah and Abtalion were scholarly authorities and teachers of Hillel (Yoma 71b).

The racial theory will surely not remain without influence on the life of our nation. Who knows whether Lord Balfour was not correct in stating that the next war will be a terrible battle between races? In the meantime, we are evidence of the victory of a warped idea over reason. The Jewish nation, the eternal scapegoat, is the sacrifice and victim of this racial insanity...

Friends in Distress
During the catastrophe that has befallen us, we must not forget the debt of gratitude that we owe to those nations who have given us valuable aid at this most difficult time. Next to England, which has publicly and forcibly expressed its indignation about the recent incidents; next to France, which has charitably given its protection to the refugees; Poland deserves the highest praise among civilized nations for defending our rights in the international arena. We

continue to be grateful to our authorities for not failing to give us support everywhere possible and necessary. Polish consulates have been a harbor for our brothers, a rock on which they could lean in moments of despair. The Polish passport has become a talisman, a good friend, and true protector on the thorny road in a strange land. On the threshold of the New Year, when we look back on the events of the past year, we express our indebtedness to the Government of Poland. A tribute must also be given to our Slavic brotherly nation, Czechoslovakia, for friendship extended to these modern exiles. "Protect the pursued; be their shield" (Jeremiah 15:3).

The only relief and joy amidst the sadness is the fact that we are not alone; that in our misery we have friends....

A Glimmer of Light

A thick fog shrouds the Jewish world. The only glimmer of light that reaches us is from the old-new land. Our brothers in America are yielding under the burden of the crisis. In Europe, hatred and suffering lie lurking in wait for us. But in the Holy Land there is a scarcity of workers. Those, who until now held themselves aloof from helping to rebuild Palestine, are now put to shame by this last plank to salvation. They are returning to Judaism, and its eternal values. After straying among foreign cultures, the erring children are gathering around their old mother. They are leaving foreign palaces in order to seek shelter in our poor hut. Welcome brothers! Welcome! שלום אתא בקר וגם לילה – Shalom, shalom to those near and far; to those from afar who are getting closer to us. Henceforth, we will not be estranged from each other. Together we will work towards a common goal!

"Watchman, what is in the night? What do you hear during the night? אמר שמר אתא בקר וגם לילה – Shortly dawn will be breaking," answers the watchman, "but humanity everywhere is prolonging the night." Let us hope that God will free us from captivity, and put a stop to our suffering.

May the coming New Year bring God's blessings, and good fortune for us all! Amen!

THE BLESSING:
OBSERVATION AT A CEMETERY[68]

"And this is the blessing with which Moses, the man of God,
blessed the children of Israel before his death"

At no time in history has mankind, and especially our sorely tired people, yearned as much for a blessing of good fortune and a cheering, illuminating ray of sunshine, as in our cloudy, present time. Our souls are weighed down by an oppressive, paralyzing feeling that the source of all blessings has dried up for us; that the gates of hope have been barricaded; that the most difficult of all eras of our tragic-heroic history is about to dawn for us. The daily feeling of hopelessness; the oppressive anxiety that constantly burdens our flaccid shoulders like a barely endurable weight, gives this hour, which unites children with parents, a melancholy feeling. It unites us, the bearers of Jewish destiny and Jewish suffering who struggle and fight against all odds, with those peacefully resting beyond all hate and haste. When we knock on the graves of our dear ones; when we stand bent before the hillocks that arch over their mortal remains, it is with a wish in our hearts to receive a maternal or paternal blessing from these holy places. In this inner experience we are similar to King Saul on that night in Ein Dor...

At the end of a tension-filled, ever-changing, and twisting life, King Saul faced the last night of his life before the decisive battle with his archenemy, the Philistines. Only one night, which would determine the entire future of his house, of all Israel, separated him from this last confrontation. As he stood helpless, he saw a vision of an abyss of destruction and ruin. What will the morning bring? How will the battle, to be fought in the mountains of Judah, end? In his despairing uncertainty and feeling of helplessness, Saul decided to call the spirit of the prophet, Samuel. In this hour of need, he wanted to beg for help from the old prophet who had once placed

[68] UGGIK #41, October 1933 7. Original in German.

the crown on his head; who had pressed the scepter of leadership into his hand; who had elevated the shepherd to the throne. When the ghost of Samuel rose from the depths, it reproachfully complained: "Why have you disturbed my rest? Why are you interrupting my blessed sleep with your petty mortal complaints?" Then Saul answered him צר לי מאד – "I feel very oppressed" ופלשתים נלחמים בי – "the Philistines are battling me, and God appears to have withdrawn from me. He no longer answers me, either through His prophets or through visions. That is the reason I called you. מה אעשה – what should I do?."..

We too address you today; you who are separated from us by the impenetrable, mysterious, veil of death. "Why are you disturbing and interrupting our rest with your petty mortal complaints?" comes the reply from the tomb of death. And we answer: "If we add a prayer for a blessing for us, the living, to our prayers for your eternal peace; if, among the tears that we shed for your death, we also shed a tear for our helpless situation, it is only because צר לי מאד – we are sorely oppressed. ופלשתים נלחמים בי – the Philistines are battling against us and the Divine strength, which has accompanied us for hundreds of years, the power of the Torah, our faith, our trust in God is no longer with us. The Prophets are silent; the seers say nothing. That is why we are calling you. מה אעשה what shall we do? That is why we stand with bowed heads at your graves, and pray for your peace and for a blessing from you for us."

וזאת הברכה – and this is the blessing. For a blessing to be effective, three conditions must be met.

The individual conferring the blessing must be worthy and meritorious although we are not to take lightly ברכת הדיוט – a benediction by an ordinary person (Megillah 15). Balak, for example, said to Balaam, not without basis: "I know that it is blessed, if you bless it."

Jacob strove with God's angel until dawn and wouldn't let him go until he had given him a blessing. "I will not let you go until you give me a blessing." He wrestles for the Angel's blessing because it appears to him that this supernatural being is capable of guaranteeing its result.

The second pre-requisite for the fulfillment of a blessing is that the recipient's motive must be pure and that he earned it. Isaac, for example, asked that his son, Esau, prepare his favorite food for him before giving him a blessing. Without effort and merit – there is no blessing! Esau first has to honor and take care of his father. He must do, work, and earn the blessing in order to prove his worthiness...

The third important pre-requisite for the fulfillment of a blessing is the time when it is given. The moment in which the blessing is given must be propitious – עת רצון. The solemn mood, the holiness and loftiness of some extraordinarily deeply experienced event, confers the blessing with a Divine and supernatural power.

We can now understand the opening lines of the *sidra* in a new light: "And this is the blessing with which Moses, the man of God, blessed the children of Israel before his death."[69] All three pre-requisites came together. The person bestowing the blessing was none other than איש האלהים – the man of God. The blessing was not given to a single individual but to בני ישראל – the Jewish people who, through a 40-year ordeal of wandering in the desert, became worthy recipients of the blessing. And the time? לפני מותו – before his death! In the hour of death when, for the last time, the entire spiritual power of a human being shines in all its splendor...

When we plead for blessings from our ancestors, we want to make sure that the pre-requisites for their fulfillment have been met. The time of the Solemn Festivals, that time of supernatural peace that radiates into our monotonous daily routine, is indeed holy. The spirits whom we summon today to request their blessing are also holy. But are we sufficiently worthy to receive their blessing? Can each of us, conscious of our own lives, come to the graves of parents, and ask for a blessing without hesitation; without blushing?

So we take leave from your graves with a feeling of shame that we have not kept all of the promises and pledges we made at our last farewell. Soon, the din and tumult of life will swallow us up once again. Privation, with its bony and ghostly hand, will once

---

[69] Deuteronomy 33:1.

again steal life's joy. Therefore, have patience with your children and with the perfume of the flowers that bloom on your graves. May we receive your blessings so that our souls may become serene and peaceful; satisfied and tranquil...

TRUE HEROISM[70]

We are tired of hero worship. We don't want to play war heroes and soldiers any more. The din of weapons, the jingoism, the Prussian generals, are repugnant to us today. Is not one Edison more valuable to us than all those famous military leaders who spilled so much human blood? Isn't an unknown technician toiling over an invention that will bring blessings to mankind, or a medical scientist trying to find the etiology and successful treatment of a malignant disease, worth more than all the heralded names of war heroes who march through history, from Epaminondas[71] and Mitaldes[72] in ancient times, until the screaming Fuehrer of our own day? We must never bow down before politicians and demagogues who, because of a whim to satisfy their lust for land, or to secure dominance and hegemony for the state they are serving, fan the flames of war fever, incite revolution, organize mass murder. We are tired and disgusted with hero worship. The romantic tales of war heroes and knights leave us, who have experienced it all first hand, cool and apathetic. We are more interested in the common man, than in those who rise to lead nations, those in high positions. The man in the street with his poverty and battles, with his anxieties over daily bread, with his hopes for a better future. The ordinary human being. How he lives and suffers. What his religious thoughts and perceptions are. How he adjusts and functions socially. That person deserves our attention today. He is the hero of our times. Those who valiantly breathe their last on the fields of slaughter are said to be our heroes. Are those who courageously and unflaggingly labor throughout their lives for the benefit of society, anything less? The ones who, in despair, struggle for their survival – aren't they heroes? And the mothers who see their children at the mercy of destitution and don't fall apart from grief; and the poor peddler with hungry eyes, with a despondent cry

---

[70]   UGGIK #45, December 1933, 6. Original in German.
[71]   Theban (Greek) general and statesman about 418-362 BCE.
[72]   Athenian general who defeated Persia at Marathon in 490 BCE.

for a piece of bread, for a livelihood; and thousands upon thousands of unemployed, their hands eager for work, the prematurely aged because they are not working – aren't they all heroes?

And yet — the heroic history, whose commemoration we celebrate at Chanukah, is eternally great and true. And yet—we cannot deny the Maccabees their due, our veneration. When it comes to them, our doubt about the value of war heroes vanishes. Who then were those Maccabees? Who were those war heroes who, to this day, have the power to rise from their tombs and stride before our eyes? Were they professional heroes? Were they strategists, kings, officers, killing experts with respectable names, with detailed, carefully thought out plans containing a firm, proposed program? Not at all! They were unknown, ordinary people, coarse and simple, firmly rooted in the soil, strong in faith, firm in loyalty to their homeland, healthy in thought and emotion...

Matathias and his sons were not aristocrats, but middle class people. It is true that they were Priests. But what did a position of Priest mean in those days, when one could purchase a position as High Priest for a few talents of silver from the Syrian king? The Festival of Chanukah is magical precisely because it is the story of common peasants who became overnight heroes. That is why this festival is so popular, so close, and so personal. It speaks directly to the heart because it doesn't celebrate kings or "supermen" but peasants. Farmers who flock to the Maccabees, flee to the desert, wage war against a well equipped enemy with primitive arms, live in crevices, struggle, die, and – triumph. An unrestrainable strength emanates from this group; an unbroken, earthy strength. These men suddenly seem to jump out of the darkness, stride onto the stage of world history, heave themselves like nettled lions on those who stole their freedom, those who destroyed their Temple, get entangled in a defiant, bitter, dogged, reckless battle and – win. Whence, you ask, does this strength come from? Whence, you marvel, does this defiance come from? Whence is this defiance of death? Man! It comes from injured pride, from desecrated honor, and from broken dignity. That, made their arms hard as steel. People who have been robbed of their honor, who have lost everything. And he, who has lost everything, either becomes a hero or comes to a shameful end. This Maccabean revolt teaches us that a people can tolerate oppression, enslavement, and subjugation for a period of time, but it also teaches us that at a specific moment, when the oppression oversteps its bounds, the cramped people's soul is roused in indignation, raises itself, revolts violently, resists heroically, and then *vae victoribus* – becomes victorious.

But why engage in metaphorical language? Why roam around in the distant past? Why don't we simply, directly and without beating around the bush call out to the hostile world with a voice that will be heard far and wide that we are prepared, nay determined, to persevere and to triumph? That we feel an inner strength to continue, to survive, and to create! That we are ready to defend our honor and to bequeath it, unblemished, to future generations, as we have done throughout thousands of years despite all of our suffering! Your world is cracking at the seams; *vestra domus ardet* your house is burning, and should we be its only sacrificial lambs?

When the shadows grow longer and the night approaches, we Jews light the small Chanukah candles. As the world sinks into chaos and disorder, we – the last Priests of the Temple of love of ones fellow man – want to renew the flame in our candles; to once more give the world a gift of a gospel, since the old one has been forgotten. A Gospel of love, of compassion, of pity...Since you have broken the old tablets we want to chisel new ones for you. New tablets with the old commandments: Do not murder, do not hate...

FOR THE DEFENSE OF THE COUNTRY[73]
To the Jewish Community in Silesia

During this week, devoted to publicity for the Air Defense and Anti-Gas League (LOPP), the Polish government is turning to each of us with a strong appeal for active participation in strengthening, guaranteeing, and ensuring its future independence by enhancing its ability to defend and protect itself. One constantly hears talk about peace and disarmament, especially in recent times, but who among us, despite such talk, does not sense that peace in Europe rests on a flimsy foundation? That any day now, we may be facing a new world catastrophe? We are all familiar with the German proverb: "He, who doesn't possess any virtues, speaks about them gladly, willingly, and often." The constant efforts of ministers from various countries to conclude treaties; the ever present secret diplomatic talks and ad hoc prepared communiqués issued to pacify public opinion; the many journeys; the receiving of national representatives; the futile, useless, and unfortunate efforts of Henderson[74] to find a disarmament formula acceptable to all parties. Aren't these loud but aimless negotiations evidence of the nervousness of those in charge; of those responsible for the future of the world; of danger lurking in the air? The warning words of Jeremiah have indeed come to pass: "They want to cure the ills of my people easily and without effort by announcing Shalom, שלום, שלום, ואין שלום – Peace, peace, but there is no peace!" A kind of curse has been cast on Europe, which has been unable to find a new equilibrium since the last world war and exists in a constant state of tension and in anticipation of big changes in many areas. Poland, which was only recently restored and rebuilt after many years of oppression and misfortune, must be ready for all eventualities. It must be armed and equipped with all types of

---

[73] UGGIK #55, May 1934, 4-5. Original in Polish.
[74] Arthur Henderson (1863-1935), British secretary of state for foreign affairs and winner of 1934 Nobel Prize for Peace for his role in disarmament.

weapons; with the latest technical advances on land and on sea.

We belong to those countries of Europe who want to defend the Versailles Treaty; who don't want to allow any revision of borders. Poland cannot surrender even one tiny bit of land granted by the peace treaty. We belong to those nations which are satisfied with our territorial possessions; which harbor no aspirations of conquest; which plot no revenge; and which don't begrudge peace or goodwill to their neighbors. Our efforts are directed solely at fortifying and consolidating our State. Our government's attention is completely devoted to solving our economic and social problems. But let us not forget that the views and desires of our neighboring countries are very different. We are surrounded by states that dream about radical changes in the geopolitical map of middle Europe; about moving borders; about a new dismemberment; about seizing new territory and enlarging their hegemony. These countries try to conceal their violent intentions and their claws. They show us only a smiling, friendly face, but they are raising their children in a spirit of war by inculcating hatred towards other nations and races and a desire for vengeance in their new generation. They glorify brutal force. They announce, write, and teach about their superiority, and the inferiority of others. Can we simply overlook this and go on with our daily lives? When they form a new educational faculty and announce in their university catalogues that a new curriculum called "Wehrwissenschaft" (military science) will henceforth be a substitute for theology, can we keep quiet? When they secretly, and now openly, arm themselves, and thus scoff at all agreements, can we passively and indifferently ignore this and allow ourselves to be hypnotized and our vigilance weakened by the empty platitudes of their propaganda ministry? Whatever success our Foreign Minister has recently had in the international arena, and the fact that countries are beginning to be concerned with Poland and contend for her friendship, is due primarily to the strength of our army, an important factor in the calculation of our enemies.

In religion we differentiate two relationships between man and God. We speak of *amor dei* – love of God. We consider love of God; being overwhelmed by a yearning for perfection and purity;

animated by a thirst for reaching the highest level of inner spirituality, the deepest expression of religion, which can be achieved by only a very few philosophers and prophets.

We are also familiar with another emotion towards God; another way for man to relate to God — fear of God; fear of God's judgment; dread before His majesty; anxiety about His punishment. This emotion plays an important role in the spiritual and practical lives of many of us. It influences our behavior by restraining our passions and softening and mitigating the impulses of our instincts.

These two emotions, love and fear also shape our social life and are deciding factors in international understandings. Our prophets, and the most worthy and noble nations, which modeled themselves on their teachings, dreamed of an era of the brotherhood of people; an era when love would link people together; an era when people would respect and honor each other purely out of love and not based on calculation or mutual fear. Unfortunately, that era is still in the sphere of visions and dreams. In the meantime, the power of an armed nation is the only measure of its significance and value in the world; the only document that entitles it to participate among the nations that constitute the Areopagus[75] of the world. In the meantime, recognition and esteem are bestowed only on those nations that, in an eventual "war game," are able to unleash armed power. On that playing field, Poland still has a large assignment. Do our neighbors love us? I doubt it. Does our relationship depend on love and sincerity? No! They don't like us but they are beginning to fear us; they are beginning to value us; to count our legions and our stocks. Oh wonder! אבן מאסו הבנים – the stone that they scorned until now, has become the cornerstone of the new Europe.

Speaking of the possibility of a future war, we cannot imagine the magnitude of the devastation and destruction; of the suffering and catastrophes, which such a war would cause with today's technical development in modern warfare. The terrain of battle is ever widening. In the middle ages, they fought only on land and wars sometimes lasted tens of years because wars were not fought

---

[75] Hill of Ares west of the Acropolis where the highest court sat, hence "court."

with such enthusiasm and obstinacy, such fanaticism and cruelty as now. The outcome of a battle was then dependent exclusively on the numerical strength of the army and the ability of its leaders. With advancement in knowledge, the conflagration of war was brought onto the sea and thousands of victims found their graves under the waves. Now, we are on the brink of a new phase in the technique of war. The angel of death will now be hiding in the clouds. The pure air that we breathe will be infected with poisonous gases that will seep into our homes, will penetrate the remotest corners, and bring with it death and decay. Air warfare will not differentiate old from young, men from women, children from adults, civilians from soldiers. We speak with great anxiety in our heart about how man abuses his ingenuity and his mind, that sublime gift from God, in order to invent ever newer and more powerful methods of destruction. But our work is not over. We must prepare ourselves, become educated, and adapt ourselves for this terrible battle. We must arm ourselves with knowledge about air defense, about defense against gas, and increase funds so that the State can build an air force.

This week of publicity about LOPP should become a week for us to become aware of our obligations towards the State; a week, during which we must awaken an interest in, and understanding of, the goals of LOPP in our public.

By defending the State, we are defending our children and ourselves. In financially supporting the League for the Defense of the State, let us remember that our ideal is, and always will be, peace and harmony, brotherhood and love. Our vision is set in the distance; our eyes are fixed on Messianic times about which our prophet pronounced:

"And they will turn their swords into plowshares and
their spears into pruning hooks"

לא ישא גוי אל גוי חרב ולא ילמדו עוד מלחמה

"Nation shall not lift up sword against nation and
they shall no longer learn war"

(Isaiah 11:4)

5694-5695 [1933-1935][76]

דע מעין באת ולאן אתה הולך
Know whence you came and where you are going

In the following brief outline, we do not intend to review all the events and incidents that occurred in the Jewish world in the course of the past year. The chariot of our history is racing forward with dizzying speed, and changes are taking place in our lives like patterns in a kaleidoscope. אין רגע בלי פגע – there is not a moment without another misfortune. Our destiny is spinning like a vortex, and the earth is shaking under our feet. When there is finally a moment of relaxation of tension and relative tranquility in one country and a dim flicker of hope for a better tomorrow is kindled in our hearts, a new flame of hatred suddenly bursts out in another corner of the world and, once again, we are shaken. But even more painful and tormenting than the constant blows and wounds, which Providence has not denied us, is the uncertainty and the instability of our circumstances; our concern and feelings of insecurity about the future. In truth, if we examine the chronology of events of just the last few days, there comes to mind the saying of our sages: "If we wanted to scrupulously write the history of our sufferings, there would be insufficient time" (Shabbat 13). Who could possibly recount all the incidents of humiliation of Jewish honor, of disgrace and slander of the Jewish name, or of denigration of the Jewish faith? In every land where we reside, the situation takes on a slightly different hue. But a few examples from recent events will have to suffice.

Deluge

Glancing back over the past year, our attention is first of all drawn to the great catastrophes that have befallen our country, which have destroyed and devastated vast areas, turned the fruits of human labor

---

[76] UGGIK #63, September 1934, 5-6. Original in Polish.

into rubbish and garbage heaps, and annihilated priceless fortunes and the hard earned property of those closest to us. In addition to the general economic depression, which hovers above us like a nightmare, bending us to the ground under its burden, and darkening the horizon of our lives with gloom and foreboding; in addition to the plague of unemployment, which grinds down the exhausted human being and forces thousands of people who pray for work into an enforced vacation; in addition to all these, unbridled nature has attacked our land. Unfettered nature with its fury and strength has dealt us an especially painful and sorrowful blow. Frothing waves have left their banks and beds and have flooded fertile, fruitful, blessed and life-giving areas of our land, our homes, and human habitations. Both humans and animals find their graves in the surging, whirling waters. At the approach of the angel of death emerging from the depth of the waves, many of our brethren cry out in despair: "Lord, God, why have you deserted me?" (Psalm 22). Colorless lips whisper in dying fear: "Help me O God, for the waters are come in even unto my very soul – כי באו מים עד נפש – I am come into deep waters, and the flood overwhelms me "(Psalm 69). Climbing to high ground, grasping onto tree limbs, searching for shelter and safety wherever they could find it, they direct their vision towards God, the only support and pillar for a person in distress and danger, pleading for salvation and deliverance. On the heels of this catastrophe follow the ghosts of starvation and misery. Where only yesterday wealth ruled, today poverty and wretchedness reign. But doesn't our tradition teach us to be thankful to God for the bad as well as the good? For punishment as well as for kindness? (Berahot 54) I ask this as a rhetorical question since I am influenced by the story of Job of how, in a specific instance, one can fulfill this obligation while overwhelmed by misfortune. But must we really thank God for sending us misfortunes, for suffering sacrificial losses, for the enormity of the destruction? Isn't it enough that we not grumble or complain at such times? That we not rebel against our Father during times of such great suffering? That, like Job of old, we don't curse our fate? Must we also thank God for the evil that He has heaped on us?

However, our teachers were not mistaken. Misfortune does indeed show us the goodness of God. Our hearts are truly filled with gratitude to God when we hear stories of the heroic behavior of people affected by the flood; of examples of true love, of individuals who, with heroic generosity, endangered their own lives in order to help and save others; of feelings of partnership and brotherhood, which enveloped everyone; of instances when Christians were saved by Jews and Jews by Christians. Tragically, this misfortune has destroyed human life and property. But it has saved our faith in man. Once again, here was proof that man is essentially good. In the face of death and the threat of common danger, all artificial divisions fall; voices of hate and discord are silenced; prejudices are dispersed; ill-will and mutual distrust disappear and the true nature of man takes their place. Feelings of pity and humanitarianism, usually hidden deep in the human heart and throttled and stifled by the daily battle for mere existence or by hypocritical demagoguery, reveal themselves. Let us be grateful to God for these sparks of light in the midst of the clouds of misfortune; for these manifestations of human goodness.

Once Again — Blood...

When we greeted the New Year at this season last year, we did not anticipate or expect that it would bring us such disillusionment; so much suffering, and anxiety. Cries and wails of despair from our oppressed brothers reaches us from almost every corner of the world, from every direction, from every place of the globe in which our nation is dispersed and scattered. Voices calling for help, rescue, and assistance, in the face of threatened extermination. מקצה הארץ אליך אקרא – sad tidings are heard from distant regions. Jews in Algiers became victims of Arab mobs. The "made in Germany" venom is penetrating the remotest corners of the earth. This madness of furious, passionate hatred, disseminated and propagated by an ignorant press, is spreading to ever-wider areas, poisoning ever more souls, and darkening the still sober minds of nations. We alone destroy order with falsehood. We alone are responsible and guilty for all economic and political catastrophes and turmoil. Just as once upon a time, in the middle ages, we were accused of poisoning wells, of spreading contagious diseases that deprived thousands of innocent people of life, so today they are accusing us of treason, of international conspiracies, and of destructive tendencies.

The warning words of the Torah have been fulfilled: "You shall grope at noonday, as the blind gropes in the darkness and you shall not make prosperous your ways; and you shall only be oppressed and robbed כל הימים – all the days ואין מושיע – and there shall be none to save you." (Deuteronomy 28:29) Our misfortune lies in the very fact that we have been plundered and oppressed "all the days"- always, and everywhere, from time immemorial. Concealed here is the answer to the question, why is there "no savior"? Why doesn't anyone intercede on our behalf? Why doesn't anyone rush to give us aid?

If a nation, living under normal conditions is suddenly struck by misfortune, everyone will give it a brotherly hand. Everyone would consider it an obligation and an honorable and ethical imperative to provide such a nation, touched by misfortune, with protection, care, and rescue. If a rich and wealthy person suddenly loses his fortune and becomes impoverished, everyone rushes to support and help him. For only recently, he was shining with the luster of wealth, success, and abundance. A sudden reversal in his luck, a sudden change in his life, a downfall from the summit into the abyss awakens feelings of pity and sympathy in the hearts of his acquaintances, who willingly offer him their help, fearing and trembling at the same time for their own luck; worrying about their own future, since גלגל הוא שחזר בעולם (Shabbat 131) – the wheel of life turns without interruption. And who knows what tomorrow may bring? If, on the other hand, we see a beggar dressed in rags, born into poverty, who has spent his entire life in misery, always dependent on other people's pity and never on his own strength; would his misery be able to move us to the same degree? Shock us in a similar manner? We walk by the beggar standing on a street corner with indifference. His cry does not move us. His misery does not awaken much pity in us. We have long ago become accustomed to the sight of this misfortune. Yesterday, the day before yesterday, from almost time immemorial this beggar has stood on the same spot, on the same corner of the street, pleading with people for help...

From time immemorial, the nations of the world have viewed us in the same manner as we see this beggar. From time immemorial, we have pleaded, begged, appealed for help, for relief, for pity. From time immemorial, we have shown our wounds, displayed our scars, cried out. In the words of Isaiah (1:5): "From the sole of the foot even unto the head there is no soundness in it; but wounds, and bruises, and festering sores... On what part will you yet be stricken?" But, like the pleading of that beggar, our cry remains unanswered. For they have become accustomed to our lamentations. They have become accustomed to the sight of our misery. The prophecy of the Torah has been fulfilled: "You will be oppressed and plundered during all the days and it is exactly because of this, that no one will help you."

Once again Jewish blood is spilled. This time in Algiers. Let us pray to God that this will be the last time that innocent Jewish blood is spilled. Once again a wound is opened on the Jewish body. May it soon be healed!

Collective Effort

For years, the will of our people has been concentrated on the feverish task of rebuilding Palestine. The worse the status of Jews in some European countries becomes, the timelier is the issue of a National Home, and the more urgent the need for its implementation. At this time, three problems are the core of our interest and stubbornly demand a rapid resolution: Free emigration, unity in the Yishuv, and finding a *modus vivendi* with the Arabs. These three problems are, in reality, linked into one unbroken totality. Only a united and consolidated Yishuv will be capable of absorbing large-scale immigration and only the numerical growth of the Jewish community will be capable of resolving issues about which various factions are engaged in passionate battle with each other. Even relationships with the Arabs will enter a peaceful track only when Jews cease being a "quantité negligeable" and come to represent a real power.

The Jewish vocabulary has been enriched during this past year by a new phrase – "illegal immigration." Masses of Jews are knocking in desperation on the closed gates of Palestine. But these gates open only for those armed with the appropriate certificate, or with a key of pure gold, which can open all doors the world over. It has, unfortunately, been forgotten that the oldest certificate belonging to every Jew is in the Bible. "And the Eternal One promised Abram...this entire land which you see, I will give to you and your progeny for ever" (Genesis 13:14-15). "Once again the Holy One appeared to him (Isaac) and promised: 'Stay in this land and I will be with you and I will bless you, and moreover I will give to you and to your progeny all these lands and I will keep my promises that I swore to your father Abraham'" (Genesis 26:2-3). "And God appeared anew to Jacob...and God promised him...'the land that I gave to Abraham and to Isaac, I will give to you and to your children after you'" (Genesis 36:12). This certificate, in triplicate, was written in the prehistoric past, before there were Englishmen in the world, and will outlast all storms and shocks, all capricious governments and transient powers. Many imperial powers will disappear into the dustbin of history and many nations will be erased from the face of the earth, but these words will always remain alive. Compared to this, what does the new phrase "illegal immigration" mean?

All parties finally agree on the need for internal consolidation and the closing of ranks. However, lasting inter-party peace will only be possible when all are willing to compromise in solving the most vital problems of the Yishuv. Peace, achieved by total victory of one party with the destruction of the opposition, is not only immoral but also dangerous since it violates and destroys the views and rights of the weaker minority and bears within it the spark of a new war. In order to protect ourselves from the ever more extreme, inflammatory, and radical claims of the various parties, we must gradually return to the elementary, common and original principles of choosing the middle path – *aurea mediocritas!*

Our increased vigor and accomplishments have helped to ignite and inflame Arab-Jewish relationship. To the list of reasons for the dislike of Jews prevalent among Arabs, must now be added a feeling of envy and jealousy at the sight of our success. Throughout hundreds of years, the land lay dead as if covered by a shroud. And suddenly, the earth, touched by Jewish hands, rises from the dead and takes on a new appearance. New settlements arise. The land loses its scowling physiognomy and smiles encouragingly to its children. Is it our fault that the people who have been here, who until now have been its only masters, did not have the will or were not capable of charming the land into blossoming? History repeats itself. Our Holy writ tells us: "And Isaac sowed in that land, and found in the same year a hundredfold; and the Lord blessed him ... And Abimelech said to Isaac, 'go from us; for thou art much mightier than we" (Genesis 26:12,16). The continued strengthening of the Yishuv bothers and frightens our neighbors. The mandatory power, in the meanwhile, takes advantage of this division, according to the old tried and true principle: *Divide et impera* (Divide and rule).

Quo Vadimus

Our outlook, at least for the foreseeable future, is foggy and our situation confused. The critical status of our people is characterized by pauperization of the masses in the east, loss of equal rights by our brothers in the heart of Europe, and a worsening political situation in Eretz. The general financial decline and the extreme poverty of so many Jews is but one link in the chain of the universal economic crisis that embraces all countries and nations. This crisis has, however, dealt us an especially painful blow since the foundation of our existence was frail even during times of prosperity. Our modest wish is that there should at least be an economic stabilization so that uncertainty may disappear. We wouldn't even dare to dream about an improvement in our "standard of living" for the coming year.

On the other hand, one would dare to hope that racial hatred in our neighboring country has reached its peak and that the frothing waves of anti-Semitism will slowly abate. The nonsense of the bloodthirsty press about the omnipotence of international Jewry is convincing ever fewer deluded people. The masses who have been led astray will soon wake with a start and will see through the false games of their ringleaders. קושטא קאי – truth finds a way to reveal itself, and is eternal.

As we cross the threshold of the New Year, we draw a warm and plaintive prayer from the depth of our heart, that God protect us and vouchsafe us in the future from persecution and misfortune; from humiliation and suffering. Let us, at last, find peace and good fortune and let our mutual wish, לשנה טובה תכתבו, be fulfilled.

HAMAN'S ARGUMENTS[77]

> "Then Haman said to King Ahasueras: 'There is a certain
> *people scattered and dispersed among the other peoples...*
> *whose laws are different from those of any other people*
> *and who do not obey the King's laws; and it is*
> not in your Majestys'interest to tolerate them."
> (Esther 3:8)

Thousands of years have passed since Haman expressed his anti-Semitic opinion in these concise sentences. He must be given credit for being the first to expound the theory of Jew-hatred in a concise and clear form, understandable even by an amateur. A modern professor, a graduate of one of today's schools of hatred would surely have presented the King with a long, annotated, "scientific" discourse. In his right hand he would hold a measuring tape and other appropriate instruments for the exact measurement of the skull and other "distinguishing" parts of the human countenance created in the image of God. In his left hand he would be clutching a Bible and a folio of the Talmud, in order to demonstrate, on the basis of false, misunderstood, and distorted citations that Jews are a foreign, harmful element in the State. Haman is modest and frugal in his choice of argument. What purpose do long speeches serve? After all, even the long speeches have the same short purpose: *Judeam dlendam esse* — the Jew will burn.

I must confess that the primitive, naive Jew-hatred appeals to me more than the phlegmatic, systematic, scientifically embellished expert theory peppered with Talmudic citations. Don't you sense how careful Haman is? He doesn't maintain that Jewish laws are worse or inferior. Only that they are different. He does not want to make a value judgment since he doesn't consider himself to be competent or qualified to evaluate the Jewish religion. He does not wish to delve into whether it is better or worse. The fact that it is "different," disturbs him. Our "learned" enemies of today are not

---

[77] UGGIK #75, March 1935, 7-8. Original in German.

content with this. They want to defame and degrade us. First, they proclaim a sentence of death for our spirit in order then, with a clear conscience, to bury our physical existence. In Haman's days, the Jew could escape his harsh reality into the world of the spirit. Here, in the spiritual world, he could be free of all burdens and distinctions. But in our day, the ghost of inferiority follows us everywhere. Every creation that owes its existence to Jewish genius is stamped as inferior. Despite the fact that the spiritual development of humanity has hung a gown of science around Jew-hatred, it stands up to critical examination as flimsily as the arguments of Haman.

Since our "friend" Haman formulated his point of view so briefly and succinctly, a commentary is not totally superfluous. He was not, after all, such a simple, uncomplicated enemy of the Jews. We must place each of his words under a magnifying glass in order to examine them carefully.

"There are a people, scattered and dispersed among the nations." Haman saw before him a people with certain ties and signs of nationhood. That could not easily be denied. And yet, among themselves they are not united. What then, holds these individualistic *golus* people together? A nation and yet not a nation! Splintered and dispersed, cleft and fissured – without a land – and yet, a nation. Where does one search for a solution to this puzzle? People who do not possess a state but nevertheless think in state-like terms, even if they don't belong to the party advocating for a "Jewish state." In their schools, they study the laws and dimensions of the Temple building as if it were still standing in all its glory. When, after his downfall, Haman is looking for Mordechai, where does he find him? In the schoolhouse. And what is Mordechai doing there? He is explaining the specifics about the Omer sacrifices and the way they used to be brought in the Holy Sanctuary in Jerusalem to his students (Midrash). As if the question had a burning contemporary reality. A most peculiar people! They speak of their King David in such a moving and animated fashion – as if they had seen him only yesterday. Space and time are strange notions for them. History tells us that Nebuchadnezzar destroyed the Temple and the altar in Jerusalem, but the Jews simply do not want to acknowledge this fact.

For them, Jerusalem remains Jerusalem! And the Temple remains the Temple! Everything remains. Just as before. That is what Haman sees. That is what Haman hears. And he cannot understand it. That is why he said to his King: "There is a nation, scattered and dispersed among the nations." Scattered, and yet, a nation. Living among the nations, and yet, itself a nation. Acquiring attributes from all nationalities, and yet, possessing its own undeniable national characteristics. A strange, unique, creation! Perhaps a religious community? A creed? ."..Whose laws are different from other nations." I have also studied their ancient historic writings, Haman asserts. Their legislation. The sources of their religion. And this also is not clear. They do not possess their own theology in the usual sense of the word. Their Torah is a compilation of religion, law, practice, government organization, morality, social ordinances, and humanitarianism. Don't they have their own jurisprudence to this very day? Doesn't their spiritual leader make decisions regarding religious as well as civil juridical matters? Their religious code, the "Shulchan Aruch," is divided into four parts that deal with liturgy and festivals; allowed and forbidden foods; laws of marriage; and issues of civil law. They are indeed more than a religious community. The concept of a creed is too narrow for them. Their laws are very diverse. Religion and law flow together. The word "zedaka" in their language means support of the poor, piety, and justice since support for the poor signifies for them an equalization of social differences and therefore represents an act of justice. Where can we find a sentence similar to one that appears in Exodus 22:25? "If you take your neighbor's garment in pledge, you must return it to him before the sun sets; it is his only clothing, the sole covering for his skin. In what else shall he sleep? Therefore if he cries out to me (God), I will pay heed for I am compassionate." There is no mention here of a threat from the executive force of the government. There is no talk of punishment by the police. Instead, there is an appeal to emotion. You have taken the poor man's garment as a pledge. See, night is approaching; he will freeze and call to God in his anguish. And God will hear him. Because He is compassionate. Therefore, give him back the garment before the sun sets. That is the argument presented by the Jewish codebook. Is this a juridical law? A religious commandment? An appeal to humanitarianism? An ethical dictum? It is all of these! It is a teaching of the Jews,"...whose laws are different from those of other nations." Haman was right. They are indeed different. How different!

We are now better able to understand the discussion between Moses and his father-in-law, Yithro. Yithro, a Midianite priest, comes to the wilderness and sees the Jews streaming in hordes to Moses seeking his adjudication of legal issues. The activity of the Jewish leader displeases the Midianite priest. "What is this that you are doing with the people? Why are you sitting here and all the people stand around you from morning until night? You, Moses, the herald of a great religion, Israel's Prophet, are occupying yourself with the small, insignificant daily quarrels of your brothers? We did not do this in Midian. When I was a priest in my homeland, I did not trouble myself with the common squabbles of the people. I was a theologian, a priest. I lived in higher regions. I stayed remote from earthly matters." "The people come to me to inquire of God. When they have a dispute, it comes before me and I decide between one person and another. And I make known the laws and teachings of God," (Exodus 18:15-16) answered Moses as if to say that the boundary between religion and law is faint for us. Our laws are indeed different...

"...And they do not obey the King's laws." That is a lie! Jews have always respected the laws of the land. We always considered the state law to be supreme – דינא דמלכותא דינא. We have never done anything, overtly or covertly, against the state. We have always placed ourselves at the service of the state, whenever and wherever we were asked. Haman is lying when he says that Jews have rebelled against the state. "God has administered an oath to the Jews that they scrupulously fulfill their obligations to the nations of the world" (Keth. 111). We have faithfully fulfilled this oath. Haman deliberately twists the truth. Don't the Hamans of the world always twist the truth?

"...And it is not in your Majesty's interest to let them live." Not perhaps in the interests of a mortal king. But it has pleased the King of Kings, who alone decides over life and death, to keep us alive. He has given us the strength to persevere, despite persecutions. May He continue to protect us and frustrate the malicious plans of Haman and his followers.

JEWISH CHILDREN AS MARTYRS[78]
On the 9th of Av

In every age, the voice of children is drowned by the energetic, pompous noise of grown-ups. Grown-ups make war. Grown-ups make history. Grown-ups write history. It is of course their interpretation, from their point of view. *They* fought. *They* made peace. *They* suffered. But no historian knows how to describe the suffering of children. They bloom like flowers and decorate our paths of thorns. And, just like flowers, they are often trampled underfoot by the relentless march of ruthless events. Quietly and without a sound. They fade rapidly because they need much sunshine and don't receive it. Everywhere, there is only haze, shade, and a sorrowful darkness...Created by adults and brought into the world through their transgressions! Their souls shatter easily because they need so much joy and have none. Everywhere, there is only sorrow, anxiety, and distress...Conceived by adults; their presence is their fault. They age early because they need so much freedom, and have none. Everywhere, – only oppression, bondage, and persecution...Pushed by grown-ups and camouflaged under a veneer of their degenerate morality! Born into a cold, joyless, and subjugated world, they carry the burdens that we impose on them. But their voice, that thin voice of children, is not heard. For grown-ups have no time. Their heroism remains unacknowledged. For, after all, no weapon glitters in their tiny hands. Grown-ups can be so easily deceived. They are certain that heroism resides only in the mouths of cannons and on the sharp edge of polished knives. "Children cannot be heroes," say the grown-ups, who make and write history. "Children can be heroes, if they are taught heroism," answers an echo from bygone days...

On this 9th of Av, we want to visit the grave of the unknown Jewish child-hero. Shh..., quiet, we are entering the ancient Jewish children's cemetery...

---

[78] UGGIK #85, August 1935, 4-5. Original in German.

I

"When you pass through water, I will be with you" (Isaiah 43:2)

A ship is on the high seas with 400 Jewish children, boys and girls who are being sent by a heartless tyrant into the unknown. Behind them is a destroyed homeland and ahead of them, an ignominious future. In distant lands, across the sea, they are to fall prey to dishonor and prostitution. Now, they are still pure and untouched by carnal, sensual pleasures. But they have already been half awakened from their youthful innocence. The disgrace into whose arms they are being led is beginning to dawn on them immaturely but darkly. Where could they flee? The waves of the ocean are motioning that they are their only escape; their only shelter. Therein lies a solution and freedom...Their childish eyes are fixated on the alluring ocean floor. They are filled with an indescribable fear. Fear of death? No! They are acquainted with death. They are no longer afraid of it. They met death on the streets of Jerusalem when it robbed them of their fathers and mothers and subdued the young warriors. No, they are afraid of God's punishment. Jewish law prohibits suicide. The following passage was impressed on them in school: "He who commits suicide, loses his portion of the world to come." Should they dash their hope of resurrection into the depths, together with their lives? Doesn't this suddenly noticed means of escape from the disgrace in store for them mean eternal annihilation and condemnation? Helpless, they look to the oldest and wisest among them. And this one frees their afflicted souls. Relying on a verse in Psalms, he predicts happiness and a reward for his companions in misfortune. "I will drag you out of the lion's jaws," says God "and from the bottom of the sea." Doubt and fear are immediately abolished. A supernatural radiance lights up their faces. Quietly, the girls plunge into the sea. They are followed by the boys. The following scriptural words are applicable: "For your sake, O Lord, we have daily surrendered our life; we are like a lamb, led to the slaughterhouse."

Bloody red, the sun sets in the west. Trembling, its last rays fall momentarily on the body of the youngest before he too is swallowed by the waves. Four hundred children's souls hang suspended against the red evening heavens. The empty ship continued into the night...(Gittin 56).

II

"Strength arises out of the mouths of children" (Psalms 8:3).

The Roman Imperator sits on his throne in a large, expansive hall. Rome's generals and famous commanders surround him. The walls are brimming with gold and war booty. The campaign against Judea has come to a successful conclusion. Jerusalem has been reduced to rubble. The Temple has been burned. Jackals howl at night where once the holy altar stood. The spoils of this war were rich.

But why does a barely perceptible shadow cross Caesar's face? Why is there a wrinkle of dissatisfaction around his lips? Doesn't he have every reason to be completely happy?

The great conqueror whom all the people hail feels that he has been beaten. His pride and vanity have been offended. It is impossible to vanquish this tiny Judean people. Hasn't he leveled their homes, plundered their belongings, and desecrated their holy places? Nevertheless, they continue to maintain the same stubbornness and tenacity. They cannot be dissuaded from worshipping their invisible God who has obviously deserted them. No power has been able to force them to worship the powerful Caesar. He knows that they respect him. But, despite being beaten and placed in shackles and chains, they remain proud and self-confident. They recognize no man as their master; their prayers are directed only to God. It would have satisfied him if, at least superficially, they showed him the same divine reverence as all the other subjugated nations. But they refuse any form of obeisance. Even their children are unbending and fight for their faith like lions. He wants to try one more time. Shouldn't he, who has conquered and held dominion over lands and seas, be able to bring the mother and her seven children, whom he has captured, to their knees? He will deal with them gently, yet cruelly. He will infatuate them and terrify them with threats. They will whimper and worship him as a god. "Bring them in, one at a time," he orders his servant.

The children stand huddled around their mother in front of the palace. The mother's face is rigid and unemotional. Will her children be able to endure the test? Will they be able to withstand the temptation? Had she planted the faith in the God of their ancestors deep enough in their hearts? Would the religious upbringing that she gave them be strong enough to withstand the seductive attractions of Caesar's court? Soon, the king's courier approaches to take them. She lifts her maternal hands, and quietly blesses her children: "May the Lord bless you and protect you.".

A Jewish child stands at the foot of the throne, facing the king. The child's dazzling beauty momentarily forces Caesar to lower his eyes. What an uncanny power radiates from the child's flaming eyes! The eyes of the Minister and the servants are fixed expectantly on this child who stands totally unaffected. Caesar collects himself. He must not become sentimental. He has to remain stern.

"Convert to our faith," Caesar's voice is both harsh and inviting.

"Our Torah states: 'I am the Eternal One, your God!' We are not allowed to worship other gods," the child answers firmly and without fear.

The constable immediately seizes the child and leads him out. He will pay for his steadfastness and faith with his life.

Six are prepared to die a martyr's death. The last one now comes before Caesar. Outside, the mother stands alone.

"Renounce your faith!" The voice from the throne is almost gentle and imploring. If only this last child could be convinced...

"We have promised our God that we will never exchange Him for another," answers the last of the seven children.

As he is led to the place of execution, his mother saw him, and kissed him. "Go, tell father Abraham that whereas he was prepared to offer one son to God, I have brought Him seven children!"

When the mother follows her children in death, a heavenly voice rings out: אם בנים שמחה – Mother and children are united in joy" (Gittin 56).

III

"Better off were those slain by the sword that those who died by famine"
(Lamentations 4:9).

Whenever suffering becomes most severe and the Jewish people plead in vain for help, the prophet Elijah appears as a comforter and holy messenger. He mingles with the starving masses that fill the streets of Jerusalem, but even he can no longer ward off the disaster since the destiny of his people has been sealed. Years of exile and suffering must follow the misspent hundreds of years of freedom. Idolatry and immorality have led the people to become degenerate. The holy places have been defiled. On every hill there are images of strange gods, against which he fought so relentlessly when he wondered the earth as a zealous prophet and seer of the true religion. But today, he is here neither to threaten and agitate, nor to battle against false prophets as he once did on Mt. Carmel. He has come to the ruins and remnants of the holy city in order to help, and to comfort...

Suddenly, a shrill cry of a child reaches his ears. He turns and sees before him a half-starved boy lying on a dung heap wrestling with the Angel of Death. Full of pity, the prophet bends over the languishing lad.

"What is your name, my child?"

The name of an esteemed family, once among the aristocracy of Jerusalem, is poised on the pale lips of the exhausted boy.

"Would you like to learn a declaration that will restore your life and your strength?"

"Yes", the child, barely audibly, whispers,.

"Then from now on, say this declaration of faith every day: "Hear, O Israel. The Eternal One, our God is one."

The child is startled at the sound of these words. He jerks and with his last ounce of strength says: "Keep quiet! Don't mention that name! I don't know this God! My parents never told me about Him."

With these words, the boy pulls an idol from his bosom, embraces it, and kisses it. As his eyes close, his soul departs. He continues to firmly hold the idol in his stiff hands, whitened by death (Sanhedrin 63).

That is how strong-willed and determined Jewish children are, even in sin. That is how persistent and uncompromising they are, even when they go astray as a result of crimes committed by adults. They die worshipping the ideals taught them by their parents.

What a terrible disgrace it is for parents, to have their children die holding onto an image of a false idol because their parents never taught them about the true God.

What a disgrace it is for a generation, to have their youth, in their very last moment, refuse to accept the truth from the mouths of prophets!

The prophet's words ring out like a last warning; a reminder to return and repent; to contemplate and to atone: "Hear, O Israel. The Eternal One, our God is one!"

The child discards this declaration. He dies with an illusion and a delusion.

"My father and mother told me nothing about this God."...

The portals of the children's cemetery are closing. Deeply moved, we take our leave of the graves of Jewish children – heroes of a bygone day. We find ourselves once again in the heart of Europe in the first half of the 20th century. Today, a Jewish child sees a world of enemies confronting him like once little David faced the giant, Goliath. His martyrdom begins in his earliest school days, where the first principles of racial prejudice are taught. He knows nothing of golden childish dreams since the childhood of a Jewish child is filled with great anxiety about the future.

Jewish children have hardly become conscious of life and joy, when they realize that they are surrounded by enemies; encircled by hatred and distrust and, like those 400 children on the ship, are to be handed over to shame. In which port will that ship anchor? Will they ever be allowed to feel firm land underfoot or will they be irrevocably condemned to perish in the wildly surging waves?

The mother stands outside, like that mother of the small martyrs, frightened and worried, and waits for her child. Will the tyrant on the throne have pity? Today, the Caesar is no longer trying to win over Jewish children's hearts. He no longer tries to convert them to his own faith. He wants to annihilate them. He knows no pity. Sympathy is a stranger to him.

And because of this, Jewish children must once again become heroes. Teach your children the affirmation of one God early, so that in their hour of distress they won't worship false gods and say: "My father and mother told me nothing about a Jewish God." Teach them to bear humiliation with pride; to accept degradation in peace; and teach them, in suffering, never to deny; in an assault from hostile forces, never to lose hope.

Hope in the enlightenment of humanity. Hope in the deliverance of the Jewish people.

II

HUMAN RELATIONSHIPS: BETWEEN 'MAN AND MAN'

Essays in this section explore the Jewish approach to human behavior and interpersonal relationships. In a series of articles on "Jewish Ethical Behavior," Rabbi Chameides emphasized the individual attitudes and behaviors that lead to greater harmony and prevent social discord within the community. Included are a historical examination of the Jewish attitudes to truth, moderation, jealousy, joy, children (written on the birth of his oldest son on September 16, 1932), gratitude, the relationship of the individual to society, and denunciation. The inclusion of the last topic, in which he reviews the Jewish attitude throughout history towards co-religionist traitors, gives one a hint of the types of problems that he had to deal with in Poland of the 1930s. In his view, adherence to Jewish rituals and laws should lead to personal improvement and social harmony. The loftiest theories alone were meaningless if they did not lead to action. He emphasized the universal application of the prophetic message and the unique value of each human being.

What motivated this communal religious leader to write so many essays on this topic? The 1930s were turbulent years for Polish Jews. The economic depression, which began in 1929, dealt the already impoverished Jewish community a severe blow. Thousands of businessmen were forced into bankruptcy, and there was massive unemployment. For example, in Warsaw, the lives of 100,000 Jews (one third of the Jewish population) were dependent on help from the Jewish Aid Committee (Joint). The situation was even worse in the smaller towns and villages. A massive migration took place as Jews were forced to leave the shtetls of Galicia in search for work, and a means of earning a livelihood. The relative stability and prosperity of Upper Silesia, with its rich coal deposits, was a natural attraction for some of these desperate people. The Katowice Jewish community experienced a culture clash between the settled, affluent, cosmopolitan local German Jews, and the poverty-stricken, Yiddish speaking, small-town Polish Jews. This expressed itself in the 1932 community elections to the Assembly of Representatives, whose results were not approved by the Governor of Silesia, probably because they represented the old German-Jewish establishment who were considered insufficiently patriotic to Poland.

The central message of the essay entitled: "And God said, 'Let there be Light,' and there was Light," is undoubtedly contained in the last sentence: "The entirety was good. The dissatisfaction of individual entities could not disturb the harmony of the whole." The message was probably aimed at these very divisions within the Katowice Jewish community.

Rabbi Chameides considered division and discord within the Jewish community the greatest calamity to befall the Jewish people. The problem was not only a local one. Jews in interwar Poland were divided by religious affiliation (religious vs. secular; Chasidim vs. Mitnagdim), political loyalty (there were many Jewish political parties vying for loyalty and votes), opinion on the Jewish future in Poland (Zionists who felt that the only Jewish future was in Palestine vs. the Bund and other non-Zionists who had a vision of a Jewish future as part of Poland), and the role of a Jewish national home in Palestine (Zionists, both religious and secular, vs. Bundists and members of the religious right). The political fragmentation was so great that in some elections to the Polish Sejm (parliament), there were as many as 12 Jewish slates. The result was an ineffectual Jewish representation. This theme is explored in "Unity" and in "And the Life and Death of Moses." Both these essays show Rabbi Chameides' ability to take a Biblical text, and masterfully apply it to problems of his day. In "The Discussion," Rabbi Chameides pleads for civilized discussion when there is a difference of opinion.

The idea of building a Community Center first surfaced in the Katowice Jewish community in 1934. It was to contain a small Synagogue seating 378 men and 230 women, a community hall that could accommodate 600 people, a kitchen, restaurant, a slaughterhouse for poultry, and a ritual bath (mikva). Building was started in 1935 but, due to a lack of funds, was not completed until 1937. "Where Is Our Community Center?" is an appeal for funds to finish the building. Internal community divisions and alienation of the newcomers are discussed as reasons for the lack of community spirit and, therefore, of funds.

JEWISH ETHICAL BEHAVIOR[79]

Ethical behavior has always been a major subject of inquiry and thought for our sages. In the vast Talmudic literature, in the innumerable tomes that contain the most fundamental teachings and principles, which influence our daily lives to this very day, we rarely find metaphysical problems dedicated solely to the consideration and solution of strictly philosophic and theoretical questions. Our sages did not revel in wide-open spaces. They did not usually dedicate overmuch attention to problems that are beyond the horizon of ordinary mortals; that are separated from our creative and suffering reality. Instead, they concentrated their entire efforts on behavior, on finding a religious and moral solution to social and legal conflicts resulting from the condition of man as an individual as well as a member of the society in which he lives and works. In the education and upbringing of the young, the words of Ben Sira (Yer Hagigah 13a; 47c) were emphasized: "Don't examine things that are not accessible to you. Don't try to investigate that which is covered by a veil. Rather, consider what is near to you. Don't get mired in mysteries!" Their attention was directed towards the ground, to the temporal world, even as their hearts wanted to soar heavenward and yearned for a coalition and union with God. For they considered it their strict obligation to protect the purity of the morals of everyday life; to help human beings to resolve life's enigmas as they struggled with the nightmares of their existence and battled their natural inclinations and foibles.

Jewish ethical behavior has a universal character. Its norms and postulates are not intended solely for the Jewish people. Its voice is a call to everyone, without regard to national, denominational, or racial boundaries, to embrace a just and religious lifestyle. Our sages had a beautiful insight into the verse from Job: "I don't allow a stranger to wait out of doors; I open the gate to the wonderer."

---

[79] UGGIK #4, March 1932, 3; #5, March 1932, 5-6; #6, April 1932, 4. Original in Polish.

They interpreted this verse as: "God does not reject any of his creatures. The gate is open, and anyone who wants to, may enter" (Shemot Rabbah 19). The prophets did not address their rebukes solely to their own people; they also addressed the pagan nations, chastising them for their crimes, sins, and transgressions. They never tired of foretelling their day of reckoning and punishment; the day of God's judgment. With great passion, their wounded and yearning souls awaited the blessed day when everyone would recognize the majesty of God, and all human oppression and persecution would cease at last. The words of the last Prophet: "Have we not all one father? Has not one God created us?" (Malachi 2:10) reveal the deep affection, which the prophets had for all human beings created in the image of God. Jeremiah defines his mission in a similar vein: "Then the word of the Lord came unto me saying. Before I formed you in the belly I knew you; and before you came forth out of the womb I sanctified you, and I ordained you a prophet unto the nations" (Jeremiah 1:4, 5).

The issue of trying to define the essence of Judaism was raised very early in our development, in our post Biblical literature. Our Sages devoted much energy in trying to distill the many lessons of Judaism into a single formula; into a brief definition that would contain and be able to express the fundamental thoughts and ideals of our religion, which is so fertile with rules and commandments. Judaism does not limit itself to an attempt to awaken religious feelings in our hearts; it is not satisfied with inculcating within us feelings of love and fear of God, or with the mere establishment of ethical principles. Its essential goal is to inspire its adherents to acknowledge the hegemony of religion in all spheres of life. It wishes to broaden its sphere of influence beyond the narrow confines of the synagogue, and to rule over life in all its breadth and diversity. Its multiplicity of rules and commandments stems from this desire. It extends its protection and supervision over all manifestations and circumstances of life. It therefore enters into nearly all spheres of existence and knowledge and, in addition to strictly ritual and ceremonial rules, it also encompasses legal and social laws. As a result, it was considered necessary, nay even vital, to grasp its spirit and thought in one catchword, in one short and concise sentence which would become a credo, a signpost in the labyrinth of life, and which would guide us in solving new ethical puzzles and problems.

The first who attempted to find such an abbreviated formula of Jewish wisdom was Hillel, who came to Palestine from Babylon around 40 BCE. One time, a pagan came to him and confessed his desire to accept the Jewish religion on condition that he teach him the essence of the religion in as short a time as he could stand on one leg. Hillel answered him: "The major tenet of our religion is 'Don't do to others what is unpleasant to you' and all other rules are only a commentary on this one" (Shabbat 31a). Hillel therefore emphasized ethical behavior as the central tenet of Judaism and subordinated all other parts of our religion to it.

There is another similarly instructive passage in the Talmud (Makkot 23b): "Rabbi Simlai said: God gave Moses 613 commandments... David contracted them to 11 rules (see Maharsha on same) saying:

"God, who shall sojourn in Thy tabernacle?
Who shall dwell upon Thy holy mountain?
He that walks uprightly, and works righteousness,
And speaks truth in his heart;
That has no slander upon his tongue,
Nor does evil to his fellow,
Nor takes up reproach against his neighbor;
In whose eyes a vile person is despised,
But he honors them that fear the Lord;
He that swears to his own hurt, and changes not;
He that puts not out his money on interest,
Nor takes a bribe against the innocent (Psalm 15)

Isaiah reduced the 613 commandments to 6 rules:
"He that walks righteously, and speaks uprightly;
He that despises the gain of oppressions,
That shakes his hands from holding of bribes,
That stops his ears from hearing of blood,
And shuts his eyes from looking upon evil. (Isaiah 33:15).

Then Micah condensed them into three rules saying:

"He has shown, you oh man what is good; and what does the
Lord require of you, but to do justly, and to love mercy,
and to walk humbly with your God?" (Micah 6:8).

Finally, Habakkuk condensed them into one rule saying:

"And the righteous lives by his faith (in God) (Hab.2:4)

Thus it is established that faith in God and trust in Him is the
last link in the chain of regulations and maxims with which our
Sages strove to express the essence of our religion. In the final
analysis, one word, *"Emunah,"* which in Hebrew means faith, trust,
loyalty, and constancy, revealed itself to be the most appropriate
and exact description of the Jewish entity.

Many sublime ethical instructions are concealed in legends like
pearls on the bottom of the sea. Hidden in the background of our
history and Biblical tradition, wrapped in a spirit of deep piety, they
are evidence that our forefathers possessed a high degree of fantasy
and a rich imagination. They are also irrefutable evidence that Jewish
ethics did not remain theoretical or the exclusive property of a few
eminent and highly valued individuals, the select of the people.
Instead, these legends connected the academy and its tightly knit
circle with the wider masses, where they awakened a lively response
in the hearts of plain people who gave expression to the same ethical
outlook, and expressed their enthusiasm in the form of legends and
beautiful stories that were passed from father to son. One such
legend with an ethical motif has been preserved for us in the Midrash
(Yalkut Noah) in the story about Lies and Calamity.

When Lie noticed the oncoming flood, and with it, the end of
the world, it turned to Noah with a request that it be taken along
with the other creatures into the ark. Noah answered: "Undoubtedly,
you have noticed that all the creatures are entering the ark in pairs.
Therefore, search among the living things for an appropriate
companion for yourself." Lie left and, along the way, met Calamity.
Delighted with this meeting, Lie begged Calamity to join it. "And
what will be my reward, if I comply with your request?" asked

Calamity. "Our friendship will bring you much benefit," answered Lie. "I will give you all the wealth that I will attain through my lies." Calamity agreed and they approached Noah, who accepted them as a couple and accommodated them in the ark. Here, Lie started to skillfully practice his profession. It lied to everyone and after a short period of time accumulated much wealth. But whatever Lie earned, Calamity took for himself. This alliance of Lie and Calamity exists to this day. Wealth gained through lies is generally consumed by misfortune.

Thus, Jewish ethics condemns falsehood and makes a harsh judgment about any gain derived from it. The Torah reminds us: "Neither shall ye deal falsely, nor lie one to another" (Leviticus 19:11). Rabbi Simeon ben Gamliel taught: "The world stands on three pillars; on justice, on truth, and on peace" (Avoth 1:18). It was not by accident that truth is the middle pillar, standing between justice and peace. Rabbi Simeon ben Gamliel wanted to emphasize that justice and peace lean on, are dependent on, truth. Neither justice, if not drawn from the spring of truth, nor peace, based on false premises and a hypocritical foundation, can endure for long.

According to the Talmud, (Shabbat 119b) one of the many causes that led to the destruction of Jerusalem and the fall of the Jewish state was a paucity of truthful people; of people willing to sacrifice their lives and property on the altar of truth. "Truth springs out of the earth and righteousness has looked down from heaven," sings the Psalmist (Psalms 85:12). Heavenly righteousness will only be bestowed on us, when truth blossoms among us on earth.

Only one thing is absolute, ideal, unchanging, ceding no concessions, accepting no deviation, and that is truth. Can we, as weak as we are, however even recognize unadulterated and authentic truth? Does it not often appear to us as a multicolored rainbow, which each of us perceives as a different hue? Our sages correctly asserted (Shabbat 55a) that "truth is God's seal"; that only God possesses pure, untarnished truth. Nevertheless we should never forget that the perfect and absolute truth, eternally hidden from mortal eyes, is the sum total of those small, almost elemental truths for which we battle in our daily lives. The mere striving towards this truth ennobles and improves us. "Man cannot perceive me and live," says God, the eternal truth, to Moses. Likewise, the mere thirst and search for truth, the yearning for it, and the waging of an incessant battle in its defense, brings us nearer to it and illuminates our lives with an eternal and divine light.

"If God were to hold all Truth concealed in His right hand, and in his left only the steady and diligent **drive** for Truth, albeit with the proviso that I would always and forever err in the process, and to offer me the choice, I would with all humility take the left hand, and say: Father, I will take this one – the pure Truth is for you alone." (Lessing[80]).

---

[80] Gotthold Ephraim Lessing, Anti-Goetze: Eine Duplik (1778) in: *Werke* Vol. 8, 32-33 (H. Göpfert ed. 1979).

MODESTY[81]

Modesty is a human ornament. The higher a person's position; the more a person towers, intellectually or socially, over others the more that person needs to preserve a measure of personal modesty, self-restraint, and moderation. The insignificance of a human being in the vast universe, his frailty and evanescence, should tame his pride, and fill his heart with humility. Rabbi Levitas taught (Avoth 4:4): "Be exceedingly lowly of spirit, since the hope of man is but the worm" (this refers to his flesh after death).

Maimonides explains this maxim. As is well known, Maimonides opposed extremism in ethics and recommended "the middle road." In his opinion, too much bravado and audacity lead to risky and dangerous behavior, and is as much a deviation from genuine virtue as too much cowardice and timid fearfulness. Between audacity, which often exposes one to danger, and cowardice, which causes one to avoid action altogether, stands the quality we should strive for, namely, judicious courage. Similarly, when attempting to achieve other goals, such as striving for success or perfection, we should act in moderation, always on guard against extremism. But when it comes to pride, Maimonides has a different opinion. Pride is an offense that deserves complete condemnation. Human beings should root it out completely and distance themselves from it as far as possible, so as to lose all attraction for it. As proof, Maimonides quotes the following anecdote from a work dealing with ethics: " A famous scholar was once asked which day was the happiest in his life. 'Once,' answered the pious wise man, 'when I was traveling on board ship at sea, one of the passengers approached me and shamefully insulted me. This inappropriate behavior and insolence from a stranger truly surprised me,' continued the learned man. 'But miraculously, instead of being provoked, I did not feel any anger toward him and I did not feel offended by him in the least. To discover such an indifference to insult within myself, such an

[81] UGGIK #8, May 1932, 3; #9, May 1932, 3. Original in Polish.

absence of pride and conceit, made me very happy and I consider that day to have been the happiest of my life.'"

Certain Talmudic teachers disagree with Maimonides' opinion. According to them, a leader, especially a scholar who heads a school or directs a community, should defend his dignity and not allow his position and authority to be diminished. Self-esteem and self-confidence are not the same as pride (Sotah 5a).

Modesty is often rewarded. When God was about to reveal Himself to Israel in the wilderness, the tall mountains started to quarrel among themselves. Each considered itself the most suitable and most worthy place for the revelation. "Our peaks reach to the very heavens," said Tabor and Carmel "and the majesty of God will undoubtedly rest on us." Mount Sinai stood aside and was silent. It did not expect that God would scorn the heaven-reaching peaks and bestow primacy on this low and relatively modest mountain. But God passed the tall and haughty mountains by and selected Mount Sinai (Midrash. Psalms 68). For thus God promises: "I am with him that is of a contrite and humble spirit; to revive the spirit of the humble, and to revive the heart of the contrite" (Isaiah 57:15). But of the proud it is said: "I cannot abide with him together in the world" (Sotah 5a).

Our sages never tired of reminding the educated person not to boast about his knowledge and education, and not to scorn his neighbor who belongs to a different social stratum. In Yavneh, the Rabbis taught a lesson imbued with a social spirit that gives evidence of their sublime worldview: "I am God's creation as is my fellow creature. I work in town, he in the field. I rush early to my work and he to his. Just as he does not boast about his work (in the soil), neither do I boast about my work (intellectual). And if one person works more than another, it is well known that it is not the amount of work, but rather its intent that ultimately determines its value" (Berahot 17a).

The work of a sage and that of a manual laborer, of a philosopher or field hand, has equal value from an ethical standpoint. God has endowed each of us with certain strengths and abilities. Our obligation is to nurse these gifts and to take great care to make sure that our motives and goals in choosing and executing our work are pure and incorruptible. Every action and each achievement is the manifestation of an idea, and the personification of the motive of the one who performs it. The superiority of the deed, regardless of the human branch of skills it belongs to, is therefore directly related to the purity of the idea and goal.

Modesty is the crown of knowledge (Dereh Eretz Zuta 8). A human being who possesses the most exemplary intellectual characteristics and the best qualities of character but is not modest, can be compared to a house without a threshold (Kalla 3). Such a house appears desolate and destroyed; its entrance is uninviting. A haughty person is similarly inaccessible; his soul is bereft of a threshold. How can one penetrate into its depth? How can one get to know it? How can one extract its collected treasures?

Let us not forget the words of the prophet: "Let not the wise man glory in his wisdom; let not strong man glory in his strength; let not the rich man glory in his riches. But only in this should one glory: In his earnest devotion to Me. For I, the Lord act with kindness, justice and equity in the world; for in these I delight, declares the Lord" (Jeremiah 9:23-24).

GRATITUDE

The kindness one receives in time of need and distress is relatively quickly forgotten. The help given by friends and compassionate people is quickly erased from one's memory. As soon as the affliction of misery ceases; the moment that the misfortune passes and fate smiles once again, feelings of gratitude are extinguished and, together with the gloominess of the past, the memory of friends and charitable individuals who rescued the individual from ruin disappear. A few exceptions here, as elsewhere, only confirm the rule.

Psychologically, this ingratitude may be caused by the humiliation we almost always feel when experiencing acts of kindness. Every grave situation from which we can not extricate ourselves through our own efforts, and which condemns us to depend on the benevolence of others, damages our innate feelings of pride, and is a symbol of defeat whose magnitude is directly related to our need for independence and self-sufficiency. It is therefore not surprising that we remember those defeats unwillingly, as evidence of our dependency. With a combination of dejection and sorrow, we attempt, unconsciously and instinctively, to banish any trace of humiliation that would recur from acknowledging another's kindness. Gratitude therefore turns into a heavy burden that threatens to overwhelm us, and that links us forever to our benefactor, that eternal witness to our helplessness and weakness; that living reminder of our injured pride.

Jewish ethics constantly wages a battle against this ingratitude, and demands that we always remember the nations and individuals who did not deny us help at times of our misfortune and defeat.

JOY[82]

An irresistible will to live has nurtured the soul of our people in all epochs of its existence. This passionate attachment to life, despite our well known suffering and martyrdom, sprang from a hidden inner fountain of creative joy; from a desire to transform and repair reality; from an ever-present consciousness that the seed for improving existence, the possibility of eliminating misfortune and catastrophe from human life, lies in the struggle against each disappointment. Our attachment and incessant flight towards the embers of life is an expression of our faith and hope that we will succeed in transforming the reality of our existence into one of general peace and good fortune; that righteousness will, in the end, triumph over barbarism, and that the light of God will finally be lit in the darkness of a gloomy world.

For us, joy of life has no connection with frivolity, with licentious gaiety and lawlessness. It is rather a quiet, cheerful, inspired harmony and inner satisfaction. "The Divine does not reveal himself to one whose temperament is one of dejection, sluggishness, or lack of restraint...but rather to one who is intoxicated with the joy emanating from the fulfillment of God's commandments" (Shabbat 30b). In order for joy not to be overpowered by the sadness of the surroundings, the Torah commands us that our joy should not be limited to ourselves, but should involve those around us. "And you shall rejoice before the Lord, your God, you and your son, and your daughter, and your manservant, and your maidservant, and the Levite that is within your gates, and the stranger, and the fatherless, and the widow that is in your midst" (Deuteronomy 16:11).

The relationship of Judaism to the world is, therefore, a positive one. Judaism does not regard the world as a vale of tears and misery. For us, the world ought to be a stage for actions; a region of

---

[82] UGGIK #11, June 1932, 4. Original in Polish.

challenges, of goals, and of responsibilities. Let us embellish it; adorn it; lead it to perfection. Woe unto us if we tear down rather than build up; if we destroy rather than create; if we rob the works of God of their beauty; if we root out the flowers from His garden and lay waste His castle! "He has established the earth and arranged it, not as an empty space, but as a habitation (Isiah 45:18). The life of man is tied to his surrounding world to such a degree that all creation shares his joy and as well as his sorrow; is happy with him and worries with him.

"A merciful person benefits himself" (Prov. 11:7). This saying was fulfilled for Hillel. Once, he said good-bye to his students. "Where are you going?" asked the students. "I am going to fulfill a divine act...I am going to bathe." "Is that a divine act?" "Absolutely, you see how much care is given to assure the cleanliness of the statues of the rulers? How then can I, who am created in the image of God not care about my personal cleanliness?" (Vayikra Rabbah 34:3).

But in truth, asceticism and abstinence were not unknown in Judaism. We had our Nazirites and Essenes. And doesn't the Torah itself demand the denial of certain pleasures, abstention from eating certain types of food, and moderation in various spheres? But let us not forget that the aim of these rules was not to suppress or stifle the joys of life, but rather to enhance our vitality, to teach us moderation and self-restraint, to strengthen our power of resistance and inner discipline. A Nazarite, who has voluntarily completed his vow to abstain from drinking wine, is called a sinner by Rabbi Eleazar Hakappar (Niddah 10a), since each person is held responsible (by God) for abstaining and needlessly distancing himself from permitted pleasures (Jer. Kiddushin IV). Rabbi Yose taught: "A person is not permitted to afflict his flesh with excessive fasting since this may weaken him, and thereby diminish his physical well-being so that he will become dependent (by an inability to work) on the benevolence of others" (Ta'anit 22b). Moreover, when the first human being was created it was said, "man became a living soul. Make sure to keep the soul that I gave you alive."

The Jewish sense of optimism was tried and tested more than once. This was especially so after the destruction of the Temple in

Jerusalem, when numbness and insensibility penetrated every joy; when sadness and mourning overwhelmed every Jewish soul. Shocked to the depths by their loss of freedom, some began to voluntarily deny themselves all delights of life, not eating meat or drinking wine. "Can we eat the meat and drink the wine, which constituted the fire offering on the recently destroyed altar of God, which has been turned into a heap of rubbish?" Rabbi Joshua answered them correctly that, using that logic, they should also abstain from and deprive themselves of the most indispensable necessities of life, such as bread, fruit, and water, which were also used for sacrifices in the Temple. Rabbi Joshua thus demonstrated that unrestrained mourning, leading to apathy and pessimism, is absurd. It feeds people's soul the poison of despair, and endangers the nation's very existence. (Bava Batra 60) Israel therefore bridled and conquered its deepest pain. We never forgot Jerusalem. The desperate question, "how can I sing the song of God on foreign soil" (Psalm 137), was never silenced from our lips, but our will to live was not weakened by it in any way. Moreover, we were always reassured and comforted by the hope that, "those who sow in tears, shall reap in joy. Though he goes forth weeping who bares the trailing seed, with song of joy shall he return, bearing home his sheaves" (Psalm 126).

JEALOUSY[83]

Jealousy is primarily caused by differences in material status or intellectual capabilities that create a subconscious chasm between people. A desire to compare oneself to one's neighbor; to win the race; to be recognized in a particular sphere as unique, and to be differentiated from the gray mass, takes a person out of the shadows to a battle arena whose ultimate goal is the defeat of one's coworkers, and attainment of the highest rung of fame and praise. The Aggadah has preserved a legend about jealousy in prehistory, when the world and the heavenly bodies were created (Hullin 60b).

At the time of the creation of the world, the sun and moon were the same size. Both illuminated the world equally. This situation did not please the moon. The moon, therefore, turned to God and complained: "It is impossible for two kings to wear one and the same crown." But instead of the expected elevation, the moon was made smaller, and was humiliated. For God dismissed its jealous and envious complaint saying: "Moon, you are correct! From now on, your light will be smaller and darker than that of the sun." Man had not yet been created, but envy was already devouring God's creation. Is it any wonder then that with the appearance of human beings, quarrelsome creatures who are forever hungry and insatiable, this emotion grew and has gained strength? "Behold how good and pleasant it is when brothers dwell together in harmony!" (Psalm 133). Jealousy knows no boundaries or obstacles. It crosses the threshold of the sanctuary and breaks into the tent of brothers. Driven by jealousy, Cain was the first to stain his hands with his brother's blood. The Holy Book (Genesis 4) notes the background of this ignominious first crime with a few words. These few words are, however, sufficient to unveil the abyss in the soul of man created by the horror of jealousy. "And in the course of time, it came to pass that Cain brought of the fruit of the ground an offering unto the Lord. And Abel also brought of the firstlings of his flock and of

[83] UGGIK #12, July 1932, 5. Original in Polish.

the fat thereof. And the Lord had respect unto Abel and to his offering; but unto Cain and his offering He had not respect. And Cain was very angry and his countenance fell.... And it came to pass, when they were in the field, that Cain rose up against Abel his brother, and slew him." Cain was unable to tolerate that his brother enjoyed a larger measure of God's respect than he. Jealousy guided his cruel hand. Jealousy proved itself stronger than brotherly love, or ties of kinship.

The destructive power of this emotion, about which the poet said, "harsh as the grave is jealousy, its flames are like those of a blazing fire" (Song of Songs 8, 6), is revealed to us several times in the Biblical narratives in all its vividness and demonic power. It can be seen in the struggle of Esau and Jacob over the birthright, and is especially evident in the hatred the brothers bore against their younger sibling, who was protected and spoiled by Joseph's father.

It did not escape the attention of our Sages, however, that jealousy can also often be the impetus to important actions and human progress. "Jealousy among the learned leads to intellectual progress" (Bava Batra 21a). Jealousy is often the incentive and impulse that drives the investigator to new discoveries and intellectual conquests, which he hopes, sometimes subconsciously, will earn him fame and praise. In this way, a human being can ennoble his deeply rooted feelings of jealousy, and transform them into a creative force.

THE INDIVIDUAL AND SOCIETY[84]

Every individual is part of the community in which he lives. He may not cloister himself in a world of self-interest, and separate himself from the community with Cain's shameful words "am I my brother's keeper?"

There is a constant struggle between an individual and his society. An individual's primary concern is, of course, his own existence, and he strives in every possible way to improve his own welfare and live his life in the most comfortable and enjoyable manner. Possessed by an innate egotism, the individual would like to acquire everything for himself and to use the wealth of the world for his own benefit, paying not the slightest attention to the rights of society as a whole, and disregarding the needs of a collective existence. Unable, however, to satisfy his own needs by himself, and gradually coming to the conclusion that without the help of others he will not be able to meet his daily needs, the individual becomes humble, gives up many of his rights in favor of the group, suppresses his impulse for expansion, restrains his selfish will, and becomes a part of a larger association of similar individuals. The struggle between the individual and the group appears to have ceased for the moment, but their coexistence is neither lasting nor permanent. From time to time, it yields to changes and reforms under the influence of social revolutions.

One of the sublime tasks of ethics is, unquestionably, to define the state of coexistence of the individual and the group, as well as their respective rights and obligations.

Communal work is considered by our Sages to be a religious obligation. One who involves himself in communal work fulfills a religious commandment (Jer. Berahot V, I). Furthermore, one is not permitted to devote oneself to communal work for the sake of personal gain; one should perform this solely out of a religious and

---

[84] UGGIK #13, August 1932, 4. Original in Polish.

idealistic motive (Avot II, 2). Misfortune tests the strength of a community. "When misfortune strikes a community, no one may say: 'I will go home, satisfy my hunger and thirst and not allow any distress to disturb my soul'...Instead, everyone's obligation is to participate in the misfortune of the community and to suffer together with others" (Ta'anit 11a).

Every erudite person, and especially anyone who has a high communal position, must in some respects accept responsibility for the mistakes and depravations of the community. "As long as a person lives for himself and does not concern himself with others, he bears no responsibility for them. However, as soon as he accepts the mantle of communal office, he dare not say: 'I accepted this rank for my own benefit but the people are of no concern to me' since the burdens of the people should rest on his shoulders. If he observes one harming another, or if someone sins and he does not hurry to aid the victim, he will bear responsibility." (Shemoth Rabbah c 27). The Midrash (Tanhuma Mishpatim) tells us that when Rabbi Ammi was on his deathbed, he started to cry. A student, surprised by this, asked his master: 'Rabbi, why are you crying? Wasn't your life a continuous series of good deeds? You avoided all schisms, and you never wanted to accept a communal position.' 'That is exactly why I am crying,' answered the ill master. 'I will be held responsible for not finding a solution to the contentious issues of my brothers.'

Hillel summarizes the interdependence of the individual and the group in a few words: "If I am not for myself, who will be for me? But if I am only for myself, what am I?"

THE CHILD[85]

In Jewish tradition, a child is surrounded with a halo of holiness and purity. Since our tradition does not acknowledge hereditary sin, no sin or transgression has yet defiled its spotless soul (Bamidbar Rabbah 4). Before a child enters this world, angels reveal the secrets of the Torah, which the child forgets at birth, and God's voice implores it to be devout and not inclined to evil. "Know that God is pure, his servants are pure, and your soul is pure. If you keep the soul, which has been given to you pure, you will be blessed, but if you don't keep it pure, you will be rapidly deprived of it" (Niddah 30b). The pious suffer for the sins of their generation. However, if a society is so morally degenerate as not to include any pious and righteous people, then the children atone for the general depravity (Shabbat 33b). Children who die shortly after birth, are rewarded and share with adults the eternal life of the world to come (Sanhedrin 110). A Kabbalistic tradition teaches us that the angel of the Torah, Metatron,[86] surrounds himself daily with the souls of children who died in their mother's womb and with school-aged children who died while learning the holy Writ, and, while leading them before the throne of the Eternal, teaches them the wisdom of the Torah (Ottioth d'Rabbi Akiba).

God loves children. He hears their prayers even when they mispronounce the words and, not having yet mastered the language, distort expressions (Shir Hashirim Rabbah 2). Even their babble is pleasant to Him. It was the supplication of children that caused the Purim miracle to occur. Mordehai was, after all, a teacher. When he discovered that Haman was plotting to destroy the Jews, he became distraught, fasted, and tearfully prayed to God. His students, who were very attached to him did the same, despite the fact that they were not yet able to understand the true reason for the grief that

---

[85] UGGIK #15, September 1932, 5. Original in Polish.
[86] Metatron is the name of an angel in medieval Jewish mystical tradition. In Rabbinic tradition, he is the highest of the angels.

overwhelmed their teacher. When mothers urged their children to eat and drink, the little ones placed their hands on the Bible, and swore that they wanted to fast together with their teacher and, if necessary, even to die. After uttering their oath, each hugged the Bible to his breast. It was only then that God, hearing the prayer of the youngsters, rescued his people (Yalkut Esther 6). After death, children protect their sinful parents from punishment and eternal damnation. They plead with God to take pity, and not to condemn their parents to eternal suffering. The children's plaintive entreaties awaken God's compassion and obtain grace and forgiveness for their parents (Koheleth Rabbah 4).

Children are the future and hope of every people. They assure the continued existence of the nation, and an uninterrupted thread of its history. Our tradition, therefore, places great emphasis on the upbringing of our youth. Parents have the primary responsibility for that upbringing. The Torah speaks to them: "And you shall teach them diligently to your children and you shall talk of them when you sit in your house, and when you walk on the road; when you lie down, and when you rise up" (Deuteronomy 6:7). The following story from the Talmud (Jer. Hagigah 76) forcefully reveals our forefathers' view about the importance of a proper upbringing. The Patriarch, Rabbi Gamliel, appointed two scholars, Rabbis Ammi and Assi, to travel to various Jewish localities to examine the children's educational standards, and to visit schools in all the settlements in Palestine. Once, when the scholars arrived in a tiny town, they requested to be shown "the watchmen of the town." The polite inhabitants fulfilled their wish, and introduced the older members of the town police force to them. But the delegates addressed them ironically: "These are not the watchmen; these are the destroyers of the town. The true watchmen and defenders of the town are the teachers and the ones who bring up the children." For a proper upbringing overcomes any inborn evil. It is the best way to disseminate enlightenment and teach good habits, a means of calming and soothing passions and hatred. Before God entrusted the Torah to the Israelites, He demanded that they give a surety that they would conscientiously fulfill its laws. "Let our forefathers be our security," promised the Israelites. "They are not sufficient," answered God. "Our prophets will guarantee for us." "That security is also insufficient." "Then let our children be our security!" "Such a security," answered God, "I like. I will gladly give my wisdom to innocent children."

ויאמר אלקים יהי אור ויהי אור
AND GOD SAID, "LET THERE BE LIGHT, AND THERE WAS LIGHT"[87]

The moment that God's command resounded in the cosmos, it immediately became bright, and light shone in all its brilliance. When it came to the creation of heaven, however, the situation was different. After the Divine words, "let there be a firmament in the midst of the waters, and let it divide the waters from the waters," the usual phrase "ויהי כן – and it was so," is absent from the text. It appears that God's command to create the heavens was not fulfilled immediately. On the contrary, we read "ויעש אלקים את הרקיע – and God made the firmament, and divided the waters which were under the firmament (the lower world), from the waters which were above the firmament (the heavens)." It almost seems as if he had to use force. Why is there a difference between how the light and the heavens were created? Why did the rays of light pour forth on the world with apparent joy, requiring only a few Divine words to unleash their radiant power, while the heavens made their entrance hesitantly, gradually? Our sages provide us with a meaningful answer to this question. The very essence of light is a blessing. There was, therefore, no opposition to its creation. Everything yearned for light. Everything eagerly awaited light. This yearning accelerated, and assisted light in making its appearance. In contrast, not all welcomed the creation of the heavens. The world below saw the heavens as an inflexible cover, which for all time would separate it from the elevated celestial spheres. Before the heavens came into existence, all creation was one entity. There was no above or below, no mortal or celestial region. Everything was still permeated with one spirit. It was only after the creation of the heavens that these worlds were separated from each other. The establishment of the heavens was the first rift in the universe, the first wedge driven into

---

[87] UGGIK #18, October 1932, 3. Original in German.

its wholeness. A Jewish tradition tells us that when the lower world was about to be separated from the upper, it burst into tears. The lower world cried. Parting from its heavenly sister was a heavy burden. Hence, the establishment of the heavens, that barrier that came between the upper and lower worlds, was a slow and an almost forced process. After the second day's work, the phrase "כי טוב – and God saw that everything was good," is absent. Not everything was good. The lower world was not satisfied. The creation of the heavens plunged it from the heights into the abyss.

At the very moment when the universe was created, there were already elements who felt insulted; whose sense of honor was wounded; who felt themselves unfairly taken advantage of; who felt discriminated against. The lower world complained that it was separated from the upper. The א, the first letter of the Hebrew alphabet, complained that God chose the ב as the first letter of the Torah, and it was only pacified when God promised that the Ten Commandments would start with an א. The moon was unhappy because God gave the task of providing light to the world to two heavenly bodies of equal size. "Despite the dissatisfaction of various components of the cosmos, the act of creation concludes with the significant words:

וירא אלקים את כל אשר עשה והנה טוב מאד
And God saw all that he had created and behold,
it was very good.

The sum total was very good. The dissatisfaction of individual components could not disturb the harmony of the whole.

UNITY[88]

ויקהל משה את כל עדת בני ישראל
And Moses gathered the entire community of Israel (Ex 35:1)

In this verse, as in verse 4, "Moses spoke to the entire community." The emphasis is on the small word כל, which indicates the totality, the entirety, the unity of the community. Rashi surmises from its location in the narrative, that this great gathering of the people took place ממחרת יהכ"פ – on the day after Yom Kippur. The question begs to be asked: Why did Moses pick this specific day to teach the people the details about the construction of the Tabernacle? Why did he gather the Jewish community and address them precisely on the day after the Day of Atonement?

Since time immemorial, we Jews have suffered from a malady, a disease that seems to be almost incurable – disunity, factionalism, and discord. We are tossed about the length and breadth of the world, constantly confronted by hatred and contempt. We seem to play a central role in all disputes and disagreements, but our greater misfortune and tragedy is that we lack internal unity and unanimity; that we have created an almost unbridgeable, and ever widening cleft between brother and brother. When Moses wanted to summon his people to erect a Tabernacle; when he wanted to call on them to join together and build a sanctuary, the great leader became sad. This Tabernacle that I am proposing, he thought to himself, should be a symbol of unity, a place of gathering together, a place of harmony. It should not become the property of one faction; a possession of one special group or of one particular orientation. No! It should belong to כל עדת בני ישראל – to the entire community. Built by all. Venerated by all. Sanctified by all. Everyone should be able to find solace, shelter, and space for devotion in the shade of this sanctuary. All should be able to rediscover their souls in the semi-darkness of this solemn place. But how can one gather these

[88] UGGIK #27, March 1933, 8. Original in German.

people together, when they are constantly striving against each other? How does one bring together these disparate groups, devoted to particularism, for one large, effective purpose? How does one pacify the malicious, ironic smirks of one, unmask the false politeness of another, and avert the reproachful remarks of a third? How does one straighten, raise, and dignify these bickering, envious, distorted, and dislocated people with slavish minds? How does one carry this out, when every spark of communal interest appears to have been extinguished?

Moses therefore called his people together ממחרת יהכ"פ – on the day after Yom Kippur. The Day of Atonement is the one day on which every Jew resolves to expunge hatred from his heart, and to search for reconciliation with his neighbor; when peace and forgiveness infiltrate all hearts. Moses hoped that on the following day he would have a chance of seeing before him כל עדת בני ישראל – a unified Jewish community.

חקת
וימת אהרן שם בראש ההר
AND AARON DIED THERE
ON TOP OF THE MOUNTAIN[89]

Aaron, the first High Priest, died on a mountain peak bordering Edom, a land inhabited by the descendants of Esau. His mortal remains found a resting place there. The inhabitants of Edom, proud of their forefather Esau, the son of Isaac, and mindful of their traditions and origins, who were ready, sword in hand, to prevent any stranger from entering their land, must forever be confronted by the grave in which the Jews buried their High Priest, Aaron. A martial people, eager and ready for battle, are watched over by the image of Aaron, the angel of peace, the advocate of love. What a contradiction! On second thought, perhaps there is a hidden message.

While wandering in the desert in the proximity of the longed-for Promised Land, our forefathers met their relatives, the descendants of Esau. After experiencing countless hardships and difficulties, after surviving dangers and privations, they, at last, find a familiar people; relatives with a common origin, and shared memories. Esau and Jacob were, after all, sons of the same father! Rebecca was mother to both of them! Despite the fact that from their earliest youth, each of the brothers had gone his own way, and each chose a different path; despite the fact that the brotherly feelings, which united them, had been sorely and gravely tried, the Jews expected a welcome and warm reception from their relatives. If, in fact, time heals all wounds, soothes pain, suppresses the memory of affliction and sorrow, why should the descendants of Esau continue to harbor envy and hatred against a brotherly nation, for a grievance once inflicted on their forefather? The Jews turned to the powerful king of Edom with a request to allow them to cross his land. "Thus says your brother, Israel. You are familiar with our suffering. Our

---

[89] UGGIK #34, June 1933, 4. Original in Polish.

father wandered down to Egypt. Egypt persecuted us cruelly. We beseeched God and He took pity on us, and led us out of bondage. We are now standing on the border of your country. Allow us, O King, to cross your land. We will not stray from the main road. We will not enter your fields or gardens, and we will not drink the water from your springs. We will not go to the left or to the right, but only straight ahead of us." The King's answer was a resounding no. He phrased his refusal in threatening, severe words. "You will not cross my land. I will greet you with an outstretched sword." The arrogance of the King's answer pierced Israel's heart like an arrow. Esau hadn't changed after all. The same intense hatred still persisted. Esau-Edom had learned nothing, and had forgotten nothing. What can be the basis for such a deep-seated hatred?

The Jews thought about the possible cause for such hatred, and they remembered the ancient quarrel between Jacob and Esau over the birthright. In a moment of spiritual weakness, the older Esau surrendered his birthright, and the cunning Jacob acquired their father's blessing with deceit. The older brother became the servant of the younger. Esau submitted to Jacob. Esau felt humiliated, wronged. He was jealous of the younger Jacob's rise in status and distinction. The more the blessing came to fruition, the greater became Esau's dislike and the more intense the hatred for his sibling. Hatred between brothers is usually deeper, and lasts longer, than hatred between strangers.

But our history also tells us of two other brothers, who loved and idolized each other, despite the fact that the younger was destined to play a larger role, and was given a more important assignment, than the older. Elevation of the younger did not diminish their brotherly love in the least. Moses and Aaron. Moses was the younger. We see the older, Aaron, standing in the shadows, on the sideline, overshadowed by the luster that surrounded the younger, Moses. Moses becomes the commander, the teacher, and the one chosen by God to free his people, and lead them out of bondage. He stands at the head of Israel. And the older Aaron submits, and keeps quiet. The older Aaron modestly acknowledges the greatness of his younger brother. He loves him. He idolizes him and happily supports him in his historic mission.

On the border of Edom, home of Esau with his jealous hatred of his younger brother, Jacob, is the grave of Aaron, who readily acknowledged his younger brother's achievements. The grave of this apostle of peace and love, eternally reminds the descendants of Esau that acknowledging the achievement of others, of younger brothers, does not diminish our own importance in the least, and in no way discredits us.

Let us imitate Aaron's beautiful example of valuing and acknowledging the achievements of all amongst us, regardless of age, regardless of status, regardless of position.

THE LIFE AND DEATH OF MOSES[90]
כ' תמוז תרצ"ג

> "And God spoke to Moses: Climb this mountain
> and see the land that I will give to the children of Israel.
> And once you have seen it, you shall die."

With these words, Moses was informed about the end of his life. He has to die without finishing his work; without achieving the goal to which he had dedicated every ounce of energy and passion since his youth. He must die in the wilderness, on the border of that dreamed-of land. His life passes before his eyes. For the last time, he reviews the long road he has traveled. He is overcome by deep sorrow. He is disillusioned. He feels that he has been cheated. Hasn't his entire life been a long series of disappointments, unfulfilled expectations, and unrelieved tensions? And now he has to die? Here, in the wilderness? He, the leader of multitudes must now be left behind, lonely and deserted, in the broad emptiness of the wilderness? A last drop determination, a last bit of energy wells up within him. No! I will not die! I will not succumb! I will continue to struggle, continue to endure, until I reach the goal, until my assignment is completed. Moses does not want to die. He wrestles with God, fights for his life. Frantically, he clings to life. He begs, he pleads, he beseeches, and he implores. Have pity! Don't let me die! Not here! Not in the wilderness! Not here, on the threshold of *the* land! His protest is all for naught! Moses has to die. The people struggle on. The leader stays behind, alone in the wilderness.

During his life, Moses experienced three traumatic dis-illusionments. Three times, he struggled with an essential life issue and three times he lost. First, he lost faith in mankind, then he lost faith in his assignment, his mission, his work, and finally, he had to abandon hope of ever knowing the secret of existence, the ultimate truth. Mankind, his mission, and the essence of God are the three poles around which his life revolved.

[90] UGGIK #35, July 1933, 5. Original in German.

I

Moses, full of confidence in life and mankind, was thrown into the real world in his youth. He spent his childhood and early youth in the court of the Egyptian King surrounded by pomp, wealth, and a *joi de vivre*. The groans of the enforced laborers, the sighs of Jewish slaves did not penetrate the palace. Its walls deflected the cries of millions. To Moses, life still appeared like an idyllic garden in which men strolled about like angels. He had not yet seen the distorted faces of the enslaved; their vacant, inconsolable stares. The dark side of life was hidden from him for the moment. Surrounded by the benevolence and kindness of the King, protected by the lovelorn eyes of the motherly daughter of the King who pulled him out of the torrent of the Nile, Moses knew nothing about human hatred and malice. Happy and full of hope, he brimmed with confidence. His confidence in humanity was still undisturbed.

One day, he left the palace grounds and wandered away from the King's court. Suddenly, he found himself in the midst of the toiling masses among the heavenward towering pyramids. All around him, he became aware of innumerable bent figures, joyless people, gasping slaves. All were stooped under the same yoke. All were driven, whipped, and persecuted by the same master. These were beasts of burden in human form. Moses became dismayed. Moses was perplexed. He was not familiar with this side of life. Is it possible that over there, in the city, people are free and happy and enjoy the bright sunshine, while outside people moan and groan under the burden of work? Is it possible that in the same world there is both dancing and crying, rejoicing and despair, and that one side does not see the heart of the other?...

He was drawn to these downtrodden figures, and found himself ever more deeply immersed in the lives of these working masses. Suddenly, he was confronted with a strange spectacle. A clenched fist is raised in a brutally threatening manner and, as it crashes down, a dark image emerges from its impact. In that instant, as if a flash of lightning had hit him, he knew that "an Egyptian was killing a brother, *his* brother." And before Moses realized what he was doing, the Egyptian was dead. He had killed him. He had struck the striker.

Agitated, Moses left the world of slavery and returned to the palace. But he could no longer find peace. For the first time, he felt out of place in the King's court. He felt that his place was with the humiliated figures, with the subjugated people. So the following day, he searched for their living quarters. והנה שני אנשים עברים נצים. He saw two slaves, two of the Hebrews, on whose account he slew an Egyptian the day before, quarreling with each other. Two oppressed, enslaved men confronting each other as enemies. This time, it was not a feeling of sympathy that Moses felt. He was not inspired with an impulse or desire to defend, to save, to stand by the weaker. Instead, he was overcome by amazement, puzzlement, an inability to understand. How? A slave striking a slave? Men shackled to the same yoke hating each other? Men pulling the same burden, forged together by sorrow, torture, and affliction, quarreling with each other? Then, oppressed by a dark premonition, Moses poses his first question to life, a question, which is still valid today, a question, which to this day disturbs the human conscience – למה תכה רעך – why would you strike your brother? Why do you torture your neighbor? He does not rebuke, he does not threaten, he does not judge. He asks a direct question. He would like to know, he would like to learn how it is possible for one pariah to strike another, for one sufferer to raise his fist against a brother in pain? Almost immediately, the penetrating gaze of the questioned striker finds its mark. A glance glowing with hatred, flashing with contempt, full of scorn, gloating, joy, evil, treachery. What? You want to play the judge here? Here, where people disappear in droves, where humanity writhes in anguish, here you expect to find justice? ויירא משה and Moses became afraid. Dread, terror in the face of such degradation seized him. Terror that a human being could sink so low. At that moment, something in Moses snapped. A chord snapped in his broken heart. His faith in humanity, his confidence in his brothers, was deeply shaken.

ויברח משה – and Moses ran away. He ran away, and was pursued by the burning look of the enslaved people. He ran away into the wilderness and carried with him a deep wound from his encounter. The first wound that life had inflicted on him. The first of his three great disappointments – disillusionment with humanity. He yearned for solitude. He wanted to be alone. Far away from people and their needs. Far away from masters and slaves. Far away from the conqueror and the vanquished. Better the wail of the jackal in the desert, than the complaints of men. Better the roar of the hungry lions eager to plunder, than the jeering gloating of human arrogance. He wanted to be alone. Alone with the mute mountains, alone with the burning sand dunes of the desert...

II

Days and weeks pass and Moses wanders around the desert with his flock. Since the incident that robbed him of faith in humanity, he feels himself drawn to animals, to his flock. He loves these docile creatures who respond to his call. He loves the freedom of the desert, the stillness of the wilderness, the twinkling of the stars, the cool of the night, the muffled echo of the vast expanses...

But his inner battle is not over. The storm in his heart has not been stilled. An overpowering longing for his brothers often penetrates his heart drunk with solitude. It draws him back to his people! He wants to be with his enslaved brothers once again! It is true that they are malicious, obstinate, and treacherous. It is true that the piercing look of that Jewish slave still burns him. Perhaps when they are freed from bondage, when their shackles are loosened, when they are raised from their deep humiliation, when the heavens open to show them the All Bountiful, the God of their forebears, perhaps then they will become better, nobler, chaster. Can he rest here by his flock while over there his brothers are waiting for their freedom? Is it not his duty to help liberate them? And as his confidence in his mission grows, he gradually regains faith in humanity. His life acquires a new meaning.

He will become the redesigner, the new architect of his people. But he is still unable to overcome his mistrust of people. He does not yet have full confidence in his brothers. "And what if they will not listen to me, and don't trust me?" But all doubts and hesitations are in vain. He must go. So Moses returns to his brothers and frees his people. His faith in his mission and his confidence in his brothers returns and grows. He feels as if he is carried on wings. A new ideal carries him. A new goal shines brightly in the distance...To lead people! To guide his people to that summit where heaven and earth come together, where he will show them the light of the world...

And then the second disillusionment of his life comes crashing down like an avalanche. He is robbed of his faith in his mission. His brothers experience freedom, light, and revelation, but their downfall comes abruptly in their shameful relapse to a strange, false god – the golden calf. And Moses breaks the tablets; smashes his work; pulverizes his mission. He has been betrayed a second time. Once again, he has been disillusioned. He loses his new life's meaning. Everything around him is empty. Once again, he is alone. He feels the reins slipping from his flaccid hands. Once again, he feels estranged from people. They don't understand him and he will never be able to understand them. And now he is too tired to start anew. He has experienced two bitter disillusionments – in humanity, and in his mission...

III

Moses has a last wish, a final desire. He wants to see God. He wants to learn the ultimate truth. He wants to explore, to understand. Why have all his dreams been frustrated? Why did his mission that began so gloriously, have to come to such a shameful end? Why?...If it is true that all creation bears witness to God's splendor, that a Divine spark glows in every living creature, then הראני נא את כבדך – show me Your splendor. Allow me to see the summit of creation, the nobility of humanity! Allow me to see your true face! I want to understand the secret of the soul of the world before I die. I cannot bear this seesawing, this up and down, this now and then. I want to see the ultimate, the source of everything. הראני נא את כבדך – give me the insight to see the dignity, the goodness of your essence!...

Moses demands too much. God cannot grant him this wish. "You cannot see my countenance," God answers him, כי לא יראני האדם וחי. "A human being cannot see my face וחי as long as he is human, as long as he lives. You have been allowed to see the secrets of the world more deeply than any other being. More than that, I cannot reveal to you."

So his last wish is not granted. His last request remains unfulfilled. Once, he walked the earth full of confidence. He was going to mold life in the image of his ideals. But reality had other plans. It proved to be too brittle, too difficult. It slipped from his masterly hand, and went its own way. He believed in humanity, but humanity proved to be impulsive and petty. He believed in his mission, and saw his mission frustrated by his brothers. Finally, he knocked on the gates of eternity, of the ultimate knowledge, and found them locked.

Now he must die. Now he has to climb the mountain, to see the land of his longings from a distance, and die. But Moses doesn't want to die. Death is coming too soon for him. He would like to see the goal, the fruit of his life's work. He loves this life, despite its disappointments. He clings to his brothers, despite their inadequacies. The Midrash tells us that when Moses saw his time drawing near, he came before God and said, "Master of the universe! Have my feet furrowed the fog in vain? Have I pranced before your children like a horse that I should now become food for worms?" "No one can escape death," answered God. Then Moses turned to heaven and to earth, to the sun and to the moon, to the stars and to the planets, and asked them to intercede with the Eternal on his behalf. From every corner came the same answer, "everything that is upright is destined to fall. You too must die!"

And so Moses died. God kissed him, and with that kiss, He took his soul. What was denied him in life, Moses achieved in death. He saw God. He died by being touched by eternity. "It is impossible for man to see me וחי as long as he is fettered to this earth," God had once said to him. Now that everything earthly had been removed, the corporeal had been cast away; he was finally permitted to see the Divine. Only in death was his final wish to be fulfilled. He saw God's splendor. The light that illuminated his last hour banished the darkness that had shrouded his life. "The pious are greater in death than in life." What had eluded him throughout his life, understanding the soul of the world, union with eternity, became his in death…

The creative Jewish spirit has never ceased to reflect over the death of its first and greatest leader. In all epochs of Jewish literature, the death of Moses has nourished Jewish fantasy and creative writing. Reflection on the last hour of our leader's life has never failed to rekindle a new Jewish faith and zeal. Moses' figure has been too deeply ingrained in Jewish consciousness to be forgotten, but the Jewish spirit has felt too guilty about its behavior towards him, to allow itself ever to be fully pacified over his tragic passing. The Jewish spirit has been restless and anxious. Did he not live for us; did he not suffer because of us?

There is a very sensitive Jewish saying: "Before Moses left this world, Israel came to him and said, 'משה רבנו מחול לנו – Moses, our teacher, forgive us!' To which Moses replied: אם תהיו אוהבים זה את זה ואם תקיימו את תורתי when you love one another and fulfill my Torah, my teaching, you will be forgiven!" Trust one another, and have confidence in working together. That is the legacy of our great teacher. That is the lesson that resounds to us from Moses' life and death! To treat each brother as a beloved brother, to feel the passion of generations that preceded us in the Jewish endeavor. That has been the secret of our existence for thousands of years, and that is what our leader and teacher demanded of us. That alone will reconcile us with his spirit, and bring us nearer to him. When fragmentation ceases in our midst. When party fanaticism vanishes. When we respect those we disagree with. When all of us work together shoulder to shoulder to fulfill the great responsibility placed on us – to use and enrich the heritage passed down to us. Then, and only then, will we be forgiven for the sins that we committed against our great teacher, Moshe Rabeinu…

שופטים
A HASSIDIC INTERPRETATION[91]

> "Judges and watchmen shall you appoint
> in all the gates that God gives you"

This verse, which opens the weekly portion, contains a directive that every city in the Jewish state must have its own judges and policemen. According to the oriental custom, judges used to sit and dispense justice at the gates of the city.

But, according to a Hassidic interpretation, this verse also contains a deeper, ethical concept.

Every human being looks out, awkwardly and self-consciously, at the rest of creation, in full recognition of his intellectual limitations. These are two worlds. Here, is my inner world. There, is the world facing me. On one side is the subject – I, on the other side, the object – the not I. Here, my interior world with an abundance of feelings and emotions – longing, desire, hopes, suffering, pain, and joy. In summary, everything, both sublime and base, that each human soul conceals. And there, the greater world outside me – heaven and earth, sun, moon and stars, seas and land, plants and animals, in addition to the innumerable inner worlds of my fellow human beings.

These two worlds are, however, not completely isolated from each other. They are connected via שערים – gates or portals of my body, bridges between my private world, and the greater, outer world.

The first שער – gate or portal that connects the inner me with my surroundings is the eye.

Images of the outer world – the beauty and grandeur of nature, the magnificent spectacles of the universe stream into my inner world through this portal. My eye rejoices in the diversity of shapes and forms, and imbibes the beauty of the world. But it is not only

[91]   UGGIK #38, August 1933, 5. Original in German.

beauty that my eye beholds. Sometimes, it encounters ugliness. The base can also find its way into my soul through this portal. That is why the Torah states, "judges and watchmen shall you install in your gates." Do not allow everything to enter your soul, indiscriminately and uniformly, through the portal of your eye. Keep your eye open to the beautiful but close it to the ugly.

Another gate that connects the world around me with my inner world is my ear!

With our ears, we can hear the eternal sounds and music of the cosmos, the never silent symphony of the universe, the edifying lessons and exhortations of our sages. But, is everything that we hear beautiful and sublime? Our ear also hears slander and vile gossip, malicious and false rumors, seductive words of hypocrisy and falsehood. Therefore, remember the words of Scripture, "judges and watchmen shall you install in your gates." The judge and watchman should guard your ear, so that nothing unworthy enters it and tarnishes the mirror of your soul.

Guard your eye! Guard your ear!

Do not forget the third portal, that שער through which our inner world can flow into the outer world – the mouth! It serves both good and evil. Divine words, as well as blasphemy, blessings as well as curses, can flow through it. Therefore, שפטים ושטרים תתן לך בכל שעריך – Judges and watchmen shall you install at all your gates!

HUMAN NATURE[92]

It seems appropriate, especially during these days of introspection and repentance, to consider the nature of human beings. Human beings hope and suffer; struggle and strain for a ray of good fortune. They can quickly become disillusioned, but, just as rapidly, they can be encouraged. They race and rush through this world at a furious pace until, struck by the arrow of death, they sink into nothingness.

Let us try to understand, and psychologically clarify, three types of personalities. One lives in the present, one lives in the fantasy of the future, and the third lives with memories of the past.

I

There is a personality type who lives in the present, who adheres to the current, who clings to the moment. He doesn't become distracted by dreams. He doesn't plan for a distant future. He despises and discards every idea or ideal that cannot be immediately turned into reality. The person who lives in the present barricades every gate to the past behind him. Anything that has flowed by, that has been swept away by the waves of time, has vanished, faded, has fallen from his tree of life like a withered leaf, has disappeared from his spiritual life, has been erased from his memory bank. But such a person of the present is also not concerned about the future. What affair is it of his what may happen some day? For him, only the present blooms. The future neither worries nor saddens him; it inspires neither fear nor hope. It is still unborn, and therefore of no consequence. The individual of the present follows the principle כי יהי' שלום ואמת בימי – après moi – le déluge.

II

The person who lives in a world of fantasy of the future is totally different! For him, the present is only a tiny bit of time, a boisterous,

[92] UGGIK #40, September 1933, 7-8. Original in German.

disappearing sound, an insignificant droplet in the sea of time. The present flies away from dreary reality to an enraptured, bright future on the wings of fantasy. We would indeed be poor, and incapable of creating anything lasting, if we did not have a fantasy – that creative power of the imagination. The architect sits at his desk, and draws plans for a building. But even before the first beam has been put in place, the building is already standing in his imagination. Would parents make so many sacrifices for their children, if images of their future happy lives, did not hover before their eyes? The idealist who dreams of a renewed world, of a better social order, has to ignite the people's fantasy with rich, imaginative pictures in order to awaken images of a more beautiful, happier time for his contemporaries. He must be able to conjure up in their mind's eye, the long awaited and hoped-for reality, in order to be able to command a following; in order to pave a path for his ideas into the hearts of humanity. And wasn't Moses' battle in the wilderness, in reality, a struggle of an optimistic leader with his eye on the future, against his unimaginative people of the present? All around them, the people saw only the present, the austere, barren, impoverishing desert. In contrast, Moses' spirit was wandering in the blooming fields of a future time, in the fertile plains of the Promised Land. He did not feel the difficulties of the road because his spirit lived in the realm of the goal. Only occasionally, did sparks of enthusiasm burst forth from the peoples' souls; only occasionally, was the leader's vitality able to drag everyone along. But as soon as the divine voice was silent, and the stirring figure of the leader was not in sight, the light of the future was extinguished for them, and once again, a cry of despair shook the camp. The people stood with their feet firmly planted in the present. In contrast, Moses' gaze was fixed on the distant future. He could see והי' באחרית הימים – the end of time.

III

Just as the person of reality is anchored to the present time, and the person of imagination is anchored to the future, there is a human personality that lives with memories and emotions in the past. The "golden years" have passed. Oh, how beautiful it all once was! How nice it would be, if the present were as alluring; the prospects for the future, as attractive. His sight is set backwards, to the enraptured past, to the lost paradise. The person of memory holds onto every past experience. In his imagination, he is constantly wandering back to the island of beauty that his ship of life has passed by. The present, and everything associated with it, seems deficient to him; seems defective, unreal. Only the past is perfect, filled with light, unblemished...His eye is constantly searching for what was lost, what is missing. And since we shall never again experience the past, the mood of the human being of memory is always one of resignation; of abandonment. כל מקום שנאמר ויהי אינו אלא לשון צער – one can sense a feeling of sadness every time it is written, "it was once."

We Jews are famous for an all too strong sense of reality. It is said, that the fact that all the cataclysms and catastrophes, all the oppressions and persecutions aimed against us did not find their mark on the mainspring of our existence, is due to our innate ability to accommodate. We Jews, it is said, belong to the present day human personality type; we understand how to yield to the present very well. Our practical, critical goal, it is said, is to establish a lifeline in the face of every danger.

This sober explanation to the puzzle of our viability is foolish and superficial. It is true, that from time to time on the battleground of life the Jew was indeed willing to sell his soul for the needs of the moment. Bowed by the burdens of life, he was occasionally willing to be untrue to himself, and court favor of the present; to become intoxicated with the here and now. However, the Jew as we see him on the High Holydays in trembling prayer cries for a solution. The Jew who, in the Avoda, draws the erstwhile magnificence of the Yom Kippur service from the ruins of the destroyed Temple; who describes how the High Priest in his splendid vestments, in his holiness, in his superhuman, spiritual beauty sang hymns of praise, and at the climax breaks out in an ecstatic call, "hail to the eyes that saw this," that Jew is not a man of the present. That Jew lives as completely in the past, as he lives completely in the Messianic land of the future. Memory and hope are intimately unified and intertwined here into a mysterious symphony of Jewish existence...

The past and the future are part of the approaching Holydays. We must examine the content of our past, atone for our lapses, correct our faults, and forget discord and hostility, which has divided us from each other during the course of the past year. For, how can we dare to beg God for forgiveness, if we affront each other, harm each other, act unjustly towards each other, and don't forgive each other? Many among us are people of the past, in the worst meaning of this word. Years after an injustice has been done to them, they cannot forget the hurt. It is, of course, even worse when one cannot overcome oneself, and beg someone whom one has hurt for forgiveness. You might think about those who once lived and suffered, of whom Koheleth says, "their love, their animosity, and their jealousy have disappeared with them."

So, during these Holy days we pray for reconciliation, harmony, and peace. Peace for our community; peace for our country; peace for our world!

THE DISCUSSION[93]

Rabbi Akiba had 24,000 students. They all died between Pesach and Shevuot
because they did not show respect for each other. (Yevamot 62)

The ostensible reason given for the death of so many appears to be inadequate. Where is it written that the penalty for lack of mutual respect is death? Did these bearers and students of the Jewish tradition have to die merely because they did not respect each other? The Jewish scholarly system is unique in having a distinction that differentiates it from all other educational systems. It is a system of long, ongoing discussions. In the academies, students fought and struggled over every new opinion, every new interpretation. This one questioned, that one answered. One compared old sources, and the other the observations of newer authorities. Traditions were pitted against each other. Opinions collided. Flashes of wit were ignited. Often, teachers and students exchanged roles. The students asked and opposed; the teachers had to answer and defend themselves. Out of this shared search for the truth, the Halaha was born; the statute was forged. The oral scholarship became the creation of the entire people, because ordinary people, the weaver and artisan, appeared in the house of study (Eduyyot 1:3), and gave testimony about practices they saw in their youth. Their testimony was listened to attentively and became part of the basis for new decisions. No tractate of the Talmud is the work of one scholar. More than a hundred names and authorities are cited in any given tractate. New scholars announce their desire to speak. Everyone is heard. All participate in shaping the theme at hand. Students and masters contend with each other in order to clarify and explain a Biblical statement.

Discussion, an unbroken dialogue is the true style of the Talmud. Scholars discuss and argue with each other over a span of hundreds of years. Even from the grave. It is said that if a deceased scholar's opinion is repeated in the hall of study, his lips move in

[93] UGGIK #53, April 1934, 8. Original in German.

the grave (Yevamot 97). He is still participating in the learning process. Such a method cannot thrive in solitude. For in solitude, discussion with a partner, the living word, would be missing (Eruvin 53). "Just as a piece of iron sharpens and smoothes another piece of iron, so scholars sharpen each other through study" (Ta'anit 7). Just as a solitary piece of wood cannot sustain a fire for long, the words of the Torah will be rapidly extinguished, if it is learned in solitude." "I have learned a great deal from my teachers, more from my colleagues, and most of all from my students." Some students are only brought to a correct understanding and meaning of the lesson by questions asked by the teacher. Discussion and honest criticism often lead us to the truth.

In order to be a productive discussion, it must include friendship, honesty, and the love of truth. There must be respect and consideration for the opponent. There is almost no personal animosity expressed in Talmudic discussions. The debate never leads to discord. והב בסופה – in the end, they treated each other with love and friendship. The battle between the students of Hillel and Shammai raged and was stormy. But their differences of opinion over their understanding of the Torah, never led to a chasm or fissure (Yevamot 14). Their disputes were considered to be מחלקת לשם שמים – ideal disputes.

Rabbi Akiba had 24,000 students. Since they did not love or respect each other, their scholarship was dead, and they no longer contributed to the development of Judaism. Their animosity brought them from the sublime heights of ideal scholarship, into the whirlpool of small personal squabbles. The currents of mutual hate carried them to the gulf of oblivion.

We continue to discuss. We are a people of discussions. The themes have changed, but the form of the dialogue has remained the same. But unfortunately, nowadays we listen only to our own voice. We pay no attention to the voices of our opponents. That's why there is so much noise; so much hatred. Every day new factions are established. The battle rages in the parties' forest of "leaves."[94] The battle goes on passionately.

Can such a discussion be called, Jewish? Is it productive?

---

[94] A play on the word "Blätter" which can mean leaf or newspaper.

מי ירפה לך
WHO WILL HEAL YOU?[95]

"This will be the law about the leper. Let him be brought to the Priest." The Priest diagnoses the illness, and determines whether the person has leprosy and must be excluded from the Jewish camp. Since the exact nature and cause of this terrible illness have not been determined to date, we are most interested in the opinions of our sages as to what this disease and its etiology might have been. "Whoever slanders others will be struck by the disease of leprosy (Arakhin 15). "Why did the Torah command us to separate the leper from the community? Since he incites discord between people, let him be sentenced to be separate and alone." God punished him with the disease of leprosy because he disturbed the social peace, caused discord, slandered and defamed others, and caused disputes and hatred. The leper was to be removed and isolated, so that his ability to instigate and incite, would be effectively stopped.

In the opinion of our Sages, it appears that a bodily illness can be caused by a moral lapse. Psychological turmoil can be a source for a physiologic abnormality. A quarrelsome person, who sows hatred and creates a gulf between people, will eventually succumb to a physical illness. On the other hand, one who guards his soul will also protect his body from various ailments. The soul is the hearth of health, the source of life. In order to reach the body, therapy must first be directed at the soul. A healthy soul leads to a healthy body. The therapeutic process begins inside a person, in the imperceptible depths of the soul, and only then, gradually, spreads to the person's entire being.

When Jews murmured against God in the desert, God sent poisonous snakes, and many died from snakebite. Then God commanded Moses to make a snake out of copper, and place it on a stick. Anyone who was bitten could look at the copper snake and

[95] UGGIK #54, April 1934, 2. Original in Polish.

survive. "Does a copper snake have an ability to heal?" asked our Sages. No! They answered. But by lifting their heads to see the snake attached to the top of the stick, they also directed their gaze heavenward, to God, and atoned for their sins. It was this return to God, which healed the effects of the poison (Rosh Hashanah 29). A spiritual change caused the body to heal.

The Talmud (Berahot 33a) tells about R. Hanina ben Dosa who was informed that in a particular neighborhood, a poisonous snake was causing people to die. "Show me the snake's hole," said R. Hanina. When he came to the hole in which the angry snake was hiding, R. Hanina placed his foot over its opening. The snake came out of hiding, bit him, and immediately died. R. Hanina, however, was spared. R. Hanina took the dead snake, brought it to his school, and said to his students, "look and be convinced that it is not the snake but sin that kills." Poisonous venom will not harm a pure, unimpeachable soul. The origin of illness blooms in the soul.

Since disease of the body results from sickness of the soul, and is only an outward manifestation of moral deficiency, it is no wonder that a Priest should be called upon to cure it. Only a Priest, radiating peace and faith, full of goodness and gentleness, could calm the soul of a sick person, bring it back to balance, and ease its return to health.

Our nation is ill, both in soul and in body. Poverty and external hatred are attacking our bodies; internal battles about different points of view are afflicting our souls. There are many Priests, each prescribing different medicines for us, but all concentrate on healing our bodies. Our souls continue to sink. Will we ever be able to find a healer – a Priest, a physician for our souls?

וספרתם לכם
COUNT THE DAYS BETWEEN PESACH AND SHEVUOTH[96]

The Pythagoreans taught that numbers are the source of all existence. Numbers have much in common with our lives. The numerical system can help us understand our earthly journey.

I

Every number is only an empty shell, a form, which only we can fill with meaning. By using numbers, the shepherd determines how many sheep he has; the businessman – his wares; the astronomer – the number of stars and planets; the beggar – his coins. All employ the same numbers, which remain unchanged whether we are counting stones or pearls. A number can convey information. It tells us whether something is expensive or cheap, rare or common, a loss or a gain. Only we can assign significance or value to a number. In gripping fear, the burglar uses numbers to appraise the value of his booty. In jubilation, the commander uses numbers to evaluate the spoils of war. In ecstasy, the artist uses numbers to blend word and melody.

Our lives resemble numbers. Life is given to us only as a form; as a shell, as an empty vessel. The content with which we fill our lives is our personal decision, an individual choice. Our allotted time on earth is the frame. We must paint the picture. If we only understood the proper balance between light and shade...

II

Every number has its fixed, steadfast place in the numerical system. The position allotted to it is constant, and unchangeable. Six always stands between five and seven. Nine and eleven always surround ten. No number can be released from its associates. With relentlessness, the later one always follows the preceding one. It is

[96] UGGIK #55, May 1934, 7. Original in German.

a follower and, at the same time, also a leader. A consequence and a presupposition. For example, the number 5 always follows 4, but is a preparation for 6.

Our lives resemble numbers. Generations follow each other inflexibly. Each generation follows the preceding one, but at the same time, is preparing the next one. Our forefathers had to leave this world in order to make space for us. We too, one day will have to clear our spot in order to free up space for the next generation's struggle for the light of life. Just like numbers, each of us is assigned a particular spot in time and space. We can neither be forced from this place nor can we abdicate it. If we would only occupy it in a worthy manner...

III

Numbers ascend from finite to infinite. The larger the number, the more difficult it is for us to grasp. The larger it is, the vaguer it becomes, and the more our fantasy and imagination have to take over. Numbers begin within our sphere of existence, and, as they increase and grow, they finally get lost in the haze of infinity, in the immeasurable. When our forefathers wanted to express an unimaginable abundance, an ungraspable quantity, they used an image to get out of the difficulty, "like the sand in the sea" or "the stars in the sky." Like Jacob's ladder, numbers rest with their lowest rung solidly on the ground of reality, but their summit reaches to infinity...

Our life is like the numbers. It begins on earth, and ends in the celestial. Its juices flow from the corporal to the spiritual world... Only at the end of the day, do we survey the road; at dusk, when space and time is slipping away. When we find ourselves between the measurable and the immeasurable; between the countable and the uncountable; on the thin border between semblance and existence; between finite life and infinite eternity...

DENUNCIATION[97]

One of the flaws and blemishes that has deformed and warped our
national character, and which, after the fall of the Jewish state and
the loss of our independence has most tormented us, was the plague
of denunciation. It has been difficult enough to have to wage an
unceasing, unrelenting war against our external enemies for a bare
existence and an elementary right to live, without the added burden
of being denounced and handed over to the mercies, or rather lack
of mercies, of our oppressors. Often, we have had to be alert against
the vigilant and spying eyes of our own brothers who, though tied
with us in shared misfortune and fate, did not hesitate to inform our
enemies about every recklessly spoken word; about every
instinctively performed, careless deed by individuals whose
freedom of action was restricted.

During our national catastrophe, when lawlessness and Roman
despotism ruled, the fate of our elite and our leaders could indeed
be pitied if they allowed themselves to express an unfavorable
opinion about imperial Rome, and if their conversation was
overheard by someone in the service of the Roman authorities.

One time, Rabbis Judah, Yose, and Simeon were discussing
Roman cultural institutions and policies. Rabbi Judah began by
praising the influence that Roman culture had on the economic and
hygienic developments of the country with genuine admiration.
"They beautified the squares and market places and built bridges
and baths," he said. R. Yose met Rabbi Judah's praise with an icy
silence. The pain inflicted on the Jewish heart by the Romans was
still too fresh; the grief for the dishonored Holy Place of Israel was
still too deep, for a scholar of R. Yose's stature to be able to accept
such a glorification of Rome. So, R. Yose kept quiet and did not
utter a word. R. Simeon replied: "Everything the Romans created
was for their own use; their motives were egotistical." Squares,
bathhouses, and bridges have become a source of income, and a

---

[97] UGGIK #59, July 1934, 4-5. Original in Polish.

means of taxing the populace. Roman civilization breathes materialism and narcissism. That conversation would not have had dire consequences, if a certain Judah ben Gerim who overheard it, had not brought it to the attention of the Roman authorities. They, in turn, did not criticize; they reacted. Rabbi Judah, who praised Rome, was rewarded with a medal and a higher position; Rabbi Yose, who kept silent, was banished; while Rabbi Simeon was condemned to death because he criticized Roman culture and didn't pay homage to imperial authority and dignity. Rabbi Simeon managed to escape and hid in a cave in the desert for 13 years (Shabbat 33b).

Judah ben Gerim, who apparently enjoyed the confidence and company of the Sages, turned out to have been a paid spy, and a lowly betrayer. He was, unfortunately, not the last Jew who, having won his co-religionists' confidence and respect with deceit, shamefully betrayed his own people.

Learning from the above-cited experience, R. Simeon (bar Yochai) changed his opinion about life and people. He had previously stated: "If I had been present at Mt. Sinai during the revelation, I would have asked God to give man two mouths, one for reading the Torah, and the other for daily use." For indeed, how does man dare to utter God's word and His lofty commandments with the same lips that he uses for secular and, not infrequently, indecent words? But, after experiencing the suffering caused by his denunciation, he exclaimed: "If human lips can cause so much damage with betrayal and slander, who knows whether the world would be able to endure if man had two mouths!" (Jer Berahot 3a).

Informers were frequently able to find Jewish teachers who violated official orders by secretly teaching the young, and nurturing and disseminating scholarship in an attempt to dispel the reigning ignorance. These informers, who themselves were Jews, accused the teachers and Sages of interrupting work, and thus detracting from activities that might benefit the state, by gathering students and zealous crowds thirsting for knowledge (Bava Metzia 86a). These teachers would then have to interrupt their lectures, and find a new hiding place in order to protect themselves against betrayal by informers who were lying in wait to deprive them of life and freedom.

We should not be surprised that the punishment meted out to informers was severe and without mercy. It was said that the fires of hell would forever consume their flesh. That even if hell ended, their suffering never would (Rosh Hashanah 17a). It is clear that our ancestors used every means at their disposal to oppose and try to neutralize the destructive work of informers. Jewish law permitted anyone with an opportunity, to eliminate informers, but it was not permissible to kill them. However, if an informer was in danger, one did not have to run to his aid and save him (Avodah Zarah 26b). Instead, every means could be used to hasten his demise.

In order to understand the hatred and contempt our Sages held for informers, it must be remembered that the Talmud considered the act of denunciation to have been the immediate cause for the destruction of the Temple. Let us briefly review the well-known story about a resident of Jerusalem who had a friend named Kamtza and an enemy, Bar Kamtza. Once, this resident gave a banquet in his home, and asked his servant to invite Kamtza. By mistake, his servant extended the invitation to his enemy, Bar Kamtza. Noticing his enemy among the guests, the master of the house asked him to leave. Pleadings by Bar Kamtza who was ashamed to leave, were to no avail. The host was stubborn and unmoved. Ashamed and humiliated, Bar Kamtza left the home of his irreconcilable enemy and decided to avenge the wrong on the entire nation. He informed Rome that the Jews were plotting and planning a revolt against them (Gittin 55b).

This story imprinted itself deeply into the nation's memory. From then on, an informer was treated with unfathomable disdain. Such a person was considered to be without religion or faith. He could not be a witness. His oath was not considered to be truthful (H. Mishpat 338). R. Shila was said to have claimed that if he ever killed a Jew threatening him with denunciation, he would plead self-defense (Berahot 58a).

During the reign of King David, Jews were known to have been pious. Yet, despite this, they were not successful on the battlefield, and lost many battles because there were informers in their midst. In contrast, during the reign of King Ahab, when Jews were idol worshippers and heretics, they were always victorious and God blessed their arms because there were no informers or traitors in their midst (Jer Pe'ah 16a).

In cursing the Israelites for not having faith in their God, Moses threatens, "your enemies will rule over you" (Leviticus 26:17). These will not be foreign enemies who don't know your secrets, but your own. They will be enemies from among your own people who know the innermost secrets of your lives (Rashi). This prediction was fulfilled, especially in the Middle Ages when Jews eked out a meager existence in the dark alleys of the ghetto in an atmosphere of pervasive hatred and scorn. Baseless accusations and groundless suspicions often sufficed to turn them over to the refined torturers and tormentors. The usual motivating factors that encouraged weak individuals to inform, were a desire to make oneself useful to the authorities, a hoped-for reward, and an improvement in ones own miserable condition. Succumbing to temptation, these traitors were covered with eternal shame, and stained their names for all time.

For a sinner, Judaism offers understanding and forgiveness; for an informer, only scorn.

ON THE MARGINS OF THE DAY:
THE SCHOOL AND THE HOME[98]

On the threshold of the new school year, our thoughts once again turn to a problem that overshadows all other current issues. All of us are troubled and concerned how to raise a new generation of Jews who are both spiritually and physically healthy. This burden rests especially on the shoulders of our teachers and educators, who are responsible for assuring the future of the Jewish people.

It is axiomatic that the major goal of all education is to prepare a child to participate in social life. *Non scholae sed vitae discimus* – the purpose of educating a child is to prepare him for the road ahead in life.

Theoretical knowledge removed from reality and not connected with the ongoing problems of our society, may influence the child's intellectual development, broaden his spiritual horizons, and increase his fund of knowledge, but its direct value on shaping the child's character is limited. Modern pedagogy tries to build a bridge between day-to-day life and education. The relationship between education and practicality has been an issue of concern for our Sages long ago. "Which is of greater merit, learning or action? Rabbi Tarphon considered action to be more important in life. While for Rabbi Akiba, theoretical learning was of greater value. This disagreement was settled, and later became part of the Jewish creed, when a majority of the Sages were of the opinion that only that theoretical learning, which leads to action, is worthy." Theory, connected with the practical; education, that will some day find application in life, and will transform itself into reality, is desirable and welcome.

School, and especially a Jewish school, is primarily a depository of the theoretical, of abstract learning. Here, by studying history and examples from the past, the child becomes acquainted

---

[98] UGGIK #87, September 1935, 3. Original in Polish.

with his obligations and shapes his mission in life. Here, the teacher tries to inculcate a love for the Jewish people and the principles of ethical living. Here, the child learns to think in national, religious, and ethical terms. But is this theory without applying it to reality, sufficient? While a child assimilates ethical theory in school, his first impulse to act sprouts in the free, unrestricted atmosphere of his parental home. In school, a child is passive; at home, he is more actively involved.

The home and the school must therefore complement each other. Parents must ensure that lessons taught at school are translated into practical deeds at home. All the efforts of teachers to raise the child's ethical level at school will be ineffective and fruitless, if parents don't set an ethical standard at home. Prayers and religious principles are taught in school, but the teacher's arduous work will be consigned to failure if the child is not surrounded with religious life at home. In school, he is taught not to lie, not to slander, etc. But if the child's sharp eye or astute ear perceives activities at home that contradict the theory taught in school, in one split second, the child loses confidence in the teacher and what he is being taught. A chasm develops between the school and the home. The teacher is not at fault; the parents are. The child's critical intellect forms a double standard. A schism between theory and action, unfortunately becomes an established fact.

Let us work together for harmony. Between theory and deed; between home and school.

WHERE IS OUR COMMUNITY CENTER?[99]

At the beginning of the New Year, it is customary for us to review all the sins and mistakes committed during the course of the past year.

In my opinion, the greatest sin that burdens us and weighs on our conscience is the fact that the Jewish community of Katowice still does not have its own community center; that we continue to be a homeless community; a homeless wanderer without shelter, without a place of refuge and asylum. Where is the community center that could serve us as a place of meeting, prayer, study, sports, recreation, and entertainment? Where is there an appropriate home for a reading room and library, which are equally important for the young, the aged, the intellectuals, and the common people, and as vital as our daily bread or the air we breathe? Where is that central meeting place, which could serve as the nerve center of our cultural and social life; from which a new energy could flow, which would revive and rejuvenate education and the spiritual life of our withered communal organizations?

Years have passed since our community became part of Mother Poland. New waves of Jews have managed, despite many difficulties and troubles, to come here, establish new albeit modest, businesses; establish homes, and become settled. But we continue to use the few institutions that we found here; institutions that previous generations built for their modest needs. We ourselves have not succeeded in building anything large, anything lasting, anything important.

Why? Are the members of our community really so impoverished that they are unable to accomplish something that all of us agree is necessary, needed, and essential? Not at all! I am familiar with smaller and poorer communities with their own community center. I know communities, where funds were collected over a period of years and which, from a modest start, finally built a building that was a credit to its members and evidence

[99] UGGIK #88, September 1935, 6. Original in Polish.

of their creative power. Why do we lack such energy and perseverance? Why don't we have such ambition and initiative?

In analyzing this unfortunate situation, I come to the conclusion that a significant part of our inaction is due to psychological factors, which somehow inhibit our energy and enterprise.

Despite having lived here for years, many members of the community are still uncomfortable here and feel they are outsiders. They are here with us in body, but their spirit is far away, in areas from which they originated. They have still not overcome their feelings of being transients. They imagine that they arrived here only yesterday and tomorrow, they will leave. It's as if they are guests here. They live in a hurry, in a rush of excitement, and, partly, also in a state of anxiety. Their ancestors are buried in other cemeteries. They spent their youth in a different environment and surroundings. They are not conscious of the fact that years fly by; that their children have become adults, and are starting to demand their independence.

This feeling of being strangers causes them to feel that the pain of the society in which they live, is a foreign pain that does not concern them at all. For, after all, they are only transients here. They think of themselves as guests. But in truth, we are the pioneers of a new Jewish settlement, which will be home in the future for those who live and work here. We are the creators and founders of a new Jewish center, and our obligation is to give form and structure to this newly established community of which each of us is a small part. We are the beginning, the foundation. We are *halutzim* in *golus*! We are responsible for the future generations that will follow us.

Aren't there at least some amongst us who would like to perpetuate their names, and become partners in an enterprise of lasting value?

The community center will be the first stage of the growth and blossoming of our community. Let us start working, as long as there is still time! Let all of us lend a hand to this cooperative effort!

Let Us Build a Community Center!

"The more things change, the more they remain the same."

COMMITTEE-O-MANIA[100]

From time to time, a certain number of community activists gather to discuss some current issue, plan a program, or find a way to cope with the evil of these turbulent times, which casts a gloomy shadow over all of us. The same people usually participate in all these meetings. They are people of good will, who are driven by a desire to serve their people, and take responsibility for carrying out decisions made at these meetings. Typically, the final decision of every such meeting is to appoint a committee, whose function it is to take further action. Unfortunately, this decision is, all too often, also the end of the committee's activity. Its participants disperse with a feeling of having fulfilled their obligations. Within minutes, each of them is already absorbed with his own worries and private concerns. It is no wonder then, that none of the decisions will ever become a reality or be put into action.

Such meetings, which accomplish nothing tangible or practical since a word doesn't automatically become a deed, are not only of no benefit, but cause us a great deal of harm; they demoralize Jewish society, and cause anarchy in the work to benefit everyone. The man in the street soon loses all confidence in these committees, which proliferate like mushrooms after a rain, and ceases to have any interest in their activities. Responsible people are repelled by these barren discussions and pointless debates, and avoid such meetings. They distance themselves from the work and social interaction of such committees, and jealously conserve their time and energy. For a moment, let each of us think of the many committees and commissions at whose birth we were present during the past year, and which have disappeared without a trace, and we will be convinced that the danger arising from multiplying

[100] UGGIK #93, December 1935, 7. Original in Polish.

committees and hypertrophied commissions is quite grave.

Our ability to council with each other and conserve our strength in order to defend our interests, is nowadays necessary to assure our continued existence. Hard reality forces us to establish committees and commissions frequently. We must, therefore, carefully consider how to prevent the multiplication of useless committees, which are of no benefit to us.

Every active member must, above all, become cognizant of the fact that belonging to a committee constitutes an obligation. It obligates him to work. A member nominated to a committee has an obligation to the Jewish community, and thereby signs a deed that he must unconditionally redeem. From the moment of his election, he becomes indebted to the community, and henceforth must unflaggingly strive to repay his debt. If an individual anticipates that he cannot fulfill his obligation, he should not accept the position. Another person, with the qualifications to accomplish the task, will undoubtedly be found.

Let every person who is active in the Jewish community, become aware of the fact that he will get no laurels for working for the Jewish community, for we have no privileges or honors at our disposal to distribute. We are a people fighting hard for its existence, constantly living in a state of siege. Only one reward awaits an active member, namely the inner satisfaction of a fulfilled obligation. Deep feelings of responsibility in our society's workers are a *sine qua non* of all productive activity.

The fewer people on a committee, the more productive it is. The larger the committee, the less flexible it is. A single, eager individual with a clear vision of the goal to be achieved is, in today's situation, better than a large number of people whom one first has to direct and motivate, and who often become burdens for the working group. This is in accord with the well-known Latin saying, *si duo faciunt idem, non faciunt* – if two are doing something, it doesn't get accomplished.

The most important requirements for communal work are commitment and continuity. An association that suffers from "senility of old age;" which has lost its imagination and vigor, and has stopped serving its purpose, should be disbanded and should disappear from the horizon. A new organization, more responsive to current needs, will be established in its place. A too conservative and too rigid adherence to obsolete institutions and forms is an impediment to progress.

May these loosely formulated thoughts about our communal work help to revitalize and regenerate our committees.

MAXIMS OF WISDOM[101]

אין אדם רואה חובה לעצמו
No human being finds himself guilty (Shabbat 119)

When human beings try to evaluate their own behavior, egotism blurs their vision and blunts their innately sharp critical powers. The spirit of objectivity, so eagerly sought and valued in others, disappears the moment people have to assess and evaluate their own deeds. As a rule, people don't see their own mistakes. People don't tend to acknowledge their own guilt. They don't condemn or rebuke themselves for their own false steps. Egoism and ambition restrain people from convicting and sentencing themselves for mistakes they have committed. They would rather imagine themselves wearing a halo of innocence, than crown themselves with a thorny crown of sins.

In contrast, people observe their neighbors with a sharp eye, and are not willing to forgive even the slightest mistake. While they try to justify their own unpardonable actions before the tribunal of their conscience with all sorts of excuses and pretexts, they do not recognize any extenuating circumstances or moments of weakness in someone else's actions. This lack of objectivity is especially apparent in the relationship between parents and children. Parents try to gloss over their children's faults by keeping them secret, all the while praising their imaginary good qualities. Blind love clouds and warps our judgment of others as much as blind hate.

A lack of objectivity is also a failing of political leaders, who wax enthusiastic about their own ideology, decry the other party's positions as nonsense, and obstinately persecute their adversaries. They are not capable of rising to a position of objectivity. Mesmerized by their own program, their own platitudes, they can't see the positive qualities in the aspirations of those not lured by their watered down slogans.

---

[101] UGGIK #114, October 1936, 2. Original in Polish.

No one accuses himself. Schopenhauer said: "Just as a person carries the load of his own body without feeling its weight, while he would surely feel the weight of another whom he carries, so a person does not perceive his own errors – only those of others. Everyone can use another person as a mirror, to see his own faults and sins. But instead, people usually behave like a dog who, looking into a mirror, barks because he doesn't realize that he is seeing himself instead of another dog." This is a terse and perhaps a little too realistic, but nevertheless apt, judgement. Goethe expresses a similar idea: "Everyone has two bags. He puts his own offenses into one, which he carries on his back. He puts other people's offenses into the other, which he carries on his bosom. He only sees, and shows others, the contents of the bag in front of him."

כי אדם אין צדיק בארץ.....

For there is not one good man on earth that does what is best and does not err.
(Eccl 7:20)

As long as human beings live in this world, striving and struggling against adversaries, they cannot avoid committing sins and making mistakes. Even if they were capable of reaching the highest peak possible on this earth, they would still fall short of perfection; they would still be sacrificed to human fallibility; they would not remain without blemish, and would still not be able to avoid the errors that hide, ready to entrap us at every turn.

When the great Sage Rabbi Eliezer became gravely ill, his students came to comfort and encourage him. The students, full of gloom and foreboding, sat around the bed of their master. The sight of their suffering teacher, whom they respected and loved so much, filled their hearts with great sadness. Only one of them retained a cheerful disposition. He was Rabbi Akiba. His face radiated peace and satisfaction. Dumbfounded by his strange behavior, the students inquired whether Rabbi Eliezer's illness didn't move Rabbi Akiba, and asked him why he showed no empathy. Rabbi Akiba replied: "When I used to see our master in the full luster of good fortune; when his wine didn't sour and his flax didn't decay; his oil didn't become rancid and his honey didn't lose its freshness; when no misfortune touched him or his property, I thought that perhaps God was giving him his full reward in this world, and that he would not get a reward in the world to come. Now, however, when he too is experiencing pain and anxiety, I am certain that real happiness awaits him, as it does us, in the world to come." Then the sick one answered: "Didn't I scrupulously observe God's commandments? Did I omit anything from the Holy Books? Why is God punishing me?" To which Rabbi Akiba replied: "You have taught us, Master, that there is no such thing as a righteous person who never sins" (Sanhedrin 101).

A poet has expressed this thought beautifully:

"Where is the human being without fault? He doesn't exist in this world;
Even perfect crystals have a blemish
There is no perfection without deficiency,
Only when I descend into the grave, will I no longer sin.
There is nothing without a defect, all of us have faults;
Crystals have blemishes and the sun has spots."

RZEWUSKI[102]

וסביביו נשערה מאד
God holds the religious responsible for even the slightest transgression.
(Yevamot 121)

A person who holds a high position and is in the public eye, one on whom all eyes are focused, bears a greater responsibility than the average person. A flaw committed by such a person, who is supposed to be an example and model for others, can inadvertently become a source of confusion and general corruption. There are few people whose philosophy of life is based on personal convictions and on independently developed opinions. More often, we imitate those whom we consider to be wise and noble. We model ourselves on them. We quote them. Those who are role models for others must conduct their lives with the greatest caution and prudence. "If a shepherd is angry with his flock and wants to punish them, he places a blind sheep as their leader" (Bava Kama 52). And

[102] Waclaw Rzewuski (1705-1799) was a Polish playright, poet, and military commander.

when God wants to punish society, He leaves its management to a "blind leader" who leads them astray. A teacher, who doesn't know his subject and teaches it erroneously, spiritually deforms the school children placed in his care.

Demokritos states: "Contrast shows. One error committed by a respected individual will draw more attention than many transgressions committed by one who is evil. Even a small stain is visible on a white cloth, while a large stain may be invisible on a black one. Besides, everyone soon forgives the scoundrel. They will say, 'this is a rascal, what else can you expect from him?' But if a virtuous person stumbles, he makes many happy as they say with pity, 'it's a shame that such a person could sink so low.'" The bad example that such a person sets has a negative impact on the entire community. "A small person going astray is akin to a broken watch – it betrays only one person. However, when a highly placed individual transgresses, he corrupts many and is like a broken tower clock, which betrays the entire town" (Lichtenberg[103]).

---

[103] Georg Christof Lichtenberg (1742-1799), German scientist and satirist.

III

RELIGIOUS RELATIONSHIPS: BETWEEN 'MAN AND GOD'

*Essays in this section explore the relationship between human beings and God. "The Call to the Prophets" is dedicated to the memory of Rabbi Jakob Cohn, the first Rabbi of the Katowice community who served from 1872 until his death sometime during the First World War. In this essay, Rabbi Chameides examines the reluctance of the Major Prophets, Moses, Jeremiah, and Isaiah, to become emissaries of God, and interpret His word to mankind, and the manner in which each perceived God. Their reluctance was due partly to their self-perception as unworthy to be intermediaries, and partly to the fact that words had lost their power, except in the hands of the poet. The development of religious poetry as **the** Jewish art form is discussed in "Art."*

He describes the tension within Judaism between ritual (Priesthood), and the highest form of ethical behavior and thought (Prophecy). He comes to the conclusion that "each of us has an obligation to reconcile Priesthood with Prophecy; to inspire the deed with pure thought and to allow ourselves to be stirred in thought by the elevated priestly act."

Our different perceptions of God, as the creator of all natural phenomena, as the director of our history, and as the one who will fulfill our dreams in the future, "in messianic times," is the theme that is explored in "The Three Attributes of God" and "The Book of Koheleth." In the latter, Rabbi Chameides dramatically describes the pessimism and lack of direction that can overwhelm a person who does not see the Divine all around him. He describes why Judaism rejected Koheleth's formulation about nature, human beings, and eternity and, despite that, included the book in the Canon.

The dilemma that hovers over several essays, namely the lack of a humanizing and civilizing effect of the Torah on world, is more fully explored in another section.

ART[104]

Religious Considerations of the Weekly Portion ויקהל

I

What is art? Poetry and painting, music and sculpture, graphic design and architecture all belong to the world of art. But what is art? Art is a world of illusion woven by human fantasy alongside the world of reality. Art is that other world, conceptualized and executed by human beings weary of reality; a world that is conceived and created during blessed hours of dreaming and yearning. The intellect and the immutable laws of nature reign supreme in the domain of reality. In the world of art, the scepter is wielded by emotion and fantasy. Art is gratification of the play instinct in man; a reflection of our desires; a momentary expression of our longing for the pure, perfect form.

Nature offers an original, primitive impulse for artistic form and demands that human beings imitate and copy it. The bird warbles its song in the air and humans attempt, in note and word, to make an identical sound expressing pain and happiness, pleasure and misery. Thus tonal art and poetry were created. The natural rhythm of the sea surges uninterruptedly before our eyes, constantly giving birth to new forms, unfolding hitherto unknown fascinations, revealing inscrutable secrets. Human beings long to hold on to these scenes, to capture them, and not to allow them to fade away. Fortune and misfortune, anxiety and apprehensive hope, flaming passion and painful self-denial, all the sensations and experiences that move or disturb us, are transformed by the creative genius into an artistic monument, carried aloft from the depths of reality into the sphere of the unique and the eternal.

II

Did art, in the conventional meaning of the word, exist in ancient Israel? Did the Jewish people, during its period of national

---

[104] UGGIK #3, March 1932, 4-5. Original in German.

independence and its flowering, give evidence of possessing its own type of art? Did it create its own unique art form? Hardly! We lagged far behind the other nations of the day in plastic arts and architecture. Art was not our domain; it was seldom the object of our national aspirations.

How can we explain this phenomenon? Were we artistically inept? No! The reason lies deeper. If art is an expression of our innermost feelings, then the Jew, from the very beginning of his history, chose and studied another way of reaching the spiritual world of yearning and emotion – by way of religion! In prayer, in its perpetual search for a relationship with God, Israel was able to find the gratification and satisfaction for those innermost urges that drove other nations towards art.

Because of this, we developed one art form, the lyricism of the Psalms and the poetry of the synagogue, to its highest perfection. Our art had its origin in religion. It is the handmaiden of religion. Bezalel, the first Jewish artist, did not create from within himself; he did not design the plan of the Tabernacle from his own intuition. He was merely an executing instrument of God's command. As is written in our *sidra*, "and Moses spoke to the children of Israel. See, the Lord has called Bezalel by name...And He has filled him with the spirit of God, in wisdom, in understanding, in knowledge, and in all manner of workmanship; to devise skillful works, to work in gold, in silver, and in brass" (Exodus 35:30-33). That was the birth of Jewish art. We received it as a present directly from God, in order to return it to Him in every new Psalm, in every intricately composed Hymn, and in our emotional prayers.

כי ממך הכל ומידך נתנו לך
For everything comes from You
Even our offerings, comes from Your hand

THE CALL TO THE PROPHETS[105]
In Memory of Rabbi Dr. Jakob Cohn[106]
(Yarzeit – 20 Nissan)

In the desert, in the mysterious twilight of a Temple Hall, at the bank of a river, or even in the midst of the thunderous noise of every day life, the voice of God presses itself on the ears of the prophet-to-be. He is being called; he is being appointed. A wide breach suddenly crashes into his ordinary human existence. For the first time, he gazes at the sublime, at the Divine with widely open and astonished eyes. He must now abandon his temporal boundary, his bodily restriction, the narrowness of ordinary mortals, in order to become an emissary; an emissary from God to man, from the creator to the created. From now on, he will no longer be an ordinary human being. Instead, he will become an intermediary, a man whose existence lies on the boundary of two worlds. His roots will be buried deep in the soil of life, anchored in the temporal, but his spirit will soar, and be in contact with the celestial, with the Divine.

The prophet, however, declines this summons from God. He does not receive the message gladly. He does not want to become a prophet. He wants to be allowed to remain an ordinary human being. He wants to remain a simple human being, a modest man, not an intermediary man. Not a human being on the boundary, not here and there, in this and the other world simultaneously. He perceives danger; he sees a personal calamity in this call to prophecy. The prophet flees from God.

Moses, Isaiah, and Jeremiah all declined to accept the position of prophet. Each sought to divest himself of the prophetic obligation.

When God gave Moses the assignment of going to Egypt to deliver a message of liberation to his brothers, he resisted. "I am not a master of words," he tells God as a reason for his hesitation. I am not an orator. I lack oratorical skills. I don't understand how to form

---

[105] UGGIK #7, April 1932, 3-4. Original in German.
[106] Rabbi Cohn was the first Rabbi of Kattowitz.

words, to build sentences. Is that really true? Moses – not an orator? Moses – not a master of style? Would he not, prior to his death, create that lofty poetic work that begins with the words, "Hear O Heaven!" that captivates every reader with its force, vitality, and deep ideas to this very day? He, who called on heaven and earth and all of nature to hear his words, could he really have been so inarticulate as to consider himself incapable of delivering a message of freedom to an enslaved people? No! Moses did not decline the prophetic call because he was not a master of the ordinary word, but because he did not consider himself to be master of the creative word. Moses says to God, "I am not a master of the creative word."

For the word, just like humanity, has experienced a long history and development. At the beginning, human beings were pure, unblemished, moved by the Divine, and at the beginning, the word too was pure, divine, creative. When God created the world, He created it solely with His word, without exertion or effort! "And God said 'let there be light' and there was light." The word sufficed to bring light into chaos. "By the divine word were the heavens created," sings the Psalmist. The word radiated creative force. It was the word that called the light, the heavens, and the entire creation into existence out of nothing. The first human being still possessed the creative power of the word. After God created animals and birds, He brought each of them to Adam so that Adam could give them suitable names. Our Sages saw this naming as the first, but also the last, creative act of the human word. When Adam, by virtue of his sin, lost his primordial greatness, his God-given splendor, the word too lost its primordial strength, its original power. The word sank to become merely a means of communication.

In the very next generation, Cain abused the word. Using words, he sought to conceal his brother's murder. He tried to conceal his sin by talking. Since then, the word has lost its nobility, and only the poet can still occasionally restore it. Only to the gifted poet, does it give up its innate, secret power.

"I am not master of the word," Moses bewails and means, "I am not master of the creative word. I am merely a creation, not a creator."

Isaiah's call proceeded along entirely different lines. He

experienced God foremost as the Holy One. He informs us about his call as follows: "And I saw the Lord sitting on a high throne. Seraphim were standing above Him. Each one had six wings. And one called to the other, 'Holy, Holy, Holy, is the Lord of hosts.' And the posts of the door were moved, and the house was filled with smoke. Then I spoke, 'Woe is me for I am undone! Because I am a man of unclean lips and I dwell in the midst of a people of unclean lips.'" The essentials that do not allow Isaiah to encounter the Kaddosh (Holy One), the holiness of God, are his personal impurity, and the absence of holiness in humanity. Isaiah experienced God as the Holy One, as the ideal of a perfect purity that will always be denied to mankind.

Not everyone experiences God in the same way. He does not manifest Himself to everyone in the same form, in the same vision. At the Red Sea, our ancestors saw Him as a warrior. They experienced Him as strong and mighty. But wasn't He also referred to as compassionate and all bountiful? Now He is the zealot who visits the sins of the fathers on the children's children, and then He becomes the helper of the weak and downtrodden, the father of the widow and orphan. To Job, He spoke out of a storm, and to the Psalmist out of the waves of the sea. To still others, He appeared veiled in clouds. He is polymorphic, multifaceted; sometimes concerned with the condition of humanity, and at other times with the state of the individual.

Moses came to know Him as the Creator. Isaiah understood Him as the Holy One. How then can he, a man with impure lips, become the prophet of holiness?

The inner hesitation that Jeremiah has to overcome when the call of God comes to him is strange indeed. A new factor comes into play in his God experience. To his eye, God manifests Himself as the ruler of history, as the disposer of nations from eternity to eternity. Jeremiah lived at a time of historical upheaval, and great national catastrophes. He saw the sudden downfall of great world powers. Before his eyes and with a premonition of its end, the newly established Babylonian empire rose to greatness. He witnessed the oncoming destruction of the Jewish state drawing near like an avalanche. Is it any wonder, then, that it is precisely a historical factor that plays such a prominent role in his God experience? History however spans time; it describes the eternal passage of time. History unravels itself on the thread of time. Each historical event lasts only from one point in time to another, only to be replaced by a new event, which likewise is only transient. Everything in history is changeable, fluctuating, fluid, temporary. Nothing in it is firm, durable, eternal. Therefore, when God, the unchangeable, the eternal, wants to make Jeremiah his herald, Jeremiah is terrified and calls out: "See, I cannot speak, for I am a mere youth." I am young, a day-old creation, a fleeting entity. You, on the other hand, are primeval, eternal, permanent. I am merely a wave on the ocean of time while You are exalted over all time. I am a slave of time, imprisoned by time, You outlast all time; You are imperishable. How can I have the power to speak in the name of eternity? "See, I cannot speak for I am a mere youth." Just like Moses, Jeremiah too complains about his inadequacy with words, but on a different basis. Jeremiah sees himself as nothing compared to God. His life comprises only a small span of time. How then, could he become the messenger of the Eternal?

Moses experienced God as the **Creator**, Isaiah as the **Holy One**, and Jeremiah as the **Eternal One**.

II

We now understand the hesitation and anguish that the prophets experienced, when the call came and they sought to decline it: Moses, because of his misgivings about the shape, construction, and creative power of his words; Isaiah, because of his feelings of personal unholiness compared to the All Holy; and Jeremiah, because of the unbridgeable chasm between the time constraints of human beings and the eternity of God. Let us briefly examine how God answered their misgivings, calmed their inner hesitations, and converted their vacillations and faint-heartedness.

As we noted above, Jeremiah saw the abyss of time that separates humanity from God; the time-limited from the timeless. Jeremiah resists and hesitates to accept the prophetic calling because he considers it presumptuous, nay – impossible, for a temporal being to speak in the name of the Eternal.

Then God called to him: "Don't say I am a youth! I chose you even before I formed you in the belly; before you came out of the womb I sanctified you." Only your corporal covering is young, your soul is as old as eternity itself, since it is part of eternity. The Midrash states that all the prophets received their prophetic abilities at Sinai. As God revealed Himself to the Jews in the wilderness, all souls hovered over Sinai. Before he ever existed, Jeremiah too, was a conception of God. He existed as a spirit long before he made his appearance in the corporal, visible world. Jeremiah's doubts were silenced when he was informed that he, a temporal being, encompasses a piece of eternity. Our visible manifestation is indeed transient, but our spirit flows from the All-spiritual and returns to the All-spiritual.

Isaiah's hesitation was answered in a different manner. With a symbolic act, God showed him that his lament, that unholiness imprisons human beings, is unjustified. "Then flew unto me one of the Seraphim," declares Isaiah, "with a glowing stone in his hand which he had taken with tongs from off the altar. And he touched my mouth with it and said: 'Lo this has touched your lips, and your iniquity is taken away, and your sin is expiated'" (Isaiah 6:6). When a human being is unholy, a fire exists that can cleanse him; a fire, taken from an altar glowing with the rapture of holiness. A glowing fire exists that can convert "a man of unclean lips" into a "Kaddosh." A glowing fire from a pure source, given to us by one of the Seraphim, can change us as it changed Isaiah who became holy enough to become a prophet when he came into contact with the pure fire of the altar.

God did not answer Moses' refusal to follow His call, either by word or by a symbolic action. The response that Moses evoked was appropriate to his extraordinary stature. Henceforth, Moses would no longer be the sole leader of the people. His brother Aaron would now be at his side. The priest would henceforth walk at the side of the prophet. The Priesthood was taken from Moses, and given to Aaron. Action was separated from thought. The Priest symbolizes the pure, pristine act; the holy, solemn service, while the prophet is a symbol of pure thought, clear knowledge. Moses became the father of prophecy; Aaron the founder of the Priesthood. Since that time, Prophecy and Priesthood have signified the two mighty but equal arms of Judaism. Religious action stemmed from the Priesthood while pure faith in God, cleansed of all dross stemmed from Prophecy. Unfortunately, these two streams did not always flow parallel to each other. Deed and thought could not always be fused into a superior unity. Prophet and Priest often stood antagonistically against each other. This conflict reached its most tragic zenith with Jeremiah who, though a member of a priestly family, as prophet, had to act against the Priesthood. An irreparable fissure rends his soul.

Tension between the pure, religious act and genuine knowledge forms the backdrop of the entire spiritual history of Judaism. It is especially evident when Jewish thought comes in contact with a strange milieu. This tension, between the "duty of the heart" and the "duty of the precept," constituted the basic theme of Jewish philosophy of the Middle Ages. A few individual personalities managed to bring Jewish action and deed into harmony in a most admirable manner. Towering among them was that beacon of light, Maimonides, who appeared to his contemporaries as a savior for their spiritual needs, carrying in one hand his legal codex (Mishna Torah), and in his other the "Guide to the Perplexed" (Moreh Nebuchim).

Each of us has an obligation to reconcile Priesthood with Prophecy. To inspire the deed with pure thought, and to allow ourselves to be stirred in thought by the elevated priestly act. This obligation falls especially heavily on Judaism's leaders whose life and activity are consecrated to the realization of the prophetic words:

כי שפתי כהן ישמרו דעת
ותורה יבקשו מפיהו כי מלאך ה' צבאות הוא
"The lips of the Priest protect knowledge;
instruction is sought from his mouth,
because he is a messenger of God"

פינחס
PINHAS[107]

Occasionally, life forces us to perform tasks in flagrant contradiction to our true nature and character. Suddenly, we are derailed from our course. Mild mannered and peaceful people are sometimes transformed into warriors and wild fanatics. That is what happened to Pinhas the Priest, and also to Prophet Elijah, the hero of our *haftara*. Both were apostles of peace. Their life-mission and work was the teaching and dissemination of a philosophy of peace. As a Priest, Pinhas was a mediator between human beings and God. Elijah's peaceful approach to life is evident from his description of God's revelation. "And behold, the Lord passed by, and a great and strong wind rent the mountains and broke the rocks in pieces before the Lord, but the Lord was not in the wind; and after the wind an earthquake, but the Lord was not in the earthquake; and after the earthquake a fire, but the Lord was not in the fire; and after the fire a still small voice." It was here that God's majesty was near. Elijah experienced Divinity in the silence, in the stillness, in the calm grandeur of peace and tranquility. But wasn't he also, like Pinhas, a zealot? Wasn't his entire life, one long and hard fought battle against the priests of Baal and the false prophets? Here we have two contradictory figures marching through our *sidra* and *haftorah*, whose souls were submerged in harmony, but whose historical appearance was accompanied by a tempest. Therein lies their tragedy. Their ever-symbolic personalities are evident in the discrepancy between their character and their action. Peaceful human beings born in a tempestuous time. In such circumstances, weak souls usually perish. The pure sound of the harp is smashed against the rugged cliffs of the times, and is silenced. Strong souls pull themselves together, and, gnashing their teeth, suppress every inborn impulse of goodness, and become warriors. However, if one

[107] UGGIK #12, July 1932, 4. Original in German.

looks deeper one sees that under their armored breast there beats a warm heart; a heart that bleeds whenever it inflicts a wound.

Pinhas and Elijah, the Priest and the Prophet, stumbled into the battle zone against their wills and against their natures. The battle is only one episode in their lives. Pinhas, after all, is given the Divine promise, "I give unto him my covenant of peace." He had to restore his peace of mind, which God had to sacrifice. Elijah too is not remembered in Jewish history as a zealot, but rather as the forerunner of the Messianic era. Three days before the coming of the Messiah, Elijah will amble over the hills of Palestine crying and bewailing: "Mountains of Eretz Yisrael! How much longer will you remain desolate, bare, and deserted?" His voice will be heard from one end of the earth to the other, and then a shout of joy will emanate from his mouth שלום בא – Peace has come to the world! Then it will be said,

הנה על ההרים רגלי מבשר משמיע שלום

Behold the messenger, whose promise is שלום (peace) strides over the mountains!

THE THREE ATTRIBUTES OF GOD [108]

ברוך אתה ה' אלקינו מלך העולם שהחינו וקימנו והגינו לזמן הזה
"Blessed are You, our eternal God, King of the universe
who has kept us alive, has supported us,
and has allowed us to reach this time! "

ה' אלקינו מלך העולם – "Our Eternal God, King of the universe!" –
Every blessing contains these three invocations. This threefold
appellation of God suggests the threefold relationship that every
Jew has with his God. ה', אלקינו מלך העולם points out the three
ways by which our spirit can reach God, and be united with Him.

ה' – This tetragrammaton name of God, which we are not
allowed to write or speak but only to allude to, is the first path to
God. It is a way of acknowledging God through His creation.
Whenever we look in amazement at everything around us,
whenever we admire the woof and weave of God's power in nature,
we are reaching out to God, we are overcome by the thrilling
experience of God's omnipotence. ה' represents the essence and
redirects human perception from the created to the Creator, from a
consideration of created beings to recognition of the uncreated, the
Eternal.

אלקינו – our God! The God who has a personal and a special
relationship with us. The God who is revealed to us in the life of
every individual human being; who is especially manifest in the life
and suffering of nations. אלקינו – our God, who stepped out of His
seclusion and other-worldliness, and concluded a covenant with us.
אלקינו is the second path to God. It leads from a consideration of
events in history to the Creator of these events, from those who are
shaped to the Shaper, from events in the lives of nations and human
beings, to the Dispenser, the Giver of all life.

מלך העולם – King of the universe. The God who, one day in
the anticipated, yearned-for Messianic days will be King of the

[108] UGGIK #16, September 1932, 4-5. Original in German.

entire world and before whom all creatures will bow down in reverence. "King of the universe" is the ideal we Jews have given to humanity as a gift. It is the main goal we strive for. It is the assignment that we Jews must fulfill. It is the essence of everything that our Prophets taught: To make God, the King of the entire world.

'ה – is the first way one can get to know God. It is the idea of the Divine that flashes within us when we delve into the mysteries and beauty of nature. It is the Divine breath that wafts towards us from field and brook, from forest and mountain. The Psalmist sings "שויתי ה' לנגדי תמיד" – I have always set God before me." God is always *before* me. When I lift up my eyes towards heaven, השמים מספרים כבד אל – I hear the heavens herald God's praise. When I stand at the seashore and cast my glance into its depths, I recognize כי לו הים – that the sea *belongs* to Him. He created it. When I step into the darkness of the rustling forest, אז ירננו כל עצי יער – I hear all the trees singing, singing that eternal song of God's perfection. And when I turn my gaze onto the mountain peaks, יחד הרים ירננו – the mountains shout for joy, and then I understand the hymn of praise that the mountains sing to God. "How great, how overwhelming are Your works, O God!" I see You everywhere; I hear You everywhere! You surround me from all sides and therefore שויתי ה' לנגדי תמיד – I always have God before my eyes, and therefore, says the Psalmist, God is always present. *He is the present.*

II

אלקינו – our God, the one we are permitted to designate as *ours*; our personal God; the navigator of our history. He, who calls to us out of the past. He, who speaks to us from the miracles of antiquity. He, about whom each of us says "זה אלי – this is *my* God," because He was also the God of my father. "Remember the days of antiquity; ponder over the time of bygone generations. Ask your father and he will make it known to you, the aged among you, and they will tell you. He found Israel in the desert, in the howling of the wilderness. He protected and shielded it like the apple of His eye. Just as the eagle hovers over its young, He spread His wings, took

Israel, and carried him on His wings. God alone escorted him without any extraneous Divine power at His side." He is our God who accompanies us on our wanderings in exile, who has been with us in Egypt and Babylonia, in Spain and in the other lands of exile, and who today continues to hover over us and protect us.

III

מלך העולם – King of the *entire* universe. God of the future messianic days about whom it is said, "and God will be King over the entire earth and in that day shall He be one and His name be one." He, about whom our poet-philosophers spoke, our singers sang, our prophets dreamed. About whom Isaiah prophesied: "And it will come to pass at the end of days, that God's temple will be firmly established, and all nations shall flock towards Him in order to walk in His footsteps. Then shall the Torah go forth from Zion and God's word from Jerusalem." During the bitterest times of Jewish history, under the oppressor's most severe yoke, we never stopped hoping for that day, praying for that time, when humanity's victims will finally find peace, when nation shall not lift up sword against nation, when no nation shall do battle against another, when God alone shall be מלך העולם – King of the universe.

'ה is the *omnipresent* God; אלקינו – the God we have come to know through our history, from our past; מלך העולם – the God who will be recognized by all in the *future*. These three attributes of God resound on Rosh Hashana, when the past, present, and future are bound together into one experience. These same three attributes are also expressed in the three words of gratitude: שהחינו, וקימנו והגיענו

שהחינו – who has given us the gift of life – is associated with the first of God's appellations in the blessing, the name 'ה, which signifies the manifestation of God in nature. As part of nature, we are maintained and supported by the same power that animates and gives life to everything that is organic. Every one of us is a small ripple in the sea of life, which is always roaring and surging and never remains still. At our most elemental level, we are related to animal and to stone. We are all a part of a continuum. Only when we are united and spiritually connected with all of creation, can we find true peace. At that point, suffering and pain will disappear. We will no longer need to cry or laugh. We will come to understand and remain still. Every tree is your brother. You will see your own reflection in every plant. *One* arm embraces you all. *His* arm. Why then despair? Does the flower cry when it withers? Does a star cry when it is extinguished? We have, unfortunately, lost this blessed concept. Each of us feels the burden of fate. Every one of us is a hero with a different life drama. Our personal experiences have separated us from nature. We have torn ourselves loose from the tree of life of all, and each of us is separately falling into his own abyss...

וקימנו – "who has sustained us" alludes to the second appellation of God. אלקינו – our God, to whom we give grateful thanks for our קיום – our continued existence. Who has helped us through national catastrophes; who has allowed us to persevere, and come through world shattering events. Our continued existence has made a mockery of the normal logic of history. From a logical point of view, we should have disappeared long ago. According to the generally accepted concepts of nations, peoples, and states, we should have lost our right to exist when our land was destroyed. That we have not disappeared in a timely fashion makes us an exception in human history. And exceptions are not appreciated. The "usual" rules the world because it does not tax our reasoning powers. It functions quietly. One can depend on things that are regular. Exceptions are uncomfortable. And not only in grammar. They demand a never-flagging state of alertness, a never-tiring memory. Hence the Jew-hatred. When we cannot grasp a phenomenon intellectually, our vanity becomes offended, and we either scorn it or admire it. If we admire it, we don't *need* to understand it, and if we scorn it, we don't *want* to understand it. In either case, we are satisfied. Our intellect remains unchallenged. We Jews are simultaneously admired and hated. Between the glowing heat of admiration and the frosty breath of hatred lies the narrow path of our קיום – our existence that leads to אלקינו our God, who suffers with us.

והגיענו לזמן הזה – we want to translate this loosely – "that we may succeed to reach that day," when the third appellation of God, מלך העולם, King of the universe, will become a reality; when the Messianic era will dawn on earth. "When Judah's harp, vibrated by the breath of Divine inspiration, awakened in the human heart the sound of the lute whose enchantment can transform the human soul into ecstasy. This melody has always been the source of our courage, of our solace, of our strength and we have sung it on all our wanderings. It is the music of the Messianic era, the triumphal hymn, which, one day, will be sung by all humanity; the true Psalm of life that will be sung by all humanity when Israel's assignment to teach it will have been completed. Its harmony is the harmony of the human family, finally united in peace and brotherhood; finally happy in its return to the one great Father." (Mendes).

THE BOOK OF KOHELETH [ECCLESIASTES][109]

> The Sages wanted to conceal the book of Koheleth
> (Shabbat 30)

Koheleth is the preacher of pessimism. His book shrouds life in a melancholy state of mind. Disillusionment, despair, and a weary self-denial cry out from his negative view of life. He did not, however, come to this view secluded in the solitude of a study. Nor is his book a harmonious philosophy of life, a polished philosophical system. Koheleth stands in the middle of life. He knows it face to face. Indeed, he clings to life, and loves it with the entire passion of his glowing soul. It is precisely for this reason that he becomes despondent about life's meaning; that he founders on the enigmas of its mysteries. The book of Koheleth is the despairing cry of a man who has fruitlessly struggled his entire life in an attempt to unravel the secrets of the world and of nature; who has pounded on the door of knowledge in vain. It is the last disturbing complaint of a delirious human being wounded by striking the boundaries of the ultimate. Koheleth pleads for enlightenment. He begs for an explanation for all the mysteries that surround him. He pleads to understand the meaning of the phenomena that surround him everywhere. But he finds himself alone. He can find no answer. There is no one to offer him a helping hand to lead him, groping and searching, out of the darkness; there is no beam of light pointing the way to enlightenment.

From the moment that the futility of his efforts became clear to him; from the moment that he realized the uselessness of his inquiries and his brooding, no sun shone for Koheleth, no flower bloomed for him, no spring bubbled for him. Nothing could enthuse or excite him anymore. There was nothing that could rekindle his courage to live. Every source of joy was dammed up. What he now wrote, composed, and preached was only the stammering of his

---

[109] UGGIK #64, September 1934, 5-7. Original in German.

contempt for life, the ranting of a fanatic pessimist who takes revenge on life by mocking it, sneering at it, and rejecting it. Koheleth had lost a living relationship with nature, with humanity, and with eternity.

I

Koheleth views the events of nature as tiring routines, as tedious mechanized processes. "And the sun rises, and the sun sets" (Eccl. 1:5). There is no emotion or sense of wonder at these sublime phenomena of nature. No expression of humility on seeing these majestic events. For Koheleth, the sun is merely a brightly shining fireball that appears on the horizon at a predetermined time and, at a specified time, disappears. While the Psalmist sings a hymn to the sun,... "Like a groom coming forth from the chamber, the sun comes forth; it rejoices like a hero, eager to run its course; nothing remains hidden from its glow" (Psalms 19:6), a tired smirk of disappointment plays on Koheleth's lips on seeing the shining sun. "Everything that is, already was." Nature has no power over him. He scoffs at its monotony. He finds the eternal cycle of events uniform and unattractive. He can discover nothing alive in it. For him, it is hopeless, monotonous, mechanical – lifeless. A windstorm, the gentle rustling of the air, the churning, cleansing power of a rainstorm only evoke a cold, critical observation from him. "The wind blows towards the south, then it turns towards the north; round and round goes the wind, turning and returning on its track" (Eccl. 1:6). He has forgotten the language of nature. "And God answered Job out of the storm" (Job 38:1). Even a pessimist like Job was capable of hearing the voice of God in a storm. "He makes the wind his messengers" (Psalms 104:4). To the poet of the Psalms, the wind is a messenger of God, an emissary of His majesty. Koheleth knows nothing of this. For him, the sun and the storm are but mute images of nature. Lost in thought, Koheleth stands before a clear stream. Silvery currents are rushing at his feet. His face is mirrored in the water flowing towards him. But almost immediately, he wrinkles his brow with the bitter reproach: "All the streams flow into the sea but the sea is not full. To the place from which they flow, the streams flow back again" (Eccl. 1:7). Koheleth doesn't hear the Divine voice rustling out of the stream. He does not call out, enraptured: "Above the thunder of the mighty waters, more majestic than the breakers of the sea is the Lord, majestic on high" (Psalms 93:4). Koheleth also remains cold and apathetic when he confronts the sea. He has lost a feeling for the Divine in nature.

Disillusioned, he turns his back on nature and directs his examining eye towards humanity, their lives, their aspirations, their ideals. But here too, Koheleth encounters the same uniformity that he sees in nature. Here too, there is the same act, the same humdrum. "For everything there is an appointed season, and a time for everything under the sun. A time to be born and a time to die. A time to mourn and a time to rejoice. A time to love and a time to hate. A time to wage war and a time for peace" (Eccl. 3:1,2,8). Everything has its appointed time. Everything goes on automatically by some preordained schedule. One is born and one dies. One dances and one mourns. One loves and one hates. Everything at its appointed time. At the appropriate age. At the prescribed hour. Again, the rigid order, the uniformity – exactly as in nature. Again the mechanical. Nothing about a volition that is alive. Nothing exciting. Nothing deeply moving. Nothing overwhelming. No escape from the boundaries that have been drawn. No possibility to flee from the daily routine, the habitual. Everything follows a prescribed course. It is made to work and is directed, instigated, and propelled by an invisible hand, by a concealed power whose source Koheleth suspects, searches for, but never understands.

Koheleth gives no hint of the pain of a misspent life. We are not confronted with a Job, a man sorely tried by fate, a man who bears a grievance and quarrels with God. No, Koheleth was a King. Koheleth had tasted all the joys and benefits of life. But, behind every one of earth's blessings, he saw only a gloomy darkness lurking in ambush to change everything into nothing. He considers the abundance and pleasures of this world as only a means of dazzling and stupefying human beings; of deceiving them about the lack of meaning of their lives. So, as he had previously seen in nature, Koheleth sees in human lives only an empty, purposeless struggle, a rising and a falling, a coming and a going, without purpose, without end, without sense...

And then a final thought dawns on him. Nature and life are both dull and desolate. Here on earth, everything is truly empty. But perhaps afterwards, when this tumultuous play ends, when the long silence of death begins, perhaps only then does true life begin. Perhaps everything here is only a dream and an illusion and only there, does the great awakening begin. Perhaps, after everything that is mortal has ended; after the deception has been stripped off; after the corporal mantle has fallen and the earthly prison overpowered, perhaps only then does pure joy, real existence, begin.

But as soon as Koheleth believes that he has finally discovered the truth; as soon as he thinks that he understands life's meaning, the long cultivated doubt sneaks out of a concealed corner of his heart and begins to gnaw the root of this last hope. He, who had previously doubted nature and humanity, will be deprived of the last consolation – the hope for an existence after death, the hope for a better afterlife. "Who knows," he asks "if a man's life-breath does rise upward, and if a beast's breath does sink down into the earth? Both came from dust and both return to dust" (Eccl. 3:21,20). With this, Koheleth's last hope is buried in the dust. Koheleth is frustrated by questions and shattered by doubts. Nevertheless, from time to time he pulls himself together and recommends enjoyment to the young before old age overtakes them. He tries to persuade the reader to enjoy a life of pleasure and happiness. But one does not believe him, that skeptic. One senses that he is searching for one final solid foothold, but that he is not really serious. Koheleth does indeed speak about God, and religious-ethical principles. But only incidentally. There are occasional sparks in the mournful atmosphere of this book but they never come together into a warming flame, into a Divine glow. Solitary and flickering, they remain submerged in a sea of darkness and pessimism.

II

"The Sages wanted to conceal the book of Koheleth"

Koheleth has no message for a people who see a defined order in the universe from its very beginning; for a people whose relationship with nature, life, and eternity is entirely different from that of Koheleth; for a people with a creation story, which states, "And God saw all that he had created and he saw that it was very good." Judaism had surmounted Koheleth's doubts long ago. Our Sages, who condemned the book from a Jewish point of view, tried to transmit this message by establishing the tradition of reading this book on *Shemini Atzeret*.[110] No other holiday answers Koheleth's doubts so emphatically, so unequivocally.

While Koheleth sees in nature only a tedious, mechanical power rather than the Divine spirit that governs it, we answer with the prayer for rain, תפלת הגשם. We answer with a declaration of faith that a perfect force, God's wish, directs the manifestations of nature. To Koheleth's prosaic consideration of the wind's whirling movement, we answer שאתה הוא ה' משיב הרוח – You O God are the one who blows the wind, causes the rain to fall, continually recreates, revives, and sustains the world.

Koheleth's view of nature leaves the Divine hidden, because he is fixated on its individual phenomena. He does not seem to be able to rise above these, and see the whole instead of its parts. His view of nature is completely different from that of Judaism. The Jew does not become lost in nature's individual phenomena. He does not allow himself to be captivated and mesmerized by the individual phenomena of nature. Rather, the Jewish view is to attempt to unify its diverse manifestations. The Jewish spirit seeks to grasp the entirety, and not to lose sight of the inter-relationship of these phenomena. Koheleth sees the sun – by itself; the stream – by itself. Not united into one entity. He does not search for the power that

---

[110] There are various customs as to when the book of Koheleth is read. It was the German custom to read it on the Intermediate Shabbat of Tabernacles, unless the eighth day (Shemini Atzereth) fell on Shabbat. It appears that the custom in Katowice was to read it on Shemini Atzereth.

penetrates everything; that flows through the sun, the stream, and the wind, and unites them. How different is the attitude towards nature expressed in the Mishnah! "When experiencing thunder, storm, or lightning, one says the blessing: 'Blessed are You, whose might and power fill the world'" (Berahot 9:2). One doesn't say a blessing for the One who makes the lightning strike, the thunder roll, and the wind blow, but rather "whose power and might fills the entire world." Our attention is focused on the whole. Storm, thunder, and lightning are manifestations of the same single force that permeates all of creation. Further on, we read: "On seeing mountains, hills, seas, and streams, the blessing 'Blessed are You who has completed the creative process,' is said." Not, "blessed are You who created mountain, hill, sea, or stream," but rather, blessed is the creator of *everything*. The Jewish attitude towards nature is cosmic. For us, each individual manifestation of nature represents one additional bond to the All-One.

This striving to achieve unity, this demand for the totality, is one of the most important characteristics of the Jewish spirit. In this regard, another Mishnah teaches: "He who says 'how beautiful is this tree, how beautiful is this field' has forfeited his soul" (Pirkei Avot III:9). A person who only sees an isolated tree; who only notices a field without considering the whole, the entire world, has forfeited his soul. He has separated his soul from unity, and has succumbed to division. Such a human being has joined the non-Jewish view of nature. Like Koheleth, such a person is confused by its individual manifestations, and is incapable of progressing to a concept of understanding the unifying force behind the many, and varied manifestations of nature.

Just as *Shemini Atzeret* refutes Koheleth's questions about the vivacity of nature, it also provides an answer to Koheleth's complaint about the lack of meaning of human life. The description of *Shemini Atzeret* and *Simhat Torah*, which immediately follows as זמן שמחתנו provides us with an exalted reason for our existence. Our life is not an unplanned, purposeless journey from a dark past into an unknown future; a journey from darkness to darkness. On the contrary, every day that we spend in the service of a higher ideal, every hour that we spend in *"Simhat Torah,"* in pure spiritual joy, is filled with purpose and meaning and serves to perpetuate and maintain this world.

When Koheleth finally dares to even cast doubt about the immortality of the human soul, Jewish tradition answers by asking us to memorialize the dead (Yizkor) on *Shemini Atzeret.* "Who knows," asks Koheleth "whether the spirit of man rises upward, and the spirit of animals goes under the earth?" No, we do not know it. But we feel it. An inner voice confirms it for us. "It does not state that Moses sang (at the Sea of Reeds), but rather אז ישיר – Moses will sing. This is a hint about the resurrection of the dead" (Sanhedrin 91). Everything does not end with our last breath. The melody of life is not yet finished. "Who knows…," cries Koheleth. But we, together with Job (19:25-26) reply, "but I know that my Vindicator lives ומבשרי אחזה אלוה – and, freed from my body, I will behold God."

The Jewish house of study has rejected the book of Koheleth. It nevertheless survived, so that we may read it anew each year, and prevail over it. To know it, and to reject it. To suppress the Koheleth voice within us.

But this is not the only reason that the book of Koheleth survived. This book also has traces of a higher, nobler pessimism. Koheleth was also granted the gift of that higher, ideal pessimism that lives in the hearts of all people who search for God. A pessimism created by tension between our desire and our ability; a pessimism that grows out of an inner conflict between the Divine and the mortal. In the lighter, blessed moments of his life, Koheleth also experienced the thrill of the sublime. A reverence for the otherworldly also pulsated through him. In addition to his mortal pessimism and gloomy worldview, he possessed that feeling of personal futility that once caused Abraham to cry out, "I am only dust and ashes" (Genesis 18:27); that feeling of personal inadequacy that caused the Jews at Sinai to say, "You (Moses) speak to us; let not God speak to us for otherwise we die." Koheleth was also familiar with that nobler pessimism that was awakened in our ancestors, when they became aware of their inability to look at the shining, unveiled countenance of Moses. That overcomes us at the thought that the pure, unclouded, primordial light will remain denied to us forever. That, when called to serve, caused Isaiah to cry out, "Woe is me because I am a man with unclean lips." Koheleth was familiar with the pessimism, which is born from a conflict between יוצר and יצר – between a yearning for God and our mortal attachment, of which Yehudah Halevi sang :

"How can I serve my creator here on earth?

I, a prisoner of my desires; a servant to my appetite."

The fact that this pessimism also found its way into his book was not, however, what saved the book of Koheleth from destruction. What saved it was that, in addition to his complaint about the ephemeral nature of everything mortal, Koheleth also experienced the pain of distance between human beings and God, "God is in the heavens and you are on earth; so let your words therefore be few" (Eccl. 5:1). Like all great people, he also suffered from human ambivalence and imperfection, since "there is not one good man on earth who is always just and doesn't err" (Eccl. 7:20).

So, *Shemini Atzeret* takes us away from Koheleth only in order to return us to it once again. It exhorts us to prevail over our mortal pessimism and to be attuned with the ideal in ourselves. We reject Koheleth's formulation about nature, humanity, and eternity but we reconcile ourselves with the Koheleth who in the end bows before God. We reject Koheleth, the doubter, but we join Koheleth the affirmant who, after long inner struggles and battles, closes his book with the confession:

"The sum of the matter, when all is said and done:

Revere God and observe His commandments!

For this applies to all mankind!"

TO LIVE MEANS TO ACT
Reflections in the Month of Elul[111]

אחת שאלתי מאת ה' אותה אבקש שבתי בבית ה' כל ימי חיי
I pray to God for one wish;
that I may remain in the house of the Lord all the days of my life

A person's character becomes most apparent in moments of deep shock, in the hour of despair. How a person behaves in times of misfortune, how he conducts himself at times of affliction, and especially what thoughts and emotions are evoked by that greatest mystery of our existence, death, is the defining and most revealing factor of that individual's character.

The entire world admires and reveres Socrates. Not so much for his life, as for his death. We view him as a sage and a philosopher, not so much for the way he lived, but for the manner in which he died. Only in his hour of death do we see him in all his greatness. He died for his convictions, courageously and resolutely. He drank the goblet of poison without fear or hesitation. He stared death in the eye, serenely and calmly. This equanimity in the face of death; this determination and courage at the moment of death, have earned him the respect and admiration of posterity, which has become convinced that this great Greek not only understood how to live well, but also how to die well.

There are many individuals throughout Jewish history who have also sacrificed their lives for their convictions. Rabbi Yehuda ben Baba immediately comes to mind.

In their effort to annihilate the mainspring of the Jewish religion, the Roman government once decided to forbid the granting of סמיכה, the authorization and designation of a scholar, as Rabbi. Jewish scholars were strictly forbidden to give their students permission to teach. Our enemies wanted thereby to open a breech in the wall of Jewish tradition, and to interrupt the chain of authorized teachers. What did Rabbi Yehuda ben Baba do? He set

[111] UGGIK #87, September 1935, 5-6. Original in German.

himself up between two mountains and there, in secret, authorized five scholars who, in turn, established new schools and places of instruction. The chain of tradition remained unbroken, but the courageous Sage paid with his life for this historical act. The Roman authorities discovered the secret meeting place in the mountains. The students managed to flee in time, but the teacher who, only moments before had ordained his students, refused to flee. He remained and was killed. He died with the conviction that his death was not a futile sacrifice...(Sanhedrin 14).

Only a few individuals are granted the privilege of sacrificing their lives for a great idea. For the majority, the following phrase applies: על כרחך אתה חי ועל כרחך אתה מת – you live in spite of your desire, and you die in spite of your desire.

I

What is the Jewish attitude towards death? How does the Jewish soul react to this final dark event, which no living creature can escape?

The answer to this question is given succinctly and clearly by the sentence that Jews say when a misfortune strikes: "הצור תמים פעלו – God's act is perfect; upright is He and without guile."

The Jew greets death trustingly and submissively. A Jew sees it as a manifestation of God's will, and of Divine justice. Even if the pain caused by death oppresses the heart severely, the Jew does not complain to Providence. With tearful eyes, he acquiesces to the loss ה' נתן וה' לקח – "God has given us life; God has taken it away. May His name be blessed!" That is how a Jew acknowledges the pitiless cycle of the earth. We understand the eternal succession that takes place everywhere before our eyes, in nature as well as in the lives of human beings. בני אדם דומין לעשבי השדה – "human beings are like plants in the field." Some bloom and others fade away. Just as flowers bloom quietly and fade in silence; just as the stars are quietly lit in the sky, and are as silently extinguished, so the Prophet admonishes us, אל תבכו למת – do not cry for the dead!" Don't cry or complain; instead, understand! Understand that this eternal coming and going, blossoming and wilting, death and life are deeply ingrained in the world order; that in death we are also with, and in, God. Understand that death is just a portal through which we reach another kingdom; a kingdom that appears dark and mysterious to us, but which in fact is simply a "hereafter," likewise ruled by God's compassion and grace just as this world; just like life....

II

Why then, does the Bible, that innate Jewish book, consider life a blessing and death a curse? If God's goodness and compassion rules equally here and there, in this world and in the next, why does a plea for life reverberate so anxiously throughout Jewish prayers? Life, life, חיים, is the cry that gushes forth! Even the most faithful among us pleads for life. Why do we fear death? Why does the Torah always promise us our reward with the phrase: "so that you may live a long time"?

Because the ultimate realization of Judaism; the fulfillment of the ethical precepts of the Torah is tied to this world, to this life. כיון שמת אדם נעשה חפשי מן התורה ומן המצוות – for outside of this life, there are no commandments or prohibitions; no morals or ethics; human kindness is no longer possible. Because all postulates of our laws have a purpose only in this world. Because the other side of life means also the other side of good and evil.

The Agadah tells us that when Moses arrived in heaven to receive the Torah, the Angels said to God: 'Master of the Universe! Give us the Torah. We want to care for it and fulfill its commandments.' But Moses countered: 'Master of the Universe! The Torah that you want to proclaim can only be fulfilled in the world of action. It contains commandments such as 'you shall not murder! You shall not steal! Are these commandments applicable here, in the sphere of the spirits and angels? Honor your father and your mother — do angels have fathers and mothers? What do angels need a Torah for? Only humans can fulfill the ideals of your Torah, as long as they are alive and can err!' The Angels became quiet and relinquished their claim on the Torah. Only here, in the world of passion, of hatred and envy, where murder, robbery, and deceit are possible; only here, does the Torah have a mission to accomplish. Only here, can it achieve its goal of purifying human passions and overcoming the evil inclination. Now we understand why it is stated מצוות בטלות לעתיד לבא – in Messianic times, the commandments will no longer be applicable (Nidah 61). Human beings will no longer require them, since their souls will be completely cleansed and purified.

So the Torah, as a molding power of life, is intimately tied to life. Hence, the great craving, the mighty desire for life pulsates through our holy writings. The Jew longs for Jewish acts. The Jew wants to do, to work. The pleading for life is due to the fact that only our world is an עולם העשיה – a world of deeds. Only here, are humans given an opportunity to perform the actions that will bring them closer to the ideal, to perfection! That is the reason for the love of life...

Only during certain extraordinary times, was a Jew allowed to disdain life; to give it up willingly. When he was persecuted for following the Law; when was forced to surrender that, which is sacred. Then, the Jew ascended the funeral pyre fearlessly. Then, he allowed himself to be led to it meekly, and without resistance, because under these circumstances, life lost all value and meaning.

We are not afraid of death. But we need life in order to fulfill our mission, in order to pass the test. We have had more than one Socrates who has died for the Law. The Torah however commands us ובחרת בחיים – to choose life! To love life! Jewish tradition gives life its ultimate meaning through death. Eternal value and meaning is given to this side, by forcefully immersing oneself in that which lies on the other side of the border of the human journey. Contemplation about death instructs us about life, teaches us to value and appreciate life; teaches us that היום קצר והמלאכה מרובה – the day is short and the work is great.

During these days of self examination, as we remember the dead, and their memory renews the pain of separation from our dear ones who have gone home, let us become aware of the meaning of our lives whose Jewish content was summarized by the Divine singer:

"Only one wish I ask of God, That I may be allowed to dwell in the house of the Lord all the days of my life."

THE POWER OF REPENTANCE[112]
On the Evening of Kol Nidre

From time immemorial, Jews have associated this evening with consolation, forgiveness, absolution, and purification from the dross of everyday life. It is an evening, whose light dissipates the shadows and dark recesses of our souls; an evening that draws ancient Jewish melodies, stifled and muffled during the year by the hubbub and tumult of everyday life, from the depths of our souls.

We thirst for purity. We hunger for holiness. May our craving be satiated, at least for this short evening. May our minds stop sinking into the mundane and the lewd, at least for this short evening; and may the inspiration of our sincere prayers give wing to our souls and turn them towards God.

For it is to God that we turn tonight. To beg Him for forgiveness for our sins and offenses; for actions committed in injudicious moments; for wrongs committed in a fit of greed and selfishness against those near to us; and for religious boundaries crossed in moments of weakness, decline, and spiritual twilight. We stand before God, beating our chests with our fists, and we say: אשמנו בגדנו, גזלנו – "we have sinned, we have deceived, we have appropriated someone else's goods." And only God, in His grace, can forgive our sins and answer סלחתי – "I have forgiven!"

The Talmud (Jer. Sanhedrin 12) cites a question once posed to Wisdom: "What punishment awaits the sinner?" Wisdom answered: חטאים תרדף רעה – "Evil pursues the transgressor." The question was then posed to Prophecy: "What punishment awaits the transgressor?" Prophecy answered: הנפש החוטאת היא תמות – "The transgressor's soul shall die." The Torah answered: יביא אשם – "let him bring a sacrifice and his guilt will be forgiven." Finally, the question was posed to God: "What must a sinner do in order to purify himself?" And God answered, יעשה תשובה – "let him atone!"

---

[112] UGGIK #89, October 1935, 4. Original in Polish.

Wisdom declares that there is no salvation or deliverance for the sinner. The awareness that he has committed an offense will haunt him everywhere and its phantoms will always persecute him. He will never be able to find peace anywhere. Wisdom, which analyzes the soul and penetrates all its mysteries and secrets, knows that the curse of sin burdens the offender eternally and always stigmatizes him. Qualms of conscience and remorse always disturb him. While others are joyful, the sinner is plunged into sadness. While others smile spontaneously, the sinner is oppressed by the burden of his crimes. The sinner, like Cain long ago, laments: "My iniquity is too heavy a burden for me to carry!" At night, when blissful sleep closes the eyes of all who are weary and worn out, the sinner rolls around in his bed, and sleep avoids him. The shadow of sin obscures and blocks his path. He laments over the unfortunate people whose blood has sullied his hands. Punishment walks in his footsteps, and he calls out in the Prophet's words: "Though they dig into the netherworld, thence shall My hand take them; and though they climb up to heaven, Thence will I bring them down...And though they be hid from My sight in the bottom of the sea, Thence will I command the serpent, and he shall bite them." (Amos 9:2,3) The viper of their conscience will give them no peace because חטאים תרדף רעה – "evil pursues sinners and transgressors."

Prophecy offers no hope for the sinner. The sinner's soul, stained by sin, will die and disappear; will wither, waste away, and perish – הנפש החטאת היא תמות. Prophecy, that Divine power that foresees the future, knows in advance that the soul of the transgressor will, in time, become callous, grow numb, become dull, and die. This criminal will jump from sin to sin, from morass to morass, sinking ever lower, and finally, falls into the abyss of depravity and emptiness. For depravity is so constituted that עברה גוררת עברה – evil gives birth to evil, until the last restraint of the conscience falls away; until petrifaction and numbness seize the soul. There comes a moment of its complete immobilization, and the soul gradually dies...

Neither Wisdom nor Prophecy has shown us a way to repentance. Wisdom has shown us a wise dictum. Prophecy drew our attention to the consequence of sin. Neither, however, showed us a way out of that magic circle of sin.

In our helplessness, we turn to the Torah, our teacher and educator, to teach us how we can repair the evil. And the reply comes: "Through sacrifice."

The Torah, whose aim above all else is to regulate social interaction, is showing us a way to rectify an evil that has occurred as a result of our faults. Sacrifice! There is no atonement without sacrifice! If you have robbed your brother, return the stolen property. If you have wronged your brother, repair the damage through sacrifice and devotion. If you have besmirched your brother's reputation, insulted him, harmed his business, undermined his welfare, taken away his daily bread, or affronted him physically, make up with him, repair the damage, and ask for forgiveness. This cannot be done through empty words and barren flattery, only through sacrifice. With your sacrifice, help him to extricate himself from the difficulties he was placed in as a result of your actions.

By offering a sacrifice, we repair damage done against people, but how about sins against God? God was therefore asked: "What should a sinner do to atone for his sins?" תשובה – I ask him only that the sinner atone; repentance, and nothing more. Just for a moment, let the sinner restrain his impulses and lust. For a moment, let him break away from the gray daily routine; let him brush off the dust of triteness from his feet and return to Me, and his soul will be redeemed.

"True, pious people need not stand in the place where penitents stand" (Berahot 34). An individual who has succeeded in mastering himself and controlling his desires, has climbed to a higher plain. According to our Sages, such a person has freed himself from the claws of sin by the force and effort of his moral strength, and has earned the crown of heroism. The only person who deserves to be called a hero is הכובש את יצרו – one who is capable of controlling his impulses; one who has waged war with himself, and has won. A narrow path leads from the swamp of sin to the sunny land of good and beauty. It is a path of spiritual rebirth; a path of moral regeneration, expiation, atonement, and repentance. Will we succeed in igniting the spark of God in our petrified hearts? Will the weak flame of our conscience be able to penetrate the hardened shell of our souls, and light the darkness of the world?

Darkness descends on the streets outside, but the interior of the synagogue is bathed in bright light. A throng of people, wrapped in *talesim* [prayer shawls] stands as one, and prays. As if from beyond, the voice of the cantor floats upwards and travels into the distance...

FAITH AND ACTION[113]

I

The moment God's voice resounded from the heights of Sinai calling, אנכי – "I am your eternal God," was both sublime and moving. No prophet or philosopher has been able to describe God; to fathom the mystery of His existence; to allow us to glimpse the source of His nature. We pronounce the word "God" with our mouths, but we are not allowed to link any image to this utterance; to attach any representation whatsoever to it. We are not allowed to personify or embody God; to ascribe any human attributes or characteristics to Him; or to attribute the contours of any earthly creatures to Him. Furthermore, all attributes and adjectives, usually used to describe Him, are to be understood only as metaphors borrowed from human language.

We can, however, affirm one thing about God without a doubt, namely, that He has not changed or been transformed in any way. The same voice has been heard in every era of our history declaring: אנכי – "I am your God!" He was with Abraham, with Isaac, and with Jacob. He accompanied their children to Egypt, and rejoiced with us during the flowering of our State. He mourned with us when a savage enemy destroyed our Holy Temple. He watched over us in Persia, Babylon, and Spain; lived in our holy places on the Rhine, on the Main, and on the Vistula. Notwithstanding the sufferings and humiliations of our times, He speaks to us this very day. As once at Sinai, the voice of the Eternal One rends the air, which today is saturated with idolatrous superstition, hatred, and the poison of racial madness, calling out: אנכי – "I am your God!" You, O man, change your views and opinions. You lose yourself in the wilderness of ever newer theories and doctrines. You are inconstant, transient, and malleable in your emotions and dispositions. You hate today that, which only yesterday you loved. You discard today that, which

---

[113] UGGIK #109, August 1936, 2. Original in Polish. For unknown reasons, this article is signed "Ch" rather than with the full name.

only recently you worshipped. You are like a plaything tossed on the waves, caprices, and beliefs of your era. I, on the other hand, says God, אנכי – was and will be, the same. אני ה' לא שניתי – I have not changed; אני ראשון ואני אחרון – at the beginning and at the end of time, I was, and will be the same.

God's law too, is eternal and unchanging. Whether we live in a time of war or peace. In a time of love for each other or a time of persecution. Of humanitarianism or barbarity. Of the French revolution, with its lofty call for brotherhood and equality, or the modern revolution, which crowns the most brutal human instincts with a halo of heroism. God's law remains the same, everywhere, always. For us, the Ten Commandments, always and everywhere, shine as a beacon with an undimmed and never-extinguishable radiance, which rises above all theories. God's Two Tablets are today, and will continue to be in the future, our constant guideposts because את התורה לא תהא מחלפת – this law will never be changed, and we shall never receive another one from God.

But is there any evidence that this law has any influence on human thought and behavior today? Is there evidence that it has had a civilizing, ennobling, influence for good?...

II

Jewish Sages have always striven to achieve a pure faith, divested of accretions, pagan superstitious practices, and idolatrous elements. But their ideal was not a contemplative faith; a faith that does not express itself in action. A faith hidden and concentrated in the soul; a faith, which does not penetrate life and influence the human environment was considered a religious experience fit only for a romantic recluse plunged in solitude, turned away from a world of concrete deeds. In contrast, the Jewish religion, which burst into the darkness like a ray of sunshine and dispersed the pagan clouds, sought to spiritualize the world, and to remove injustice, force, cruelty, and bestiality from society. It therefore devoted more attention to establishing the norms of ethical behavior than to dogmatic faith.

Every action consists of an external shell, the actual physical act, which can be called the body of the act, and the hidden intention or volition of the person performing the act, which may be called the soul of the act. Faith and good will alone, not manifested by a deed, is like a spirit carried in the clouds. On the other hand, an act without of a noble intent is like a soulless body, dead, because it does not radiate warmth; is not pulsating with life.

The world is currently divided into two camps. In one are people of action, and in the other, dreamers with noble intentions but without the strength to transform their dreams into reality. On the one hand, the ideal but bodiless faith. On the other, the crude deed. And in the middle is a gaping abyss, swallowing a never-ending supply of new sacrifices.

We hope for a day when that chasm will disappear. When action (the body) and faith (the soul), will unite! That will be the dawn of the day of liberation for tragic humanity...

IV

NATIONAL RELATIONSHIPS: BETWEEN THE JEWISH PEOPLE AND THE NATIONS

The anti-Jewish propaganda and actions that prevailed in Germany during the 1930s gradually crossed the border, and found fertile soil in adjoining countries. This was especially palpable in Katowice, which was so close to the border with Germany. Jews were bewildered at their ever growing isolation, and the distortions of their history, religion, and way of life. Jewish sources were slanderously misquoted to show that Jews considered themselves to be superior, more worthy than non-Jews, and that the Jewish holy books encouraged contempt and hatred for Christianity. An openly anti-Jewish periodical, Błyskawica (Lightning) made a series of slanderous accusations against Judaism and its holy texts, especially the Talmud. On the basis of complaints by the Jewish Community Administration of Katowice, the Public Prosecutor confiscated issues of this weekly three times. The Administration finally sued the editor for slander. Rabbi Chameides was the Jewish Community's main expert during the trial. The essay, "Jewish Attitudes towards other Faiths," is signed only Kalonymus, Rabbi Chameides' Hebrew name, and probably summarizes his court testimony. The editor, Chowański, was found guilty and sentenced to nine months imprisonment, a fine of 200 zł in damages to be paid to the Jewish community, and court costs. The universalism and inclusiveness of Judaism is also stressed in the beautiful essay "Pirkei Avoth."

In the essay, "And a New King Arose in Egypt who did not Know Joseph," Rabbi Chameides discusses the historical ingratitude of the nations for Jewish contributions to the welfare of their native or adopted lands. While writing it, Rabbi Chameides undoubtedly had in mind his wife's uncle, Josef Königshöfer, who was killed while fighting for Germany during WW I. He was awarded a posthumous medal by Germany, with a written assurance, given to his mother, that "his great sacrifice will never be forgotten by the fatherland." Barely 20 years later, his brother, Isaak, Gertrude Chameides' father, showed the medal to the Gestapo who came to arrest him, to prove the family's loyalty to Germany. The Gestapo threw the medal out of the window, just before they took him to Buchenwald concentration camp.

In the essays, "Religion and Nationhood" and "The Tents of Jacob," Rabbi Chameides tries to show that anti-Semitism is incompatible with true Christianity. Puzzled by the fact that countries that profess Christianity can nevertheless be anti-Semitic, he points out that these countries were previously pagan, and Christianity was forced on them. As a result, there has been a constant inner tension between their faith and their nationhood. In contrast, Judaism became a nation and a faith-community at the same time, and therefore avoided this tension.

בסכת תשבו
"YOU SHALL DWELL IN BOOTHS"[114]

On the festival of Sukkoth we leave our comfortable homes, and move to rapidly erected huts. The entire year, we cling to our possessions; hang on to temporal value and quality of our lives. One time each year, however, we leave ownership and comfort behind, and move into a plain, primitively constructed shelter.

The foliaged hut is an apt symbol of our history. We Jews have built flimsy huts for centuries. As homeless wanderers from land to land, we did not know a permanent residence. Instead, we often had to be content with a hastily constructed, and therefore just as easily destroyed, shelter. "You shall dwell in huts!" This has been the motto of our dispersion; the tragic rule of our exile. We have had to dwell in booths for centuries, not only for seven days. During the long night of exile, our very existence was comparable to a flimsy, unstable hut. Every gust of wind threatened to destroy it. With a pilgrim's staff in our hands, we have been constantly at the ready. Constantly on the move. Always unsettled. Only occasionally, did a ray of hope shine like a star into our hut, and only occasionally, did a whispering wind bring tidings of redemption from distant lands...

"You shall dwell in huts!" Hasn't our weak Jewish hut outlasted mighty empires and glorious, sturdy palaces? Any other people in our situation would have been subdued long ago; would long ago have disappeared from the face of the earth. We have persevered, precisely because we did not build houses, but instead we built light, portable huts. For us, the curse of never being bound to the earth, of being rootless in the soil, has been transformed into a blessing. As soon as we were banished from one land or province, we pitched our tents in another. In insecure times, those who possess nothing are, in fact, the most secure. Not burdened by the ballast of property nor bent by the weight on their backs, they can more easily find refuge for their bare bodies, when the earthquake erupts.

A Talmudic tradition tells us that at some future time, God will

---

bring the states and nations to justice. The Romans will be the first to make an accounting of their deeds and accomplishments. "What have you accomplished?" God will ask Romans. "We built roads, constructed markets, amassed gold and silver. But we did all of this for one purpose only – to make it possible for the Children of Israel to occupy themselves with study." The Romans hoped to justify themselves by claiming that they placed their civilization in the service of culture. "No!" answers God. "You did it all for your own comfort; to make your lives easier and more beautiful. Your civilization was an end in itself for you. The strict organization of your state was a product of your egoism, and your lust to conquer. The protectors of my ideals and the watchmen of my truth, derived no benefit from your expansionist policies." The Persians and all the other nations will follow suit. As soon as the heathen nations saw that they were condemned, they asked God for another chance, and requested to be taught the truth once again. Henceforth, they would obey the commandments scrupulously. "I have one commandment (Mitzva)," God said, "whose fulfillment entails only a small expenditure of energy and cost – the commandment of the foliage hut. Fulfill this one commandment and you will be forgiven!" The heathens quickly built themselves foliage huts. In order to test their intentions, God caused a scorching sun to shine. The nations did not pass this test. They destroyed the huts, thereby losing their last opportunity to receive Divine mercy.

The heathens could tolerate and endure anything else. But living in huts in an unsettled condition, in *golus* – in exile, that they could not bear. The test, which God presented to them through the commandment of the foliage hut, brought them failure and ruin. They could not get used to a homeless state. Dispersion is a nation's bitterest fate!

On this festival, we therefore pray that our Jewish huts ultimately become permanent and firmly established.

הרחמן הוא יקים לנו את סכת דוד הנפלת
May the Almighty once again raise up David's fallen hut

ויקם מלך חדש על מצרים אשר לא ידע את יוסף
"And a new king arose in Egypt who did not know Joseph" [115]

Unfortunately, most statesmen and politicians of Jewish origin discover this fate. Their accomplishments seldom get the recognition they deserve. Even those who, through great effort, self-sacrifice, and rare merit, achieve the respect of their contemporaries are soon forgotten after their death. Their names stand mute in the raging sea of history, and posterity weaves them no garland. They might have sacrificed the ripest and most beautiful fruit of their effort and ability on the altar of their fatherland. Every heartbeat, every moment of their lives might have been devoted to society, but as soon as the first insignificant tremor of the old order was felt, they were the first to be sacrificed; the first to be forced to leave the arena of the past. They were mercilessly swept away before every new wave. Every new wind blew them into darkness. Their sudden fall from the pinnacle of power into the abyss of contempt and slander usually swept their co-religionists along into the grave. Joseph's fate in Egypt is typical, and has often been repeated in Jewish history.

God directed Joseph's journey miraculously from prison to the highest rung of the Egyptian throne. With boundless energy, he threw himself into the service on behalf of the powerful pharaonic state. He saved the land from a severe economic crisis. He implemented a number of economically necessary preventive measures, and introduced agrarian reforms. He raised the country's productivity, and paved the way for an era of prosperity and economic boom for its rulers.

What did this stranger, who traveled the long road from prison to power, expect as a reward for his efforts and diligence? Nothing! He harbored no illusions. He expected neither thanks nor reward. He feared, and an inner voice told him, that despite his great achievements, and in spite of his deep attachment to his new

---

[115] UGGIK. #24, January 1933, 4. Original in German.

homeland, he would always remain a foreigner in the eyes of the people. Before he closed his eyes in eternal sleep, he made his brothers swear – פקד יפקד – "When one day God leads you back to your homeland, don't forget to take my mortal remains with you." He expected nothing from the Egyptians; not even a permanent tomb. With his clairvoyant vision, he foresaw ויקם מלך חדש אשר לא ידע את יוסף – that one day a king would ascend the Egyptian throne who would not know Joseph's accomplishments; who had no desire to know them, or to recognize them. His premonition came to pass soon enough. A new regime had barely come to power, and Joseph and his achievements were all but forgotten. Many future Jewish statesmen shared Joseph's tragic fate. They helped pave the way for their fatherland to achieve greatness and glory, and, instead of receiving the thanks due them, they harvested shameless ingratitude.

In our imagination, let us now leap forward several thousand years, and stop in the 16th century. At that time, there was an influential government official in the Sultan's court in Constantinople by the name of Don Joseph Nassi, a fellow-sufferer of the Egyptian Joseph, with whom he had more in common than just his name.

Joseph Nassi came from a rich *converso* family in Portugal that owned a banking house with widespread interests. With the introduction of the inquisition, the lives of the conversos, who outwardly converted to Christianity but inwardly remained believing and inspired Jews, became a hell on earth. The Nassi family, therefore, decided to turn their backs on the country of their persecutions, and to immigrate to Constantinople. Here, Nassi openly acknowledged the faith of his fathers, and gained entrance to, and increasing influence in, the Sultan's court. Because of his broad education and his diplomatic skills, Joseph Nassi soon won the confidence of Sultan Suleiman. He used the far-reaching influence and connections of his important position to help and protect his persecuted brethren in all European lands. A true disciple of his namesake Joseph of Egypt! One of his significant projects was an attempt to rebuild the ruined city of Tiberias and seven villages in its vicinity in Palestine, and to develop them into a Jewish settlement, where the fleeing Jews from Europe could find their cities of refuge. Joseph Nassi publicized his plan to

Jews in Christian lands, and urged them to go to Palestine. Immigrants gathered in Italy, and were to sail from Venice on ships arranged for by Joseph. Joseph Nassi's very efficient plan was, however, frustrated by the opposition of the Arabs, and the fact that Nassi was stretched to the limit by his many activities and had no time left to devote to it. Nassi's reputation grew daily throughout the orient, until he controlled all European contracts. No great power could negotiate with the Sublime Portal [Turkey] without going through Joseph Nassi. The German Kaiser, Maxmillian II, ordered his delegate to Turkey to ask for Nassi's intercession. The Polish King, Zygmunt Augustus, also had close contact with this Jewish dignitary. But Joseph Nassi's luminous star would soon be extinguished.

ויקם מלך חדש אשר לא ידע את יוסף. A new king, who did not know Joseph, ascended the throne. With the death of Sultan Selim, his influence waned. Selim's successor, Murad III, had no use for a Jewish statesman. Joseph Nassi withdrew from his productive activities at court, and redirected his energies to the intellectual pursuit of the humanities. Henceforth, he devoted his life exclusively to study. His former patrons deserted him. In the last years of his life he was alone and lonely. His accomplishments on behalf of the state were soon forgotten. His name lives on in the annals of history, but he did not earn a place in the consciousness of the nation for whom he accomplished so much. That was Joseph Nassi's lot. That has been the lot of all Jewish statesmen from Joseph of Egypt until this very day. Like a meteor, Jewish energy, Jewish enterprise, Jewish genius bursts forth and just as suddenly, just as abruptly, is extinguished.

May we, despite this ingratitude, always feel the blissful feeling which permeated Joseph's whole being כי למחיה שלחני אלקים – that God has sent us here to promote life and spread happiness; to stand by the needy and serve humanity. May the words, which God spoke to our patriarch, Abraham, always light our way and, despite disappointments, always keep human goodness and a willingness to help alive in us:

והי' ברכה ונברכו בך כל משפחות האדמה
"Be a blessing – and all the family of man shall be blessed because of you"

PIRKEI AVOTH[116]

On the Saturday after Pesach we begin to read a tractate called "Chapters of the Fathers,"[117] which contains moral lessons and ethical principles taught by our teachers and sages. Each Saturday, we read a different section of this beautiful and edifying book, which is Jewry's treasure of sublime thought. During the most beautiful season of the year, when nature is resurrected, and the rejuvenating breath of spring reawakens everything to a new, creative, and powerfully pulsating life, a yearning for spiritual rebirth and rejuvenation of the traditions of our forefathers grows stronger in the heart of the believing Jew. Spring in nature has a counterpart in our souls. Nature puts on a splendid, variegated attire of flowers and plants. A refreshing and reviving stream nurtures every blade of grass; penetrates every life-thirsting bud. Should the human soul alone remain numb and deaf, and not be reawakened to new and noble impulses; to soaring heights? Our bodies are chained to this world, but we can reach heavenward with our souls. We are a connection, a bond, between the temporal and the eternal; a bridge between this world and the one beyond. As we observe beauty and bliss pour over the physical spheres of every creation, and, with its magic charm, take possession of our physical existence, our souls are overwhelmed, and try to slip away from the pernicious embrace of the pain of everyday existence to the deep thoughts and wise lessons of Pirkei Avoth, which remind us of our spiritual mission.

Nature is not governed by ethical principles. It functions strictly according to its assigned laws; according to inviolate norms established by the Creator. Next to, or rather above, this limited world, imprisoned in a net of eternal laws, we mortals create our

---

[116] UGGIK. #30, April 1933, 7. Original in Polish.

[117] Pirkei Avoth (Ethics of the Fathers) is traditionally studied in synagogues between the Sabbath afternoon and evening prayer services during the spring and summer months (from Passover until Rosh Hashana).

own world, which operates according to the principles of free will and an unhampered ability to choose between good and evil. Every Saturday, therefore, the Jew turns his attention from the inexhaustibly rich and dazzling forms of nature, to free himself momentarily from the prison of reality, and surrenders to thoughts of his assignment as a superior being. With the magic wand of his free will, he creates a beautiful world of purity and holiness out of the misty chaos of his passions, his dreams, and his contradictory inclinations.

At the beginning of every section, there is a citation from the tractate Sanhedrin (90a), which serves as an introduction to the lessons that follow: כל ישראל יש להם חלק לעולם הבא – "every Jew has a share in the world to come." The intent of this introductory phrase, which is repeated like a mantra at the beginning of each of the six sections, is to show us the ultimate aim of our earthly pilgrimage, and the reward that awaits us if we observe these principles of morality. It also reassures the sinner who wants to repent, but who might despair about saving his sinful soul when he notes his many failures. The phrase כל ישראל, gives us hope by teaching us that everyone has the capacity to achieve the highest perfection. A spark of God hidden in every human being, even the most degenerate, needs only to be revived in order to be transformed into a noble flame. This phrase should, therefore, be understood as stating that every Jew possesses a חלק, an element of goodness, a germ of purity, which makes him worthy לעולם הבא, of a portion of the world to come!

The phrase כל ישראל is not intended to exclude the righteous followers of other religions who, like we, are assured a share in eternity, as long as they live a pure and moral life. Our teachers explicitly emphasized this principle, extending it even to the pagan. It is written: "The wicked shall return to the nether-world; even all the nations that forget God" (Psalms 9:18). Rabbi Joshuah taught: "It does not state that all nations will sink into the abyss, but rather those nations that forget God. From this, we conclude that the pious of other nations will have a share of the world to come" (Tosefta Sanhedrin 13). Rabbi Joshuah's opinion was sanctioned by

Maimonides (Teshuva 3 #15), and thereby became a part of normative Judaism. In the same spirit, Rabbi Yehudah Hanassi (135-200 CE) answered a question from his friend, the Roman Caesar Antonius, as to whether he would have a share in eternal life. Yes! Rabbi Yehudah answered, because the complete destruction that our forefathers prophesied regarding the house of Esau (Rome was often compared to Esau) applies only to those who imitate Esau's acts (Avodah Zarah 10b). The phrase *kol yisrael* thereby loses the character of exclusivity, and encompasses all people who, by the manner they conduct their lives, deserve God's grace without regard to religion or origin.

JEWISH ATTITUDES TOWARDS OTHER FAITHS[118]

Like a bolt of lightning[119] from a bright blue sky, we were hit with the news that a party, using the tactics of fascism and anti-Semitism flourishing on the other side of the border, has been established on this soil. This group is mimicking and imitating the methods of leaders of a movement, which proclaims a motto in its banner calling for the annihilation of Jewry; which solemnly, and with almost religious fervor, announces and propagates a program of exterminating Jewry. This movement, which has thrived on foreign soil under totally different conditions, has principles and goals that are fundamentally opposed to the soul and historical traditions of the Polish nation. But our homegrown ringleaders don't concern themselves with such trivial details. For, according to them, every means is fair and every action is allowed, as long as it achieves their goal and assures victory. And what exactly is their lofty goal? To slander Judaism, to disseminate hatred throughout society, and to incite and instigate peaceful citizens. By these means they hope to acquire positions of control, to achieve influence over the masses, and, finally, to exploit this influence for their own gain.

In an issue of their newspaper carrying a bolt of lightning like a mark of Cain on its forehead, these "experts" on Jewish issues tackled a scholarly subject dealing with the character and contents of our religious books. On the basis of false citations, misquotations, and ad hoc reasoned opinions, they conclude that our religious books should be confiscated because they teach contempt and foster hatred for Christianity.

Since this, as well as similar nonsense, is quite frequently disseminated in a variety of forms, I deem it appropriate in a modest way, to inform our public and objectively show that these accusations and charges are groundless.

In truth, I do not even dare to hope that I will succeed in

---

[118] UGGIK #39, September 1933, 3. Original in Polish.
[119] Play on the name of the anti-Semitic paper, Błyskawica, which means lightning.

convincing our enemies of the absurdity of their statements, or of the damage caused by their destructive journalism. And even if I were successful in documenting and proving the complete absurdity of their thesis and in tearing to shreds the pseudo-scientific attire in which they are attempting to dress up their hatred, can we really expect to awaken their conscience, and change their erroneous ways?

These people don't really want to see the truth, because they are only looking for a pretense under which to carry on their destructive ways. Since, for the time being at least, we have no hope of convincing them, we must use the strength of our facts to educate our own society and other people of good will who are not yet infected with the venom of hatred, and who cherish truth above all else.

We will endeavor to clarify three issues:

1. The relationship of Judaism to paganism.

    It is important to emphasize very clearly that there is almost no mention of Christianity in the entire Talmud. In dealing with people of other faiths, our sages use the term עכו"ם (Akkum), an acronym for עובדי כוכבים ומזלות – worshippers of stars and planets. This term cannot be applied to Christianity, which, like Judaism, considers the heavenly bodies as creations of God and never as deities deserving worship.

    Whoever therefore quotes a statement from the Talmud or the Shulchan Aruch containing the word "Akkum," and considers that word to include today's Christians, either reveals his ignorance or his ill will. In either case, he causes us harm, and our obligation is to teach him in the first instance, or to fight him, in the second.

2. The relationship of the Christian church to paganism.

    We intend to show that our teachers and Sages treated pagans in at least as humanitarian and cautious a fashion as our Christian brothers.

3. Our relationship to Christianity

JUDAISM AND PAGANISM

Pagan Prophets

"Seven prophets from among the nations of the world prophesied:

Balaam, his father, Job, Elifaz from Teiman, Bildad from Shuach, Tsofar from Naam, and Elihu the son of Berachel from Buz" (Bava Batra 15b).

The Talmud, therefore, acknowledges that prophets and seers did exist among the pagans. If today, one nation can consider itself "a nation of poets and thinkers," and another can think of itself as "a nation of ingenious inventors," and each considers itself justified to this title and honor because of its special gift, then surely the Jewish people could proudly point to prophecy as a one-of-a kind manifestation of Jewish genius, and see its prophets as heroes and propagators of its eternal spirit. But the Talmud is objective, tolerant, and modest. As we see in the cited passage, it clearly and gladly acknowledges that prophecy existed among pagans. One does not have to be a "pure Jew," in order to share the honor of prophetic ecstasy...

"Eliahu said: I call heaven and earth as witnesses that a Jew or a pagan, a man or a woman, a male or female slave, can all acquire the holy spirit, according only to the merit of their conduct" (Seder Elia-Rabba 9).

Human actions, rather than religious belief or social class, are recognized as the sole criterion by which human beings are to be measured. Even a slave deprived of his freedom, or a pagan, can still become a participant in the holy spirit to the degree that his behavior merits.

Do you see scorn and hatred of pagans in these opinions?

Moses – Balaam

"There never arose a prophet in Israel equal to Moses. Not in Israel, but among the nations of the world [there existed a prophet equal to Moses]. And what was his name? Balaam, the son of Beor (Sifre Devarim 34)."

Every nation glorifies its leaders. In its easily aroused enthusiasm, it may even attribute virtues to its leaders that they did not really possess. Love blinds. Blind zeal and enthusiasm lead to fanaticism, and fanaticism leads to intolerance and conceit.

We Jews also surrounded our first leader with a halo. The Holy

Writ asserts that no prophet ever arose in Israel to equal Moses. Moses was the first and greatest prophet in Israel. The Midrash, therefore, in saying that the pagan Balaam was equal to Moses in his prophetic gift, gently tries to diminish the luster of his halo. How magnanimous! And where, in this, do we see the proverbial Jewish conceit?

The Egyptians – God's Creatures

"At the time the Israelites crossed through the sea, the angels wanted to sing hymns in praise of God. The Eternal One spoke thus: 'My creatures [the Egyptians] are drowning in the sea, and you want to sing hymns?'" (Sanhedrin 39b).

Our protecting angels were not even allowed to rejoice over the destruction of our worst enemies. Even the enemy does not stop being God's creatures. Thus teaches the Jewish Talmud. During the War [WW I] "pure raced" nations, were murdering each other as they were singing war marches. Anno 1914. Where was that famous love of one's neighbor, which the Jewish Talmudic religion apparently does not posses?...(To be continued)[120]

---

[120] The remainder of this article has not been found.

Religion and Nationhood[121]

The memory of Israel's exodus from Egypt, and the giving of the Torah to the Jews in the desert are recurring themes in our liturgy and religious books. These two experiences imprinted themselves deeply on the memory of our nation. They crystallized our psyche; they shaped the Jewish soul for all time.

The liberation from the Egyptian yoke was a defining moment of our nationhood. A horde of pariahs and slaves was transformed into a unified nation. The giving of the Torah to our ancestors at the foot of Mt. Sinai was a defining moment of our religious existence. Brought up in spiritual and physical slavery, the children of Israel met their God.

The festivals of Divine revelation at Sinai (Shevuot), and of our ancestors' national liberation (Pesach) are linked and joined in our liturgy by the ancient custom of counting the days (Sefirat Haomer). By counting the 49 days that separate the festivals of Pesach and Shevuoth, we give expression to our view that our religious and national experiences are closely and inseparably connected to each other. The national and religious roots are linked with each other in the Jewish consciousness to form one unified totality. The exclusion of either one of these two roots, by the smothering or weakening of the religious rhythm in our soul, or by the dimming of our national consciousness, causes a narrowing and constriction of the Jewish horizon. Early in our history, we did not differentiate between nationality and religion. This terminology comes from foreign sources, and is evidence of our spiritual assimilation. An individual who does not conform to his nation's traditional life style, who does not participate in the celebratory and sublime moments of its communal life, who does not take part in its happy as well as its sad experiences, is torn from the maternal bosom and condemned to wither and disappear. The liberation of the Jews from the

---

[121] UGGIK #52, March 1934, 5-6. Original partly in German and partly in Polish.

Egyptian yoke and the Divine revelation at Sinai are, in some measure, both a beginning and an end, a prologue and an epilogue, of one deep spiritual process that transformed our ancestors' soul in the desert and gave it a new physiognomy, a new face...

II

The Divine revelation on Mt. Sinai made a powerful mental impression on our ancestors. Moved to their depths at this extraordinary phenomenon, full of dread and fear before God's majesty, the Jews begged Moses to speak to them since, as ordinary mortals, common people, they were not capable of listening to words emanating directly from the Eternal. "You speak to us and we will listen. Let God not speak to us lest we die."

The question immediately arises: Was it only Jews, the immediate witnesses, who felt the impact of this deafening and stunning impression, caused by the Divine revelation that made people fear for their lives, or was it also felt by other nations? How did the other nations of the world react to the revelation at Sinai? How were they influenced by the commandments?

An old Talmudic tradition relates that before God gave the Torah to the Jews, he first offered it to other nations. But they refused to accept it. The ethics of the Torah were foreign to them. They did not yet possess that spiritual intensity, preparation, and quality to be able to accept a newly revealed Torah. Although the pagan nations did not want to renounce their idolatry, they did not remain completely indifferent to the sublime event at Sinai.

A Midrash tells us that when God revealed himself to the Jews, his voice could be heard throughout the world. Nations became very frightened and trembled. In their despair, they turned to Balaam and asked: "What is that voice that penetrates the world? Is it announcing a new flood or heralding another catastrophe?" Balaam answered: "God is giving a Torah to his nation." To which the nations replied: "May God bless His people with peace."

It is appropriate here to present a difference between Judaism and other religions. Our religion never aspired to attract new believers with fire and brimstone. We never used force or violence to conquer the world. We never forced other nations to accept our religion. We restrained ourselves from propaganda; we did not try to entice others to us.

When thunder and lightning on Mt. Sinai heralded the Revelation, and the earth trembled with a din and crash, the nations were overcome with fear and alarm. They were dismayed and frightened because they thought that a religion, revealed to the accompaniment of such sounds and miracles, must surely be a conquering religion, one that aspires to convert others by force and oppression; a religion that would mercilessly exterminate people of other faiths, and intolerably persecute other religions. But Balaam pacified them and dispelled their fears by saying: "God is giving the Torah to his people." The Torah was given to the Jewish people. Our point of view is contained in the prophetic phrase: "Let everyone adore the name of his god"; let everyone follow the path taught by his religion. On hearing this, the nations were relieved that this new religion teaches tolerance and peace; recognition of the sublime ideals of other nations; and resistance to any conquering impulse within itself. Joyfully, the pagan nations answered him: "Let the symbol of this new religion be peace and harmony, brotherhood and love of ones neighbor." Peace and tolerance, love and brotherhood were the lamps that have lit the historical path of our nation.

III

If we want to understand and correctly grasp recent events, we must be constantly aware of a basic difference between Christianity and Judaism. Christianity came to already established nations. It was forced on them with fire and sword, or through the controlling words of its apostles. Judaism remained within the narrow sphere and boundaries of its followers. It rejected expansion of its sphere by force, violence, or deceit.

Only a worldview that develops from the depths of our soul remains our property. What is applicable to our mortal property is equally applicable to our spiritual acquisitions. Only that for which we have struggled and which we have earned, remains our eternal possession. What we have acquired without earning it; foreign treasures that managed to come into our possession, trickle through our fingers with the same ease as they were acquired. The "erev rav," the Egyptian people who, out of fear and dread, joined the Jewish people during the exodus from Egypt, soon deserted their newly chosen religion. They formed the Golden Calf in the desert. They created all the spiritual crises that our forefathers experienced in the desert. Their attachment to their new religion was loose, superficial. The Jewish religion was emotionally foreign to them. They acknowledged it because at the time it was victorious, triumphant. They were mere followers; insincere proselytes. Inwardly, they remained chained to the old philosophy.

It appears that the battle between Judaism and paganism has not yet ended. It appears that deep down, many nations have not yet accepted Christianity, especially its ethical components, drawn from the old Jewish sources. In their hearts, these nations have remained heathens. The intellect was Christianized; the emotion remained pagan. Their instinct remained rooted in the animal sphere. Love of one's neighbor continues to be preached, but hate of one's neighbor has not disappeared. That is why we are witnessing the birth of a new paganism in Russia. That is why the insight is dawning in the heart of Europe, that Christian ideals are not suited to the people's character. The more they dwell on origins and bloodlines, the more they find the spiritually foreign to be disturbing. Human beings and their worldview are separating from each other. The rift appears to be irreparable...A national church is the vision, the hoped-for ideal...

IV

We Jews are in the fortunate position to possess a national religion. Religion and nationhood are so intimately woven together; they penetrate each other so thoroughly, that every religious Jew, consciously or unconsciously, is a nationalist. Every national Jew, one who has lost his religious attachment, declares with his actions that knowledge of Judaism is foreign to him.

In reality, I have used false terminology because a division of Judaism into nationality and religion is quite un-Jewish. Our forefathers never knew about this division. This two-component system – religion and nationality is only appropriate for people who accepted their religion after they had hundreds of years of experience as a nation. First came the community. The religion was brought in afterwards, from the outside. For us, nationhood and revelation came together; together in time and in space. On Mount Sinai we became a nation. At Sinai, we became a religious community.

Henceforth, we will speak of Judaism as only one indivisible, whole entity; as a community held together by multifarious ties. A society that is bound together by world view and mission; by destiny and suffering; by an unbending striving for life, and a never wavering faith in the victory of light, of freedom, and of love in the world!

THE TENTS OF JACOB[122]

As I see them from the mountain tops,
Gaze on them from the heights,
There is a people that dwells apart,
Not reckoned among the nations
(Numbers 23:9)

How fair are your tents, O Jacob,
Your dwellings, O Israel
(Numbers 24:5)

How can I damn whom God has not damned,
How doom when the Lord has not doomed
(Numbers 23:8)

I

In a certain distant land there lived a very wealthy, highly respected, and influential man. He had children and lacked nothing. But despite his material wealth, the respect that he commanded, and his marital bliss, he was unhappy and did not escape bitter suffering. For he had prodigal sons who, pampered and brought up in luxury, went astray and lead a life of revelry paid for by the good will and wealth of their father. The bitterness this caused the father was victorious in his internal struggles, and he finally decided to leave his home, his beloved wife, and his children and go to a distant, foreign land. This was intended as punishment for his prodigal sons who had robbed him of his happiness, respect, and even his possessions. Moreover, he wanted to see whether he could once again become successful in another environment. He lived with the hope that one day he would return, and find that his sons had improved and become more serious; that they had become aware of their goals and responsibilities; that they no longer lived day-to-day, and were no longer primarily dependent on their father's wealth. He was, however, troubled by the fact that he was deserting his beloved wife

---

[122] UGGIK #107, August 1936, 2-3. Original in Polish.

and leaving her poor and destitute. He called his sons together and ordered them not to forget their deserted and poverty-stricken mother; to treat her with love and respect; to support her; and above all, to make her happy until the day of his return. The sons, with tears in their eyes, promised to carry out their father's wishes to the letter and never leave or forget their beloved mother.

The father had hardly left, however, when the sons forgot their promise. Some were ashamed of their mother's indigence; others claimed that they were so busy with their own children that they simply didn't have any additional time to care for their mother. Still others completely forgot their mother, and didn't even bother to look for an excuse. Only those few sons, who themselves lived in the most dire poverty, remained true to the promise they had made to their father. They helped their mother to the best of their ability. They tried to support her spiritually, and encourage her by reassuring her that father would return safely. Only this small handful remembered their bygone splendor, the years of their youth, and the love their father showed for their mother and children.

Years passed. The mother became weaker and more vulnerable as a result of her longing, and the older she became, the more abandoned she felt since her sons, no longer expecting their father's return, completely forgot her.

One day, news was received of the father's imminent return to his land and family. Suddenly, a miracle occurred. All the sons, without exception, began to try to outdo each other in the love they showered on their mother. They showed affection and respect for her on every occasion. When the old lady became aware of this, even she began to hope that her husband would return to her, and that conditions would improve for her. She then said to her sons, "love your father like your brothers who, during his absence, did not forget me. For only that love was genuine, and only it kept my spirits up in my time of solitude."

II

Our beloved Zion has been deserted, neglected, and forgotten for almost two thousand years. Her own children, whom she had brought up, educated, and embraced, forgot her. Zion therefore complained that God had deserted her; forgotten her. But when God left Zion, He commanded His children: "Remember Jerusalem, even more in exile." And the children answered with one voice: "May my right hand wither if I forget you." Nevertheless, Zion was deserted, forgotten. No one tried to repair the wrong done to her. And how did her children behave? Only a small handful remained faithful to the father's admonition. The remainder, were busy seeing to their own welfare. They even convinced themselves that their father would never return, and they therefore lost interest in their mother. Only a small group of faithful children awaited their father's return, and showed their beloved mother an undiminished and unremitting love.

Suddenly and unexpectedly, the children started to gather around the decrepit, deserted old lady. And a voice was heard: "Look around you, mother. All have come around you; even those who until now have stood afar have come to help you, to raise you up. And the mother embraces her children with love. For is there a mother in the world who would not cuddle her repentant, returning children? The mother, therefore, takes her children in her ancient arms, and cuddles them against her old, aching heart. And she says to her children: "Do you still remember what father told you? 'I will only consider you as my nation when, as faithful children of your father and your mother, you will no longer perform those deeds that forced me to abandon you.'"

III

This week we entered a period of sad commemorations in Jewish history.[123] The enemy attacks. There is no harmony among Jews. Resistance weakens and finally causes the destruction of the state and a loss of independence.

As we study this segment of Jewish history and compare it to the present Jewish situation, we must conclude that little has

---

[123] The date corresponds to the commemoration of the period of mourning for the destruction of both Temples and the end of Jewish sovereignty.

actually changed in the course of several thousand years. The only difference is that the ancestors of those who attack us today, once suffered just as we did, and at the hands of the same tyrants. Today, this is taking place in the name of "Christianity" despite the fact that it is precisely Christianity, which proclaims absolute and limitless love, whereas anti-Semitism is an expression of hate. The root of anti-Semitism is not intrinsic to Christianity; it is anti-Christian. No good Christian can be an anti-Semite.

Christianity and Judaism, the Old and the New Testaments, both have a common principle on which all morality is based, the principle of love. "Love your neighbor as yourself" is, according to Christ's word, the essence of the Old Testament, and it is also a summary of the New.

Is it even possible for a modern human being to be an anti-Semite? There can be no Jewish problem for a person who is a liberal in fact, and not only in name. Such a person must acknowledge the complete equality of Christians and Jews in our country without restriction or reservation, as a necessary result of our entire cultural development, and as a basic legal requirement of our legal-political system.

The anti-Semites are trying to promulgate a policy of not buying from Jews, but somehow they never want to ask the public not to sell to Jews; they have never been known to reject orders from Jews. Frequently, the very publications, which call for boycotting Jews, also feature advertisements from Jewish businesses.

IV

Jewish history shows that even when the Jews were still wandering in the desert, anti-Semites used a variety of methods to try to harm them. They even called on several prophets to curse the Jews. But these prophets blessed them instead. They could not do otherwise, since, with their prophetic vision and their enlightened intellect, they could see that this nation is being wronged; that it is being unjustly attacked; that this nation lives apart, i.e., that it does not want to disturb anyone, and merely wants to be left alone and given an opportunity to earn an honest livelihood.

We are therefore hopeful that all attempts by our enemies to destroy us will be unsuccessful because after cloudy days, the sun must shine. The Father will once again return; the mother will once again embrace and cuddle her children.

ועמך כולם צדיקים לעולם יירשו ארץ
וכל בניך למדי ה' ורב שלום בניך

V

COMMUNAL RELATIONSHIPS: BETWEEN THE JEWISH PEOPLE AND POLAND

Beginning with the first partition of Poland by Prussia, Russia, and Austria, Poland began disappearing from the map of Europe as an independent country, a process that was completed with the third partition in 1795. Polish independence was regained 123 years later (1918), as a result of the Treaty of Versailles. Part of the conditions for Polish independence, was a guarantee by Poland of minority rights. In the essay, "Anniversary of the Resurrection of the Polish State," Rabbi Chameides expressed gratitude to Poland for sheltering Jews for nearly a thousand years, and for the support by the Polish delegation for protection of minorities at the deliberations of the League of Nations. He reminded Poland that Jews had repaid their debt by their loyalty to the State, and by their many contributions, including the building of its cities. Turning to the problems of the day, he made the following prophetic statement almost six years before the German invasion of Poland: "We have not yet been able to come to terms with the idea that the enlightened 20th century could give birth to the middle ages, a dark era of pain and suffering. But are we going to be the only sacrifices to that dangerous insanity? Doesn't that megalomania contain within itself the spark of a new, bloody world war; a spark of bellum omnium contra omnes? ... We have a common enemy who lies in wait for our destruction and who, at the first opportunity, will not hesitate to lift its sword against the freedom of Poland, the freedom for which the nation has suffered so much and fought so hard."

The mood is very different in the essay, "National Holiday," written on the same occasion two years later, in 1935, when he reminds Poland that it is easier to win freedom than to keep it, and that freedom cannot exist in a divided society, in a society where one segment is scheming against another. The Jewish position in Poland had changed significantly in these two years. The spread of Hitler's racial hatred across the border with Germany, and the death of J. Piłsudski in 1935, made the Jews of Poland feel very vulnerable.

Józef Piłsudski (1867-1935) was a Polish hero who fought for Polish independence, and was twice arrested by the Russians and banished to Siberia. He organized the Legion, which fought on the side of the allies during WW I. He became Poland's first Chief of

State (1918-1922) and, as First Marshall, led the Polish army in the Russo-Polish war (1919-1920). He returned to power in a coup d'etat in 1926. Despite the fact that he destroyed the parliamentary system and, towards the end of his life, established a dictatorial regime leaning towards fascism, the Jewish community reacted with genuine sorrow and fear when Piłsudski died. By consolidating his power, he managed to keep the viciously anti-Semitic Endencja (National Democratic) party in check. This party held Jews responsible for the deepening economic crisis, stimulated anti-Semitic riots at universities (1931), renewed a call for a numerus clausus in higher education (1932), and, in 1933, started a campaign in the Sejm (Parliament) with the slogan: "There is no place for Jews in Poland." Piłsudski's death, therefore, coming shortly after Poland signed a non-aggression treaty with Germany (1934) and renounced its obligations under the Minorities Treaty (1934), spread fear and a feeling of impending doom in the Jewish community.

"Ritual Slaughter" is an attempt to logically answer an assault against one of the basic tenets of Judaism. There were a number of attempts in the Sejm to ban shechita, the religiously mandated slaughter of animals. Arguments against shechita were based on a supposed compassion for animals and economic concerns. In fact, any increase in the price of meat was borne solely by Jews. Legislation to ban shechita had been introduced in the Sejm in 1923 and 1928. It was once again brought up in 1935, stimulated by a pamphlet, "Kosher Slaughtering According to the Bible and the Talmud" by Father Stanisław Trzeciak, who attempted to prove that ritual slaughter of animals was not required by Biblical law. A bill to ban ritual slaughter was again introduced in February 1936, but an amendment allowed a limited amount of ritually slaughtered meat to be available. This, as well as the strict controls placed on the industry, caused many thousands of Jews in the kosher meat trade to become unemployed. A bill, calling for a total ban on shehita, was again introduced in 1938 and 1939, but the outbreak of the war, prevented a vote.

In describing Jacob in "Anniversary of the Resurrection of the Polish State," one cannot help but wonder whether Rabbi

Chameides was reflecting on his own life and the break with his home: "As long as he was in the restricted environment of daily routine, surrounded by the solicitous shelter of his father and the protecting eye of his mother he could neither dream nor have visions. He could not yearn nor could he cross the threshold of his narrow area of existence. Only in exile, did the gates of heaven open up for him. Only on foreign soil, with a wanderer's staff in his hand, did his spirit mature; secret powers awaken within him; did his soul strengthen and his imagination grow."

The outpouring of national feeling and support for Poland present in these essays may come as somewhat of a surprise to the modern reader. Some of these feelings were undoubtedly genuine, but it must also not be forgotten that government officials were often present during synagogue celebrations on national holidays. It was prudent for Jews to constantly remind these officials of their loyalty. Between the lines, in expressions of unity and love, one can sense the deep anxiety of an embattled minority fighting for its rights and against the increasing evidence of discrimination.

Anniversary of the Resurrection of the Polish State
A Celebratory Service in the Synagogue[124]

On the occasion of the 15th anniversary of the restoration of the Polish State, a large celebration took place in our Synagogue in which a large segment of the Jewish public participated. After prayers, sung by Cantor Dembitzer, Rabbi Chameides gave a moving address suited to the occasion. We hereby present, in an abbreviated form, the text of Rabbi Chameides' speech, which made a deep impression on all who heard it.

Hardly 15 years have passed since Poland was resurrected, and its existence is so taken for granted today that we cannot imagine a consolidated Europe without it. In the course of this relatively short period of time, the whole world has become convinced that a powerful and strong Poland is the best guarantee for peace and security in the east, and that Poland is not a transient, temporary entity, but rather an organic, durable, and indestructible creation.

During the past year, we have honored the memory of three Polish kings each of whom deserves our homage, respect, and admiration. Each of them continues to serve as an example of virtue and nobility worthy of imitation. First, we commemorated the coronation of Casimir the Great to whom, we Jews, are especially grateful. When hatred raged in the west, and our ancestors were threatened with almost certain extermination, Casimir the Great opened the doors of his state to us, giving the persecuted and hounded Jews asylum and shelter on Polish soil. This act testifies to his feelings of pity and Christian love of one's neighbor as well as his enlightened thinking, intelligence, and political maturity. He recognized the benefits and blessings that this humiliated Jewish people might, in time, bring to the State economy. He recognized the creative energy, the potential contributions to economic development and flowering of the State, and the capabilities in

---

[124] UGGIK #44, November 1933, 5. Original in Polish.

manufacturing and trade that lay hidden in our old, tired nation. And his expectations were fully realized. The Jewish nation, which took refuge under the wings of the Republic, became its faithful son devoted to serving it. The frequent accusations of our enemies are actually the best proof of our contribution. Among other things, we are reproached for concentrating in Polish towns; that towns and cities are filled and populated by Jews. That we have stamped our "foreignness" on Polish culture. But these critics forget that these same cities are in fact monuments to our creativity. Just as the Polish peasant has stood guard over, and tilled the soil of Poland, the Jew has developed and enlarged its cities; established its towns and new settlements; and nursed their progress. Through our work for the welfare of the State, we have repaid, and continue to repay, a debt we owe to King Casimir the Great. Modern Poland is following in his footsteps by caring for the poor and the oppressed, by protecting our brothers on the other side of the border, and by extending us a saving hand at this time of despair and distress. On this festive day, we want to extend our heartfelt thanks to the Republic of Poland for their support, and especially for help given us at the League of Nations where our government repeatedly stepped in as an advocate of justice and equal rights for all nations and races. Poland remembers its old traditions. Poland, the noble and chivalrous, has remained faithful to the principles of its men of vision, to the ideals of its tolerant kings. Our attachment to the fatherland has been immeasurably strengthened and deepened by recent events. Even our brothers, who for years have lived outside the borders of Poland – in America, in Palestine – have not cut the thread that binds them to the old homeland. Polish Jews are famous throughout the world for their patriotism and close ties to their country. We recently saw proof of that once again, when our government turned to its citizens with an appeal for a subscription for a national loan. All segments of the community, we among them, rushed to the aid of the fatherland. Not only we who live in this land, but also Jews who have lived abroad for years, came forward voluntarily to fulfill their national obligation.

King Casimir the Great gave us, the foreign newcomers, life

and affection. Another king whose memory we honored this year, gave us strength by demonstrating that a person with a different religion and background is spiritually and honorably capable of becoming part of a culture foreign to him. That such a person can adhere to a foreign state with all his soul; even to become its leader and defender; to bring it honor and glory despite the fact that his cradle rocked in a different land; despite the fact that he came from distant lands and that his roots were planted in other regions. King Stephan Batory is excellent proof of this. Despite the fact that foreign blood flowed in his veins, he became king of Poland. He was a heroic king, and fought courageously for the honor, for the greatness of his new freely adopted fatherland! When God created a human being, He gathered dust from all the corners of the world so that a human being may feel at home everywhere; so that he may easily acclimate himself, and get used to any environment. Our relationship with the Polish nation is not artificial or superficial. Instead, it is based on a shared fate and shared fears; on our long-standing shared experiences, convictions, and suffering. Any theory imported from abroad that threatens the relationship between one segment of the community and another; that threatens to loosen this connection and brotherly love; to disturb the peace that reigns in the land, threatens the unity and cohesion of the nation, and creates an abyss of hatred and discord among brothers."

On the basis of the history of Joseph as told in the Bible, who, despite belonging to another nation, brought blessings and benefits to the Egyptian state, the Rabbi demonstrated that he who is faithful to the God of his fathers and is not ashamed of his origins, is able to be a good and faithful citizen of the country in which he is living. He then pointed to various historical figures (Abarbanel, Disraeli, Samuel Hanagid) who offered sacrifices on the altar of love for their fatherland.

Some nations and world powers are nurturing strange and dangerous themes. Instead of promoting international cooperation, of strengthening mutual relations, of searching to find points of agreement and common concern, these nations are excluding and separating themselves. They are locking their country with seven locks, meticulously examining the pedigree of each of their citizens, and segregating and excluding valuable individuals only because they cannot prove their ancestry with an appropriate certificate. Human history teaches us that at times of great catastrophes, no nation can rely on its own strength. It cannot resist a threatening danger, alone. This is exemplified by the immortal and heroic deed of Jan III Sobieski at the gates of Vienna, with which this Polish king saved western culture from destruction. This is the third Polish king, whose memory is dear to us as well as to other nations. The first Polish Marshall, Joseph Piłsudski, prostrated himself in the presence of the President before the ashes of this great king, thus accepting with this gesture the principles of Sobieski: The unity of nations and mutual aid. The dazzling heroism and courage of Sobieski's accomplishment, a victory won over a common enemy, points us in the direction in which resurrected Poland needs to proceed. We should not shut ourselves off hermetically, like our neighbor to our west, nor should we, haughtily and pompously, immerse ourselves in our own fiction of strength. Instead, we should search for support from other nations. To establish contact with anyone who can serve and be useful to us and, at the same time, to submit to a higher ideal and to activities that enlighten all of humanity.

Soon, we will be reading passages from our Holy Writings in our synagogues that deal with Jacob's flight from his parents' home. Hated by his biologic brother, his life endangered by a desire for vengeance, Jacob leaves his parents' threshold where he spent his early years; where his flowering life blossomed, and where he had barely awakened from the sleep of childhood. Suddenly, he stood on the brink of a new and mysterious period of his life. He could not foresee when his wanderings would cease; where this pilgrimage would lead him. An indescribable fear gripped his heart about the uncertainty of the morrow, and anxiety about his future. But, despite his inner torment and concerns, his spirit was lifted to heavenly heights with the appearance of a prophetic dream, which momentarily removed a veil that covered his future with a haze like a shroud. With a supernatural dazzling light, the majesty of God made its appearance, and a voice, calming his pain and suffering, said: "The land on which you are lying will be a possession owned by your descendants." This was Jacob's first vision; the first prophetic dream of his life. As long as he was in the restricted environment of daily routine, surrounded by the solicitous shelter of his father, and the protecting eye of his mother he could neither dream nor have visions. He could not yearn, nor could he cross the threshold of his narrow area of existence. Only in exile did the gates of heaven open up for him. Only on foreign soil, with a wanderer's staff in his hand, did his spirit mature; secret powers awakened within him. Only then did his soul strengthen and his imagination grow.

The era of subjugation of the Polish nation also included dreams and God's vision. As once for Jacob, the era of subjugation kindled a beautiful fire of idealism and yearning within the Polish nation; it extracted, as if by magic, a secret, hidden source of strength; it hastened and enhanced the mental powers; and it deepened and tempered its desire and thirst for its own national life. The time of political decline was, therefore, also a time of inner blessing; a fruitful and fertile time of monumental spiritual activity. Like a ray of sunshine out of dark clouds, the victory of the spirit over the martyrology of the body shines for us from the Polish tragedy. An inner, never silent voice, was constantly calling the nation to freedom and independence from the tormenting claws of the enemy. A voice calling, like once to Jacob: "The soil on which you are resting, shackled and chained, will belong to your descendants."

Today, we are celebrating a happy 15th anniversary of the restoration of Poland, an anniversary of the realization of this vision, this God-given dream."

Finishing his speech, the Rabbi touched on current issues, saying:

The tragedy that has befallen our brothers in Germany overwhelms us like a terrible nightmare. Even though several months have already passed since the outbreak of this terrible insanity, that sudden mania that overcame that once great nation of "poets and thinkers," we are still dazed, wounded, and mute from the blow that has been delivered to us. We have not yet been able to come to terms with the idea that the enlightened 20th century could give birth to the middle ages, a dark era of pain and suffering. But are we going to be the only sacrifice to that dangerous insanity? Doesn't that megalomania contain within itself the spark of a new, bloody world war; a spark of *bellum omnium contra omnes* [a war of all against all]? Indeed their theory of lower and higher races, their false measurement of the value of a human being is in opposition to a basic principle of the Church, scoffs totally at all religious views about the mission and purpose of a human being. Consequently, we have a common enemy who lies in wait for our destruction and who, at the first opportunity, will not hesitate to lift its sword against the freedom of Poland, the freedom for which the nation has suffered so much and fought so hard. It is true that it is difficult to attain freedom, difficult to win the battle for freedom, but it is a hundred times more difficult to keep and assure this hard won freedom and independence, which was so laboriously attained at a cost of so much spilled blood.

Let us therefore be aware of our obligations to the future. Let us be unceasingly mindful about the development and growth of the Republic, and let us have hope and confidence that God will deign to give us his blessings for ever and ever. Amen.

An Echo of Mourning[125]

A speech delivered at a service of mourning in the Synagogue in Katowice on Friday, 17 May 1935 after the death of the late Józef Piłsudski.

ויהי לאבל כנרי
ועגבי לקול בוכים

So my lyre is given over to mourning
My pipe, to accompany weepers.
(Job 30:31)

O mourning community! Pain and deep sorrow have crossed the threshold of our synagogue, of our holy place, a place where we usually bare our souls before God, a place in which we bare our hearts and reveal its most hidden secrets. Today, a genuinely sincere pain envelops our hearts. Today, a black shroud of mourning hangs over the entire country. Today, each of us is plunged into an inconsolable sadness because of the sudden death of our beloved leader, our dear chief of the nation, the reviver and First Marshall of Poland, the late Józef Piłsudski. He is no longer in our midst...He has gone far away from us into the beyond. He, who for so many years, was our faithful protector and patron, a rock of nobility and justice, a source of hope and strength, an example of heroism and boundless patriotism.

I still remember and can hear the words I spoke only recently, on March 19th, the anniversary of his birth, about his contributions. On that occasion, I mentioned the words of a certain philosopher who compared great souls to mountain peaks that reach to the heavens. It is easier for us to breathe there. There, on the mountain peaks, the air is pure; the view is magnificent; and our eyes can take in scenes of distant fields and gardens. People should make a pilgrimage at least once a year to such a peak in order to come closer to God; in order to reinvigorate the heart for the battles of our daily lives. From this place, we have made such a virtual pilgrimage every year to the peak whose name was Józef Piłsudski. Each year, on the solemn occasion of his birthday, we too have been

---

[125] UGGIK #80, May 1935, 3-4. Original in Polish.

invigorated, as we have probed his significance for resurrected Poland; we ourselves have been strengthened by bringing his accomplishments into focus, and by examining the influence that he has had on shaping Poland. Today, I have been given a sad assignment – to give a eulogy over the grave, over the still open grave, of Józef Piłsudski. Today, in orphaned, lonely Poland we look helplessly, searching in vain for him on whom we have always depended in times of depression and sadness, in times of momentous decisions. One of the most beautiful and strong personalities in Polish history descends into the grave. With Marshall Piłsudski's death, an entire era of struggle and battle, superhuman effort and sacrifice for a free Poland, a strong Poland, a powerful Poland, comes to an end. As it is said about the Biblical Joseph (Exodus 1:6), וימת יוסף וכל אחיו וכל הדור ההוא – and Joseph died and all his brothers, and with him an entire generation.

An English philosopher tells us that the entire history of humanity, everything that humanity has accomplished in this world, is in reality the history of great leaders. For they were the foremen and the chiefs of humanity; they led it to the heights of their destiny with pillars of fire. Everything that is sublime and excellent, everything that exists thanks to human ingenuity, is in fact nothing more than the realization of ideas and dreams born and developed in the minds and hearts of great leaders. The history of every nation is saturated with the spirit of its heroes, leaders, and visionaries. Just as poets are recognized by their poems and creations, so nations are recognized by their heroes. The spiritual state of the poet, his dreams and emotions, his point of view, and his soaring ideas, are all expressed in his poetry. Similarly, the deepest emotions of the nation, its pain and success, its joy and despondency, its infamy and yearning, are expressions of that nation's heroes. Alexander the Great, Philip II, Napoleon – these are not only names of individuals. Each represents an era; expresses a period in human history. So strongly were they identified with their times; so tightly was their life bound and joined with the events of their country, that the mere mention of their names suffices to awaken in us an image of their era. They remain, for all time, a symbol, and personification of their nation.

In this spirit and with the same symbolic significance, we mention the name of Marshall Józef Piłsudski, whose untimely death is plaintively mourned today by thousands upon thousands in Poland. Piłsudski is not just the name of a person, but the substance, the very essence, the meaning of a whole generation. This one name encompasses and contains the secret and the miracle of the recent phase of Polish history. When, many generations hence, a Polish child will utter the name of Piłsudski, his young heart will experience the suffering and toil, failure and triumph that the great leader of the Polish Legion experienced. For that reason, the day on which the Marshall gave up his ghost will become progressively more solemn every year. It will penetrate ever deeper into our consciousness as a day on which the nation pays homage to its redeemer, expresses its deep gratitude to its leader, its affection and admiration as well as its steadfast wish and readiness to continue working to complete the task that he began. An old Jewish tradition comes to mind. "Every year, on the anniversary of the destruction of Jerusalem, a fissure appears on the remaining wall, from which drops of blood and tears fall as from an open wound. Every year at midnight, on this day of mourning for Israel, one can hear, amid the cinders and ruins which rise like an eternal monument in place of the bygone glory of Judea, wailing and crying, an echo of the lament of Jeremiah, the sound of the last sighs of the Jewish heroes who fell for freedom and their fatherland." Every year at this time, when we remind ourselves of our great national loss, when we once again realize that inexorable death has suddenly and prematurely robbed us of a leader, whose life was a holy sacrifice offered on the nation's altar, the wound will once again open. We will once again experience the breech and emptiness in the ranks of warriors for an independent Poland left by his death. His life, dedicated to the restoration and rebuilding of the State; intended to bring together and unify the vital forces of the nation with the aim of increasing Poland's luster and splendor, and to blot out the stigma of her long years of bondage was, however, only one in a series of sacrifices and heroic deeds by the Marshall.

Only a future historian will be in a position to evaluate the significance, greatness, and importance of the life of Józef Piłsudski.

Only then, from a historical perspective, will the full magnitude of his accomplishments illuminated by a halo of heroism and victory be revealed. But even today, we can discern two main forces in his character: determination, and faith in his own destiny. With perseverance and stubbornness, he was able to draw from a deep well of faith in his mission, from an inner conviction that Providence destined him to accomplish a great assignment for the history of Poland. Today, when pain overwhelms us; when a wave of sadness flows from Belweder[126] across all of Poland to its most remote borders and corners; when it is difficult to free ourselves from the thought that he is no longer with us; when we realize that the staff has fallen out of his strong hands; that his commands are forever silenced; that his heart is forever stilled; that this great solitary figure standing watch over Poland has gone to an eternal sleep; on this day we again open the book of his rich life; we stare at the abundant fruit of his tiring, but blessed work; stage by stage we review the blossoming of his accomplishments from the hardly perceptible beginnings to his current greatness. And we are overwhelmed by astonishment and a feeling of humility. In the face of this inexhaustible energy, in the face of this vital creative force, in the face of this powerful determination and deep faith that illuminated his path in life, we realize our own insignificance and weakness.

Determination and faith were characteristics already evident in his youth. The words of God to the prophet: "Before I formed you, I selected you; before you knew the light of day, you were destined for your mission" (Jeremiah 1:15), were equally applicable to the Marshall. As a schoolboy, he instigates against the invading authorities. As a young man, he conspires, secretly plots, publishes pamphlets, smuggles illegal publications, schemes. As a grown man, conscious of his mission, he forms an army, sets out for battle. He, a leader of a small group of soldiers against the mighty armies of oppressive states. Hard labor, prisons, Siberia, Magdeburg – suffering and torture are insufficient to weaken his resolve. No obstacle can restrain him from carrying out his life's mission assigned him by Providence until, from the political prison, from

---

[126] Belweder Palace, in Warsaw, was the Marshall's residence where he died.

Siberian exile, he becomes the leader and commander-in-chief (Hetman) of his nation. The vision of the poet has been fulfilled; the prophecy of Wyspiański[127] has been fulfilled:

"I am nothing but a fantasy
I am nothing but a poem;
I am nothing but a soul.
But after me will come a power
emanating from my words,
a power that will crush the fetters,
that will once again revive the State."

That power did come. That power revealed itself. The lustrous and honorable symbol and expression of this power was Marshall Piłsudski.

The secrets of his accomplishments were faith and determination. In death, he bequeathed that faith and determination to us. And just as his word, his command, his majesty, the luster of intelligence and experience reflected from his face united and consolidated us during his life, so may his death, the sorrow that moves us to our very depth, the gratitude that all of us feel towards him, the tears that are being shed for him by millions, unite us today into one harmonious community. For, Marshall, it is not only your daughters and your faithful life companion who walked hand in hand with you along the thorny path of suffering to the highest rung of triumph, who now cry over your tomb. Millions of school children are crying; your faithful comrades-in-arms are crying; all who saw chivalrous, noble, free Poland – a good mother to all its sons personified in you, are crying.

You bequeathed your heart to the town of your birth to which you were tied with bonds of deep love. You bequeathed your brain to scholars. Your mortal remains will rest in the Royal Tombs of the Wawel.[128] And who would dare to ask which of these gifts is the

---

[127] Stanislaw Wyspianski (1869-1907), was a Polish playwright, painter, and poet.
[128] The Wawel is a hilltop in Kraków of great national significance. It is home to the Royal Palace, armory, and Cathedral, and the final resting place for many Polish heroes. Piłsudski is buried at the Wawel, except for his heart, which according to his instructions, was buried in an urn next to his mother's remains.

greater? Your heart, which contained so much goodness and so much spiritual character? Your brain, which to the last moment of your life, did not stop being concerned with the future and welfare of Poland? Your mortal remains, which frequently were bent under the yoke of adversity, and were an external cover and mantle for the holy embers and fire of inspiration that glowed within you? There, where rest the remains of Polish kings and prophets, in the Pantheon of the nation, there too you shall find rest!

In this hour of solemn mourning, permit me also to express our gratitude and admiration to the great one, now deceased. The gratitude and admiration of one of the oldest nations in the world; the gratitude and admiration of the nation of the Bible and the Prophets; the most esteemed and yet the most persecuted nation on the face of the earth. Accept, Marshall, words of homage, words of genuine affection flowing to you from all Jewish communities in Poland, from the mouths of spiritual and secular representatives of our people. There is no personality in the entire expanse of Polish history, to which the hearts of plain, God fearing Jews, as well as the hearts of the most secular of Jews are as devoted as to Marshall Józef Piłsudski. I don't know where that affection came from. I don't know how it arose. I don't know when it was born in our hearts, nor when it germinated and grew to such exuberance. But I do know that whenever I have heard a plain Jew in the street speak of Piłsudski, his eyes would brighten; an internal happiness would spark within him as if to say, "he belongs to me also..."

Exactly how our nation will perpetuate his memory, and pay homage to him is still unknown. But at this moment, I am already certain that, just as there are settlements and forests in Palestine today bearing the names of leaders of other nations such as a Masaryk settlement, a George V forest, a King (Yugoslavian) Alexander forest, so in the near future, a Piłsudski forest will undoubtedly be established in the Holy Land. Despite the supposed Jewish wealth, we are a poor nation. But we are a grateful nation, and we want the names of our benefactors, the names of our friends, always to exist among us. May a beautiful Piłsudski forest soon bloom in Palestine, and when a Jewish child, whose ancestors once lived on the banks of the Vistula, asks in the future who Piłsudski was – we will tell him: He was, my child, a great hero from a great nation!

And now, open your gates Wawel and receive the remains of a great leader for whom our affection will last forever, and whose memory will never be extinguished amongst us. When Słowacki's remains were brought to Poland, you, Marshall said: "There are people and their accomplishments so mighty and powerful that they defeat even death!" And you have defeated death! Your spirit is immortal! Your accomplishments – indestructible! And so we bid you good-bye with an old Jewish blessing – לך בשלום – Eternally blissful peace to your soul! Amen!

HOLIDAY OF THE SEA[129]

The period of national mourning for the late Marshall Piłsudski has just ended. The outward symbols of mourning, the black flags and the armbands have disappeared, but all of us still feel the same loneliness and anxiety in our hearts, a feeling that overwhelmed us on hearing the distressing news of his death. However, אל תבכו למת – we must not allow ourselves to become overwhelmed by sadness. We must not allow sorrow to sap our energy; to interrupt our creativity, even momentarily.

Piłsudski's order of 1918 sounds short and terse and yet strong and decisive: "I order the formation of a Polish navy." We have not yet completely carried out this order. The fulfillment of this order is still in its first stage. An old Jewish maxim teaches us מצוה לקיים דברי המת – it is a duty, a religious obligation to see to it that the wishes of the dead do not remain dreams; one should fulfill them as quickly as possible.

Providence has given us a great assignment. It is our fortune to live in an era of the rebuilding of the nation from its very foundation. We are the first free generation to live in a free Poland. It is well known how difficult it is to be the first. The first must create יש מאין – something out of nothing; to charm reality out of emptiness. The first is a pioneer, a conqueror. The first, laboriously and with self-sacrifice, paves the way for those who come after. And just as our ancestors, who wondered and roamed through the desert for forty years and there, in the desert sands, found their graves without ever reaching the border of the yearned-for and dreamed-for land, prepared a better future for their descendants with the sacrifice of their lives, their labors, and their sweat, so we too are, in some measure, pioneers in all the activities of statehood.

We found a veritable *tohu vavohu* in every part of our work. There was no tradition to light our way. Our ideal and profound faith in victory was our only signpost. Inspired with a Divine

---

[129] UGGIK #84, July 1935, 4-5. Original in Polish.

creative spirit, we called out יהי אור – let there be light! And a bright light appeared! We called out – "let a mighty Polish army appear" – and it appeared. Let a Polish national idea bloom in every heart – and it bloomed, beautifully and exuberantly. Let a Polish port be established on the Polish sea – and wasn't beautiful Gdynia established? This was the most forceful evidence of the creative power, the determination and energy that nurtures the resurrected Polish nation. And now, the nation calls: "Let the sea be the front! Let us conquer the sea for Poland! Let us conquer Poland for the sea! Let us create a Polish merchant marine, a Polish navy, Polish maritime positions, and a Polish coast guard." And, we are sure that this appeal, this call to the nation, will also be answered!

Let us briefly remind ourselves of the significance of the sea for the nation and the State, especially from the cultural and economic standpoint.

History teaches us that only nations with a relationship with the sea; masters and rulers of the sea, reached a high cultural standard. A nation with access to the sea possesses a wider spiritual viewpoint, and an unlimited intellectual horizon. The sea is a window on the world. Who knows whether Palestine, relatively small in size and area, would have become a cradle of religion; a cultural center that influenced practically all enlightened nations; a center of interest and adoration for the whole world, if it did not have access to the sea? Whether its very geographic location on the Mediterranean Sea did not predestine it for its role as teacher of humanity? Whether human ideals born on the holy soil, such as brotherhood and the uniting of all nations, the unity of the human race and eternal peace, messianism and salvation, which have exerted such a profound influence on the works of Mickiewicz in the era of towianizm,[130] whether all these lofty ideals are not imbued with the atmosphere of the sea, which connects nations and peoples? Isn't the expanse of the sea reflected in them, endless waters reaching into infinity...?

Isaiah predicts that in the Messianic era, quarrels and dissension

---

[130] The creed of Andrzej Towianski (1799-1878) making Poland a messiah among the nations.

between people would disappear because "the earth will be full with the knowledge of God, כמים לים מכסים – as the sea is full of water." This comparison hides a deeper thought. For on the bottom of the sea, there are summits and craters, mountains and valleys, heights and depressions. But the water smoothes out all these irregularities. The sheet of water covers and hides the ragged sea bottom, which, at least from the surface, appears to be smooth. In the depths there are, to be sure, irregularities. In reality, there are rifts, and even dangerous chasms at the bottom of the sea. But standing on the shore and looking out on the surface, we see before us only a smooth and even watery surface. Likewise, in the depths of human souls, there are psychological differences. Each of us has a different point of view. Everyone thinks differently, reacts uniquely, and strives for something different. The Prophet foretells that in the Messianic era, all these differences will be covered up and mitigated by the knowledge of God, just as water covers the variegated bottom of the sea. A shared ideal will overshadow differences of opinion and points of view. Among us, too, there exist differences of opinion and outlook about the best method for governing the State. We do not agree on everything. But there is a common goal, which all of us can and must work for. And this goal is the conquest of the sea. The sea is our common wish! The sea connects all of us! The sea is one of the most important links in the chain of tasks that we must accomplish in the near future.

From an economic point of view, the possession of even a tiny piece of seacoast represents, without a doubt, an incalculable asset for us. Let us remind ourselves of our situation immediately after the war, when we tried, in vain, to find markets for our country's products. The large Russian market was closed to us. Contact with other overseas markets was made extremely difficult. We were, moreover, dependent on the intervention of others, who quite often looked at us with a jaundiced eye, and did not make it easy for us to reach our goal. Adding to our difficulties was the customs war with our western neighbor. At that point, the sea became a matter of life for us. We were forced to transport goods by land to the sea, and then by sea, to overseas customers. And thus, we gradually built up the port of Gdynia whose activity arouses general admiration, and whose equipment satisfies the needs of the most modern ports in the world.

Historia magistra vitae. History is a good teacher. And history teaches us that the Polish nation, despite our yearning for the sea did not, in the past, have a deep understanding of its importance. We also did not appreciate the importance of possessing maritime colonies for our emigration as well as for our country's goods. Let us, therefore, learn from history and let us not repeat the mistakes of the past!

We Jews, in addition to our pure patriotic feelings for Poland, hope that perhaps in time, the development of Polish seafaring may become a link between Poland and the new Palestine. The ship "Polonia," carrying thousands of Jews from Poland to Palestine, represents the ideal synthesis of the Polish spirit with the new Palestine reality in miniature. The ocean waves link Polish emigrants, in the distant lands where they have settled, with the mother country. They carry greetings from parents to children and good wishes from children to parents. מקלות מים רבים אדירים מבשרי ים אדיר במרום ה' – from the depths, the waves of the sea carry a beautiful song in praise of God, אשר לו הים והוא עשהו – who is Master of the earth and the sea. May He grant us the strength to carry out our duties, everywhere and always, for the good of the State and of all humanity!

NATIONAL HOLIDAY[131]

Sermon Delivered on November 11

Today, in an atmosphere filled with gravity and anxiety; in the face of struggles and challenges, we are celebrating the anniversary of the resurrection and renaissance of the Polish state.

On the occasion of these festivities in the first years of Polish independence, we usually described our feelings of joy and attempted to strengthen our patriotic attachment. We reminded ourselves of the importance of the historical experience of the resurrection of free Poland. Despite the battles and suffering, sacrifices and blood, we gave thanks to Providence for leading us on a path from prison and servitude to a land of independence and self-dependence. The experience of becoming independent was so shocking and powerful, so stunning and unique, that it was always in our thoughts. Our view, constantly focused on the past, was entranced by the sight of the miracle; dazzled by the heroic exploits of the Legions. We were so mesmerized by the past that we could not see the reality of our daily lives, and the ever-emerging new political and economic crises, except through the prism of this miraculous experience. We could hardly believe our own eyes. It took a long time for the consciousness of the existence of the Polish state to penetrate the most secret recesses of our souls; for us, but especially for other states and nations, to become accustomed to Poland as an indisputable, achieved fact, as a state with a capacity to survive, sanctified by the will of God and historical events; for the Polish nation to become an important and constructive factor in the world, a state that cannot and must not be scorned. It has taken a long time for this psychological change to have an effect on us and especially on our neighboring countries.

Now, however, that time has passed at last! Because *cogito ergo sum!* We think, we function; we are working and creating in every

[131] UGGIK #92, November 1935, 1-3. Original in Polish.

field and endeavor. We sail our ship of state independently. We occupy the highest positions in the areopagus of nations. We have, once and for all, stopped being a state in the process of birth, a Saisonstaat, a fleeting state destined for a short life.

Now, we are inaugurating a new era in Polish history. After a period of intoxication, enthusiasm, and sudden awakening; after internal and external battles, and persevering over great difficulties and obstacles, there now follows an era of straightforward, sober, and ordinary activities of daily life. The Polish nation must prove to itself and to the world that just as, in its time, it was capable of dying for Poland on the field of battle and buying victory with death, it is now able to live for Poland and serve it with its life. We must transform ourselves, psychologically and physically, from a nation fighting for its freedom into a nation guarding its freedom. And sometimes, it is more difficult to preserve and guarantee freedom than to win it in battle. It is sometimes more difficult to protect and strengthen the existence of the State with day-to-day unremitting work, than to lay down its foundation. It is more difficult to keep one's balance and remain on the peak, than to climb it. We, therefore, now need a new, a different spiritual strength than before in order to pacify, calm, and soothe the raging and agitated ideas of the long clandestine battle for freedom and transform a revolutionary and conspiratorial citizen into a citizen-farmer who patiently cultivates the soil of the fatherland; into a citizen-craftsman, worker, and merchant who watches over the growth and development of the State's welfare. We have conquered Polish soil. Now we must conquer and, perhaps totally remake, the Polish persona; to cleanse it of the accretions of bondage; to fill its soul with Polish essence; and to implant it with Polish feeling. How can we accomplish this? What must we do? The Bible tells us.

Adam, Noah, Abraham, three prominent Biblical figures who have recently been subjects for our consideration and thought, represent three stages on the road of development of human ethics. They are like three pillars of fire that illuminated the primitive world and scattered the darkness of the then prevalent moral licentiousness. We can see a progressive ethical development in them, as the human character became stronger and gradually inured itself in the battle against temptation. How human beings gradually freed themselves from the shackles of instinct and dark impulses, and thus acquired ever-greater self-control and mastery and the ability to subjugate the emotions that drive them. This process, as exemplified by these three Biblical figures, occurs in each one of us. Everyone experiences this process of moral maturation that begins as a battle against our instincts, and ends when, with complete free will, we acquire awareness and moral responsibility. What were the individual phases of this process?

At the very beginning of Biblical history, we meet Adam who easily falls prey to temptation and lust, and is unable to resist and oppose the incitement of his life's companion. His will is still weak, brittle. He doesn't yet have his own opinion as to what is good and what is evil. He allows himself to be beguiled and drawn into the net of sin without hesitation or the slightest resistance.

The second personality, Noah, to whom the Bible devotes a separate section, is more independent. He lives in a corrupt, depraved, and unbridled environment devoid of all restraint. His spiritual will is, however, already mature and strong enough, so that the ubiquitous corruption has no influence on him. The entire world is immersed in sin; he alone avoids evil. All are intoxicated with sin; he alone remains sober. Noah is a classical example of an informed individual who goes his own separate way and does not acknowledge or take part in the contemporary mania; who has the courage to think independently and to live in harmony with his own convictions. Whereas Noah undoubtedly represents a higher ethical stage than Adam, since he has an independent opinion and refuses to bow down before the idols of his day, it cannot be said that he was an excellent person, that he reached the highest ethical standard. He did not succeed in convincing others that his world view was correct. He did not succeed, and worse still, he didn't even attempt to root out and remove the error of others. He saved and protected himself. But he was neither teacher nor mentor for others. And when the flood overwhelmed the earth, he locked himself and his family in the ark. He separated himself from his environment;

everything outside the ark was destined for destruction.

Abraham, the forefather of our nation, is the first person who deserves to be called perfect because he was a man of solid character and deep faith. He worked untiringly to convince his contemporaries to accept his belief that all should abandon paganism and idolatry and bow before God's majesty. He was the teacher of his generation.

Adam, Noah, and Abraham can serve as models for us even today. First of all, every one of us should strive to fulfill his obligations to the State as an individual and then, using Abraham as an example, teach others. The mission of educating others in the spirit of the State rests on each one amongst us, regardless of party affiliation. Everyone is called upon, and is obligated to be involved in the revival and the spread of "Polishness" in his surroundings. Everyone has to work on himself and to encourage others – to encourage, but not to force or supervise. To encourage is the only appropriate method. A bad educator and worthless pedagogue is one who, incapable of kindling a love and interest for his subject in the hearts of his students, has to resort to force in order to get the students' attention. One can achieve greater results by being a good example and by having informative and educational material, than by dull propaganda, which makes demands without showing a method for turning theory into action. Tolstoy says: "It is easier to write ten volumes of philosophy than to turn even one solitary maxim into practice."

All of us are very much aware of our difficult assignment to try to make this scrap of land on which we live Polish, and to eradicate all foreign influences from it. We are all aware of our great responsibility to future generations and to Polish history. Who would dare dispute the fact that we have a responsibility to efface and blot out the last traces of the bygone subjugation of this southern part of Poland; that, in place of the foreign conqueror's culture, we must plant the beautiful tree of the native culture; that we must create forms and structures of social and communal life; to speak, think, and feel, in ways that are compatible with our obligations as citizens of the Polish State? Who disagrees with this?

Who would argue with this? Who could oppose this truth? I wouldn't think anyone! But there do exist among us differences of opinion about the best way for bringing this about. Some want to take the evolutionary road; others, the road of revolution. History teaches us that revolutions have indeed been successful in achieving far-reaching changes in the direction or the psychology of nations. But it also teaches us that these changes have, for the most part, been transient, short lived, and not durable because they did not reach into the depth of the soul and did not take deep root. Only gradual, evolutionary, and systematic education can furrow the soil of the soul; can fundamentally transform an individual. Only with patience, brotherly love, tolerance, and mutual understanding will we be able to improve the national agenda, and the future of the Polish nation.

And the Polish nation is currently facing serious and important problems. A significant change has taken place in the political situation in Europe since the late Marshall Piłsudski left this earth. The hope that peace can be maintained in the world and that world humanity will be able to breathe easier, has proven to be illusory and, in view of recent events, very much weakened. The shadow of war is once again looming on our horizon. A feeling of uncertainty about the morrow once again pervades the nation. In these turbulent times, we must be all the more vigilant about the welfare of the State so that it is not drawn into the whirlpool of events and catastrophes. Only a nation strengthened by work and peace of mind, in which everyone defends truth and righteousness; in which everyone fulfills his duty and obligation and serves the common good; in which there is dedication and a readiness to sacrifice, and in which love for everything that is beautiful, worthy, sincere and pure has not disappeared, only such a nation will be able to withstand and successfully persevere through storms and cataclysms. Such a nation will have the capacity to overcome all hardships and win recognition and respect even, from its enemies. Let us therefore, first of all strive to improve our moral and intellectual qualities in both our private and public lives, to increase our storehouse of true knowledge and true virtue, and then let us entrust ourselves to God, so that He, who has not deserted us in so many sad and difficult times, will continue to protect us with His grace.

If we study the beginning activities of the new government and the newly elected Sejm, we must come to the conclusion that the major goal of our leaders is to achieve a balance. We are striving to achieve a balance; to achieve equilibrium in all aspects of our public lives. Balance in the State budget, balance in the relationship between village and city, balance in the equitable division of services and taxes to the coffers of the State. But we often forget the balance that is most important for us all, spiritual balance. Until we achieve that balance, all of our work will be for naught. But spiritual balance can only reign if the national community includes all classes and parts of the nation; if harmony and mutual responsibility draws individual citizens closer to itself; if one segment of society is not scheming ignominious plans against another.

"Why has your nation been granted the strength to be restored?" asks Mickiewicz in the books of Polish pilgrimage. "Not because your nation was powerful, since the Romans were mightier and they disappeared and were not restored. Not because your republic was old and glorious, since Venice and Genoa were older and more glorious and they did not survive nor were they restored as nations. Not because your nation was enlightened by scholarship, since Greece, the mother of philosophers, disappeared and lay in her grave until she forgot all scholarship...But you will be awakened from your grave because you believe, love, and have hope."

The words of the national poet have been fulfilled. The Polish nation has arisen from the grave, not because it was powerful, not because it was glorious, and not because it was intelligent. But because it "believed, loved, and had hope." Woe to us if these three attributes stop existing in our society. Woe to us, if a lack of faith and skepticism creeps into our hearts; if, instead of love, the raucous voice of hatred is heard amongst us; and instead of hope, we are conquered by defeatism and pessimism. Then, in one moment, this magnificent edifice built by the Polish nation with the effort of its blood, will lie in ruins. For the world is sustained only by love.

The words of Mickiewicz are a source of consolation and comfort for us, Jews, in these sad times. Despite our affliction and pain we have not ceased being a nation of "faith, love, and hope." Others, in our position, would long ago have been spiritually broken and long ago would have lost the last spark of hope in the possibility of escape and rescue. We, however, still believe, love, and hope. We believe in the eternity, immortality, and the indestructibility of the spirit of our prophets. We love the ideals of peace and justice and thirst to serve them. And we have a profound hope that Poland will follow the path illuminated for it by its great son and First Marshall, who is sleeping the eternal sleep on the Wawel, a path paved by love and cooperation of all its citizens leading to happiness and the glory of free Polish nation.

Ritual Slaughter[132]

A wave of compassion for poor animals has swept over all of Poland. Amidst the poverty and misery experienced by a large segment of Polish society, our "noble" leaders and representatives have suddenly reminded themselves about an apparent injustice against our domestic animals that has been caused by the ritual slaughter practiced since time immemorial. We are not surprised that ritual slaughter has become the sensation of the day, and, at this moment, is the major topic of discussion and consideration. Indeed, it represents an especially attractive prey for every type of movement searching for an escape valve for their party passions and racial hatred. It also offers an opportunity to raise the so-called Jewish question; to attack Jewish ethics, to threaten the livelihood of thousands of Jews, and to deny them a last economic opportunity, all under the guise of mercy. One can oppress the Jew, the scapegoat of all time, and still have a feeling of performing holy work, of serving a higher ideal.

Something that we never expected to happen has in fact occurred. The issue of ritual slaughter has been added to the daily agenda.

Since I am working on an extensive, annotated treatise on this subject, I would like in the meantime to bring attention to the following authentic documents, in order to help to elucidate this issue and pave the way for the truth.

1. Declaration of the Director of the Veterinary Section of the Public Health Department of Germany in 1930. (Reichtagsdrucks. Bericht Sitz. 123 des 21 Ausschusses vom 14.II.1930 Seite 6)

    "The Public Health Department has taken the position over many decades and continues to do so today, that ritual slaughter, performed according to law, cannot be considered as cruel to animals."

---

[132] UGGIK #98, February 1936, 2. Original in Polish.

2. The Ministry in Sachsen at one time forbade ritual slaughter. But after some time, the Ministry rescinded this prohibition. The order of December 20, 1910, (Dresdner Journal "Koenigl. Saechsicher Staats-Anzeiger" Nr. 296 of December 22 1910), which once again permitted ritual slaughter, states:

> "In today's issue, the Ministry for Internal Affairs presents a new order once again allowing ritual slaughter, thus rescinding the order of March 21, 1892 regarding the stunning of animals..... For a long time, many scholarly and practical leaders have strongly expressed their opinion that slaughter performed according to the ritual code cannot in any way be considered as cruelty to animals, and, in recent times, it has been restored with an identical order as a result of the opinions of competent administrators. The basic order prohibiting ritual slaughter in Sachsen became increasingly more difficult to justify inasmuch as the Jewish religion prohibits the eating of animals killed in a manner not in accord with ritual. As a result, Orthodox Jews living in Sachsen were forced to import meat from outside of Sachsen, if they did not wish to give up eating meat entirely."

3. Pronouncement of the Reich Chancellor of September 24, 1917 (Reichtagsdrucksachen der 13. Legislaturperiode 2. Session 1914/1917 Nr. 1039):

> "A prohibition against ritual slaughter is not foreseeable. The acquisition of blood for human nourishment, which is now wasted because of the incision used in ritual slaughter, is not sufficiently significant to justify religious persecution of Jewish Orthodox fellow-citizens and penal interference (by the Government) in the religious regulations of a faith recognized in Germany.

It should be noted that this decree was published in war-time when the issue of nourishing the population was very important in Germany and had a decisive influence on the outcome of the war.

4. The opinion of the well-known scholar and German Minister, Radbruch, is extremely significant. He maintains that even if ritual slaughter were an inhumane method of slaughtering animals, which cannot be stated by any means, protection of animals should not legally take precedence over freedom of conscience and religion. It is worthwhile to quote Radbruch's opinion in his own words:

> "The degree of pain inflicted on an animal during slaughtering will never, in the final analysis, be resolved beyond doubt. The issue must therefore be examined from a different vantage, namely, that one segment of our citizens claims that its conscience unconditionally requires a particular slaughtering procedure. The spirit of this issue is dealt with in article 135 of the Reich Constitution, which guarantees freedom of religion, as long as it does not violate the general state statutes. But this very statement also means that state laws must not interfere, to the degree possible, with religious regulations."

The Polish constitution also guarantees freedom of religion. Since in Germany, with barely 500,000 Jewish inhabitants and a long standing policy of stunning during non-ritual slaughtering, the government, as long as it was cultured and liberal, has complied with Jewish desiderata, we cannot imagine that in free and tolerant Poland, three and a half million Jews will be deprived of meat and that a religion, considered holy by all nations of the world, will be defamed. No! It will not come to that! Contra spem spero!

VI

'BY THE SWEAT OF HIS BROW'

The economic depression, which began in Poland towards the end of 1928, impoverished the Jewish community and caused massive displacement. Jews were primarily small businessmen, petty traders, and peddlers and thus especially vulnerable to economic downturns. Because of long-standing exclusionary guild practices, there were few artisans among Jews. The Association of Jewish Craftsmen tried to reverse this. The essay, "Handwork in Judaism" tried to point out that creative handwork is an honorable Jewish occupation.

In "The Holiday of Pesah," Rabbi Chameides tried to comfort those Jews of his community who were beaten by the economic hardships of the day. His words of comfort give us a glimpse of their sufferings. At the end of another article detailing the many Pesach laws,[133] Rabbi Chameides adds a paragraph, which graphically depicts the desperate economic plight of Polish Jews: "We want to conclude our factual discourse with a quotation: כל עדת ישראל יעשו אתו – the entire Jewish community should celebrate the Pesach holiday. But as we utter this phrase, a bitter question is already poised on our lips: Will the entire Jewish community indeed celebrate this holiday? Will all who want to, be able to celebrate it? How many families are there who, this year, are overcome by privation? How many are there who, only a year ago, could give to others; lend a helping hand to others in similar circumstances, and who, today, are victims of the economic catastrophe? Who, this year, will say הא לחמא עניא – this is the bread of poverty, with a breaking voice and tears of despair? Therefore, permit me to appeal to every member of the community. Look around you, among your acquaintances, employees, and coworkers; search out the most poverty stricken and help as much as you can!

For, מה נשתנה הלילה הזה מכל הלילות – how different is this year's Seder evening! Everywhere – suffering and poverty! And therefore, I ask you, this year as never before, to join with each other, to comfort and encourage each other, so that we will be worthy of that magnificent day when the call will resound: כל עדת ישראל יעשו אתו – a unified free Israel celebrates its festival of liberation!"

---

[133] UGGIK #28, March 1933, 4-5. Original in German.

In an attempt to help the victims of the economic depression, the Jewish community of Katowice developed an interest free loan bank, money for which was solicited throughout the community. This is highlighted in "David's Harp," "The Interest-Free Loan Society," and "On the Margins of the Day: Operation CKB."

HANDWORK IN JUDAISM[134]

On the occasion of the 20th anniversary of the establishment
of the Association of Jewish Craftsmen.

יגיע כפיך כי תאכל, אשריך וטוב לך
You shall enjoy the fruit of your labor;
You shall be happy and you shall prosper
(Psalms 128:2)

One of the most important obligations that Judaism imposes on us is that of *imitatio dei*, of emulating God. A human being should strive to resemble God in his behavior and in the conduct of his life; to always set those qualities that are metaphorically attributed to God as a model and an ideal to strive for. "You should be holy for I, your God, am holy" (Leviticus 19:2). The path of your life should be illuminated by a reflection of God's grandeur and holiness. "Imitate Him! Just as He is merciful and compassionate, so you too should be merciful and compassionate" (Shabbat 133b). "Follow your God," calls the Torah to the Jew. But is it really possible to follow God? Is it not said of Him that He is an all-consuming fire? The true meaning is that you should imitate His pure and sublime qualities. That you should clothe the naked, visit the sick, comfort the bereaved, and bury the dead. For was it not the Holy One, blessed be He, who gave clothing to Adam, visited Abraham when he was ill, comforted Isaac after the death of his father, and buried Moses?" (Sotah 14a)

This thought is beautifully expressed in the following Midrash regarding the fact that it is forbidden to sacrifice an animal obtained through robbery or theft. "What can this be compared to? To a king who, together with his entourage, once passed by a customhouse in his kingdom. The king said to his servants: 'Pay the toll for me!' The servants were astounded. 'Doesn't the entire toll belong to you, O King? Why should we pay the toll for you?' The king replied: 'I

[134] UGGIK #5, March 1932, 2-3. Original in German.

wanted to set an example for others! May all my subjects pay the toll as conscientiously as I! In the same fashion, God says: 'I hate a sacrifice that is stolen. May my children also shun theft and robbery." (Sukkah 30a)

The story of creation, at the beginning of the Bible, will be seen from a new perspective if viewed through a prism of emulating God. The creation of the world and the gradual formation of everything gives us a glimpse into God's workshop; allows us to see God as an energetic, hard working, productive, and creative spirit. His creative word calls forth the dead, chaotic, and formless matter out of nothing in order to tear away its *tohu-vavohu* in six days of work and to give it life, to form it, and change it into something significant. This portrayal of the appearance of the blossoming world in a stepwise fashion out of a mysterious nothingness is not there merely to satisfy our thirst for knowledge, or broaden and deepen our understanding of the origins and beginnings of the universe. The Torah is a book of jurisprudence, and as such, should rightfully have started with an elucidation of prohibitions and commandments (see Rashi's commentary on the first verse of Genesis). But in reality, doesn't the detailed description of the six days of work contain one of the most important commandments, namely the command to work? Doesn't the section about the creation of the world contain a challenge to humanity to match the Creator; to imitate Him and carry on the battle against lifeless matter in order to unlock from it ever new forms, to extract ever new formations? Man should become like God. He must become a creator. For this reason, the Ten Commandments, which summarize the wisdom of God and His impenetrable being, also includes the commandment about work: "Six days shall you labor and do all your work." Work is part of the Master. Work is one of God's attributes and should therefore also become a human attribute.

This explains the direct religious attitude of Judaism towards handwork. The sages of the Mishnah and the Talmud frequently practiced a trade in addition to their studies. While Plato and Aristotle had reservations about granting rights of citizenship to artisans, our sages enjoined Jewish fathers to teach their sons a trade (Kiddushin 30b). "One who doesn't teach his son a trade is considered as if he is raising a thief" (ibid). Rabban Gamliel taught (Tosefta Kid 1): "One who has a trade is comparable to a garden that is enclosed and surrounded by a fence which animals cannot trample underfoot. In contrast, one who does not have a trade is comparable to an open, fenceless garden whose fruit will be destroyed by cattle and wild animals." Of our sages, Hillel was said to have been a wood cutter (Kesef Mishna on Rambam Talmud Tora 1:9), Rav Huna – a water carrier (Ketubboth 105), Zakkai – a butcher (Jer Megillah 4:1), Rabbi Yehudah – a baker (Bava Batrah 132a), Rabbi Joshua – a blacksmith (Berahot 28a), and Nahum – a scribe (Pe'ah 11:5). The Midrash (M. Rabba Emor 26:9) tells us that a certain stonemason, by the name of Pinkus, was invested with the position of High Priest. When the priests delivered the happy news, they found him working in his difficult occupation. Whenever someone turned to Rav Huna, who was a water carrier, with a rabbinical question, he would request a substitute who could replace him for the duration, and carry out his work responsibilities. In the famous synagogue in Alexandria, every guild had its own area. There were spaces for gold- and silversmiths, for weavers, for copper workers, as well as other occupational associations (Sukkah 51b). The purpose of this arrangement was to easily enable a stranger, who happened to come into the synagogue, to meet his occupational colleagues and feel more comfortable. Handworkers were also given certain religious concessions. For example, they were freed, while engaged in their work, from rising before a passing sage (Kiddushin 33a). The voice of a learned handworker found a welcome response in the house of study (Eduyot 1:3).

The persecution of Jews during the last century, forced them to engage in petty trading and money transactions. As a result, handwork by Jews gradually declined. In eastern Poland to this very day, the artisan, unfortunately, still does not enjoy the respect due him, despite the fact that in recent years the social position of handworkers has substantially improved. The profound economic shock waves, which are convulsing Jewish society with an unusually severe impact, will undoubtedly give the trades a new Jewish vitality. But the individual associations have a difficult assignment. They must mobilize the young Jewish handworkers, kindle within them a love for Judaism and its venerable traditions, keep awake a desire for self-improvement, strengthen their self confidence, and give new life and substance to the old maxim: "Beautiful is the Torah when it is combined with a worldly occupation." These are the goals that the handworkers' associations must strive for, and which will serve them well in the future. The occupational upheaval within Jewry, as well as the general economic turmoil, demand extreme vigilance and unselfish devotion to an ideal on the part of all leading segments of Jewry, if we are to preserve our leaky ship from damage as it is heaved over the tempestuous waves of the sea of time.

May our unshakable trust in God and His wise guidance be a signpost like a lighthouse in the darkness, and may the words of the prophet be fulfilled for us:

"When you pass through water, I shall be with you;
Through streams, they shall not overwhelm you.
When you walk through fire, you shall not be scorched;
Through flame, it shall not burn you.
For I the Lord am your God,
The Holy One of Israel, your Savior" (Isaiah 34:2,3)

THE HOLIDAY OF PESAH[135]

"And thus shall you eat the Pesach offering: With your
loins girded, your shoes on your feet, and your staff in
your hand" (Exodus 12:11)

"With your loins girded" – for battle against the hardships of life, in order to conquer and vanquish the innumerable difficulties that loom on your way. Never before, has life demanded so many sacrifices and such harnessing of all our physical and mental strength, as at the present time. Heroes on the armed field of battle have always been praised and lauded. Their names and deeds have been recorded by history in indelible syllables, in order to perpetuate the memory of their battles, and preserve it for future generations. But who will remember and remind others of the countless deeds of the heroes who are quietly exsanguinating in the dark haze of life? Of the silently suffering knights, wounded a hundredfold with poisoned arrows? Who will count the tears of pain and shame of these unknown soldiers; these lonely warriors battling for a bite of bread, for the bare means of existence? Today, therefore, the voice of the merciful God calls to you, beloved brothers, and martyrs of life, "with your loins girded"! Do not lose courage; do not lose hope! Be brave in battle and have confidence in the future!

"With your shoes on your feet," always inclined to progress, and to march forward on the outstretched road leading towards enlightenment and perfection. The tumult of life and everyday anxieties often smothers any perception for our obligations and our calling. Satisfying our material needs should, in reality, only be preparation and a means to enable us to fulfill a higher mission, but, unfortunately for us, it has become the summit of our dreams and the essence of our endeavors. We have descended from the heights of idealism to the depths of gray, ruthless, reality. The waves of a

---

[135] UGGIK #7, April 1932, 1. Original in Polish.

stormy life have tossed our ship far from its destined objective! Let us remind ourselves of this, at least during these holidays. Let us tear ourselves away during these rare blissful moments of respite and rest from the misery of daily life, and direct our souls towards higher spheres. Let us not stand still, but rather let each of us at his sentinel nurture the growth, development, and blossoming of beauty and goodness!

"And with your staff in your hand." That is the last and only remaining support for humans in moments of doubt. That same staff, about which God commanded Moses, "and thou shalt take in thy hand this staff, wherewith thou shalt do the signs" (Exodus 4:17), is the foundation of a deep unshaken faith in the justice of God. I know that for many of us, even this last fountainhead has dried up; that the soul is empty and deaf; that it resembles a temple in which there is no God. However, I also know moments of inner rebirth. When humanity in the deep yearning of a shattered soul cries, "God, my God, why have You abandoned me?" the Shechina cries with us and, embracing us with her wings like a mother her sick children, bestows God's blessings on us...

DAVID'S HARP[136]
In connection with the relief work of the
Interest-Free Loan Bank – "Gemilat Hesed"

The Talmud tells us that a harp hung above David's sleeping area. At the stroke of midnight, the north wind blew over the strings producing notes and sounds. King David would immediately arise from his couch, open the holy books, and begin to study Torah. He studied and sang the Torah's words until dawn. When morning came, the elders of the people came to the palace and addressed him: "Sublime majesty! The poverty of your people is great; its source of subsistence is exhausted!" The King answered them: "לכו והתפרנסו זה מזה" – go and support each other."

As nice as this *aggadah* sounds, its basic message is gloomy. Let us examine the soul of this splendid and God-graced singer of the Psalms, King David. His agitated life was rich in meaningful turns and transformations. In his youth, he had to flee from Saul to save his life from the ambushes and pursuits of the elderly suspicious king. On his flight, he was often hungry for a piece of bread and thirsty for a refreshing sip of water. But he never allowed despair to become his master. Hope and faith were always his true nourishment. They accompanied him on all his trouble-filled wanderings, and threw a shaft of light on his thorny path. From his earliest youth, he had tasted the bitterness of poverty. His sensitive, sentimental, love-starved soul must have felt more deeply and with greater pain the vindictiveness of his enemies. Despite the fact that the hearts of the people beat with love and reverence for him, he was left alone, abandoned by all in the decisive and perilous moments of his life. As a result, he was able to record the whole range of feelings of the human soul in his Psalms. He was qualified to interpret human suffering as well as human happiness. Untold numbers of distressed and helpless people have found comfort and

---

[136] UGGIK #26, February 1933, 3-4. Original in German.

exaltation in the Psalms. To this very day, they remain a source of edification and support for the innermost torments of innumerable people. Soaring above this marvelous book is a sense of optimism, most beautifully expressed in the words השלח על ד׳ יהבך – leave your worries about your livelihood to God, and He will support you." When David became old, he had to bear the bitter lot of banishment yet again. His own son rose up and conspired against him. He left his home and concerns about subsistence had to trouble his hoary head once again. And yet, at the end of his life, he could say: נער הייתי וגם זקנתי – "I was young and I became old but I have never seen a righteous man forsaken, or one whose children had to beg for bread." So he was always filled with hope. A harp, whose music of promise was never stilled, hung above his bed. The words of the poet, "wer nie auf seinem Bette weinend sass, wer nie sein Brot in Traenen ass, der kennt Euch nicht, Ihr himmlischen Maechte" (he, who never sat crying on his bed; he, who never ate his bread through tears, cannot know You – You heavenly Power), did not apply to him. A serene, confident mood reigned wherever he sat. Whenever gloomy apprehensions banished sleep, the strings of his harp began to stir, and new hope lit up the darkness of the night...

Who of us, however, is so deeply anchored in piety that he is spared hours of doubt and anxiety? They even creep into King David's camp. "As soon as midnight came, the north wind blew over the strings of his harp." As soon as an ominous darkness came over the Jewish people; a darkness that concealed any prospect of improvement from the horizon, a cold north wind glided over the strings and coaxed a sad melody out of the harp. In Jewish literature, the north symbolizes nourishment. "By the north wind the golden rays emerge," says Job (37:22), and the table with the showbreads stood on the north side of the Temple (B Bathra 25). The north wind, the struggle for daily bread, lay like a stubborn hand on the strings of David's harp. Slowly, the howling north wind, the storm of awakened worry and anxiety, stifles the last melody of hope. "David immediately arose and studied Torah." He immersed himself in the section of the Torah that tells about the Manna, the Jewish miracle food, about which our sages stated: לא נתנה תורה אלא לאוכלי המן – the fulfillment of the Torah was easiest for those who sustained themselves with Manna, and who did not need to worry about their daily bread. King David could identify with the Manna section because, during the midnight hour, he became conscious about the economic plight of his people. When our forefathers were in the desert, God spoke to Moses: "See, I will cause bread to rain from heaven in order to test whether or not you will go in my ways." You will live without worry. You will not need to cultivate or sow anything. You will have no further concerns about your source of nourishment. A precise amount of Manna fell from heaven. Not in abundance – עמר לגלגלת – an amount equal to an *omer* was provided for each person. If a larger amount of Manna was gathered, with the intent of saving it for the following day, it immediately spoiled and became inedible. Everyone received only as much as was needed to maintain him and his family. God, however, did allow a small pitcher of this Manna to be kept for the future; as a reminder for future generations. When, in the time of Jeremiah, the Jews complained and bewailed that poverty prevented them from fulfilling the Torah, the prophet picked up the pitcher of Manna saved by Moses, and held it up before the grumbling people. His message was: "Didn't your ancestors live in similar circumstances in the desert? Did they have reserves for the next day? Didn't they too live from hand to mouth? And, despite this, didn't they receive the Torah in the desert? And didn't they, gladly and willingly, accept responsibility for serving the Eternal and Supernatural...?"

"The King studied until dawn." It gradually became light. From unfamiliar worlds, a ray of hope beamed on his tired countenance, and smoothed out the wrinkles of worry. The people over whom he ruled lived correctly, always with one eye on the pitcher of Manna. Its future was never assured. Its determination was to live with the times, but also above the times. Every moment was devoted to recapturing access to the Source of Life. They were pushed and squeezed from all sides, but, nevertheless, they did not become discouraged. Suddenly, the elders of the people called the King from his dream world back to reality עמך ישראל צריכין פרנסה – "Your people, Sir, need a means of subsistence! God has granted your majesty the power to escape the gloomy everyday, and look into the future. Through your ideas, you are able to lift yourself above the desperate reality. But your people need help promptly. The visionary view of your lofty spirit will not satiate its hunger. Give us bread!" Then King David answered them: לכו והתפרנסו זה מזה – "Go and support each other." The last lifeline in our time of need, remains mutual help – Gemilas Chesed.

Today, interest-free loan banks serve that ideal in all Jewish communities. More than ever before, the words of Hillel אם אין אני לי מי לי – if I am not for myself, who will be for me, apply to our times. The capital, placed unselfishly at the disposal of small businessmen by the interest free banks so that they do not collapse under the burden of the crisis, is the best evidence of Jewish self-preservation. It shows the world that a mutual feeling of community continues to live in us, Jews, and that above the grumbling, which the storm of the times coaxes out of David's harp, a song of confidence and hope continues to direct our poor nation...

THE INTEREST-FREE LOAN SOCIETY[137]

One does not need to justify, or make any theoretical arguments for the existence of benevolent institutions like the BKP [Interest Free Loan Society]. We will not cite Jewish sources to unequivocally prove that benevolence and charitable work, usually encompassed by the beautiful phrase, Gemilat Chesed, is one of the pillars on which our Jewish world rests. It has always been a mainstay of our communities and a credit to Jewish society. Whoever has delved deeply and analyzed it, or has even superficially examined our world view, knows that help given to a destitute brother; support given without a bitter taste of pity or sad melody; a gift, given in a kind manner so as not to offend feelings or honor, to someone standing on the brink of disaster is one of the prime obligations and elementary duties of every Jew.

Never before in our rich history, has the individual been so tightly bound to his environment; been so interdependent with the entire nation. Outside of Jewish society, a person does not seem to have a place or even a right to exist. No one can avoid the fate of the Jewish community. No one can escape the sword of Democles suspended over us. No one can protect himself or hide from the moral and material catastrophe that has fallen on us with a great weight. In the old days, a person could save himself by running away, by cutting the cord that bound him to the rest of the nation. An individual could flee from ruin; leave the camp of the suffering; jump the ship sinking into the waves of the sea. But today, there is no way out, even for those who long ago separated themselves from Judaism. There is no gate through which one can escape because, on the other side, contempt and hatred lie in wait. For this reason, the icy armor of indifference and neutrality is gradually melting away from some of our brothers, those wilted leaves on the Jewish tree. All of us are searching for mutual support. We are all looking

---

[137] UGGIK #50, February 1934, 5. Original in Polish.

for a brotherly hand to protect us from falling down. We expect help from those to whom we are linked by shared misery and suffering.

Never, however, has the welfare of people been so unsteady, so wavering, so deprived of any solid foundation as now. At one time, prosperity and wealth lasted generations. It was transferred from father to son, from son to grandson. Material stability and security; an ability to save acquired wealth, guaranteed a certain material tradition and continuity. How fortunes have changed today! We are witnesses to blood frozen in the veins of tragic families. Businesses that we thought could withstand any storm are being destroyed. Solid businesses disappear from view before they are able to reach maturity and gain strength. People who a year ago were donors and generously shared their wealth, are today dependent on the kindness and help from others. Some of these people are themselves forced to knock on doors of welfare institutions, the most important of which is indisputably the Interest Free Loan Bank. BKP serves all segments of our community, and is often the last saving plank and support for those who fall under the burden of poverty.

Let us therefore not forget our obligation to this organization. Let no one dare to exclude himself from participating in the activities of the Interest Free Loan Bank.

ON THE MARGINS OF THE DAY[138]
OPERATION CKB[139]

The emigration of several active members has caused a temporary halt to the self-help activities in our community. It will soon be resumed since the appeal of our brothers, crushed by poverty, cries out to us ever more loudly from every corner of our land.

For a long time, overseas Jews have rushed to our aid. Our brothers in America have given us a hand, thus temporarily averting an economic catastrophe. Today, however, the nightmare of a crisis oppresses everyone, and poverty rages threatening even those, who only recently, were affluent. Today we are dependent on our own initiative and on ourselves.

Overseas Jews expect evidence that the economic crisis has not succeeded in breaking us spiritually, or annihilated our vitality. We must all become aware of the significance of this self-help operation, whose organizers plan to start supporting poverty-stricken families materially and establish new businesses, as soon as 1,000,000 zł has been raised.

Let us hope that our efforts will be successful, and that members of our community will participate fully in operation "CKB," which will once again resume in the next few days.

---

[138] UGGIK #87, September 1935, 3. Original in Polish.
[139] CKB (Cekabe) were the initials of Centralne Towarzystwo Popierania Kredytu Bezprocentowego i Krzewienia Pracy Produktywnej wśród Ludności Żydowskiej w Polsce (Central Society for the Support of Free Credit and the Spread of Productive Labor among the Jewish Population of Poland). In 1935, this organization announced the establishment of a self-help fund of 3 million zł for Jewish economic rehabilitation.

VII

'REMEMBER THE DAYS OF OLD'

The essays in this section deal with the present as reflected in the mirror of the past. The "foreignness" of Joseph in Egyptian society, despite his high office and status, is masterfully explored in two commentaries on the Torah portion, ויחי. Several essays are devoted to the destruction of the Temple, the destruction of Jerusalem, the loss of freedom, and the Babylonian dispersion. These essays emphasize the many similarities between those days, and contemporary times. The similarities include the pernicious effects of factionalism, the placing of the interests of the individual above the needs of the entire people, assimilation, despair, and an attempt at national independence including the many enemies trying to frustrate it.

In "Hero and Martyr," Rabbi Chameides contrasts the heroism of the Jew in Eretz Yisrael with their martyrdom in Europe. He writes: "Here, [in Europe] we must be prepared to suffer for our Judaism. Our surrounding world demands this sacrifice of us. Here, we must often pay for our Jewish existence with our happiness and that of our children." But the absence of physical joy and happiness is more than compensated for by the deeper spiritual joy, as described in "Four Coins."

However, Rabbi Chameides comes to the sad conclusion that spiritual strength, a will to resist, and joy are also absent. In "The Flaming Message of the Hanukkah Lights," he writes: "Now is a time reminiscent of the times of Hiskiyah. Sleep with folded arms reigns. We cannot fight. We don't want to fight. We have unlearned this skill. We can't even defend ourselves. After all, they have superior strength. We are a small handful. But even the song and music is gone from us. The songs are silenced. Here and there, someone still mutters a prayer in time of danger. The word dies on the lips. Like Hiskiyah, we sink in our encampment. You, O God, fight for us. Our strength is depleted. Alone, we sit in the night staring out into the darkness to see whether a savior is coming..."

The 800th birthday of the great Maimonides, affords Rabbi Chameides an opportunity to teach his community about him. In many ways, the times were similar. Both, lived in an era when there was an effort to fuse general knowledge with Judaism. Both lived *in an era of Jewish persecution, apostasy, and flight. In this essay, Rabbi Chameides discusses the Iggeret Hashmad in minute detail, and one can't help but wonder whether he believes that it is especially applicable to Europe of the 1930s. He states that "towards the end of this treatise, Maimonides nevertheless recommends that all who have the means, should leave the country in which their human conscience is violated, in which the most elementary rights of people are trodden under foot, and that, regardless of the sacrifice, they should move to a country where one is allowed to live according to the precepts of the Torah. The world is surely wide enough!" Was that deliberately paraphrased because of its relevance to Poland of 1935? Unfortunately, despite the comment at the end of the essay "to be continued," the continuation does not appear in the 118 issues we have found.*

5693 [1932-1933][140]

למנות ימינו כן הודע ונביא לבב חכמה
Teach us to count our days and we shall acquire a heart of wisdom

This quotation forces us to pose a question: Is it really so difficult to count days and years that the Psalmist has to beg God to grant him the wisdom to do so? Can't even the simplest person, let alone someone with an average amount of intelligence, master the counting of days, and add up the years of our meager lives? "Teach us O God," prays the Jewish poet "to count our days and the heart will be filled with wisdom." Do we really need instruction from God, a revelation, and a wise heart in order to count the number of our passing years; to place the short period of our lives in a numerical frame; to be able to count days and years?

In order to understand this puzzling sentence, we must acquaint ourselves with the essence of the Jewish calendar. Our history has experienced many eras; the calendar has undergone many changes and metamorphoses. During its existence, our people have repeatedly changed and transformed the underlying principle of its calendar. In the beginning, in the dawn of our nation's history, Israel counted time from the Exodus from Egypt; from the overthrow of the yoke of the Egyptian Pharaohs, the Egyptian oppressors. In the Holy Writ, we therefore often encounter the familiar expression, "this occurred in such and such a year after the Exodus from Egypt."

At that time, the Exodus from Egypt was the cornerstone of the Jewish calendar. The attainment of freedom after the suffering and humiliation of bondage, stirred the soul of the nation so deeply that it considered it a watershed of our history, and it was decided to use it as a starting point, the beginning of a new era. With the passage of time, new far-reaching, decisive epochal events arose in our history. The Exodus from Egypt faded in our nation's memory, and our ancestors concluded that freedom alone was not the only

[140] UGGIK #16, September 1932, 6-7. Original in Polish.

attribute of a nation aiming for more lofty goals; that the Exodus was the important first, but by no means the final link, in the chain of historical events. So when Solomon built the national Temple on Mt. Moriah in Jerusalem, thus fulfilling Israel's most sublime religious dream, that became the commonly accepted beginning of a new era, and years were counted from the establishment of that holy sanctuary, a symbol of our creativity and our mission. Then came a catastrophic turn in our history. The Temple was destroyed; an abyss swallowed the previously holy place, and all that remained were ruins. Was it likely that the years would continue to be counted from the building of the Temple? As a result of this painful blow that touched the entire nation, the year of the destruction became the basis of the Jewish calendar. Still later, the year 312 BCE, when Alexander of Macedon defeated Darius, became the beginning of a new era. Every historical event disturbed our equanimity. We were deeply affected by every unusual event. When then should we have started to count time? Which tragedy was most worthy to be remembered in this manner? Which played a decisive role in our lives? What is the beginning of our unique Jewish destiny? Which moment most determined our future? The Psalmist searches in vain through the breadth of our history for support for the Jewish calendar. Because of the many shocking events in our people's history, he begs God to show him the correct point in our past, which will help him recognize the reason for our existence. "Teach us to count our days"! Our ancestors were convinced that they would become the toys of capricious times and incidental events if they continued to make the calendar dependent on the illusory foundation of the eternally unbridled waves of history. So, they finally dissociated themselves from historical events and attached themselves to the very source of time, the creation of the world. We thus made an alliance with eternity, and declared war on time. We associate every New Year with the creation of the world. We are thus united with the Creator, and free ourselves from the prison of the temporal and evanescent. We conquer the power of time and by touching the source of eternity with our souls, we acknowledge the miracle of rebirth and rejuvenation.

As we cross the threshold of the year 5693, we fully realize the threat that faces the entire world, and especially our oppressed and generally despised nation. Each New Year that we welcome has its face hidden by a veil of mystery, but awakens within us a sense of new hope and courage. This is also true of 5693. We hope that it will bring alleviation to the suffering of humanity, and end the pain and exile of the Jewish people. We pray that hatred will finally cease, and that all oppression on earth will come to an end...

ויחי[141]

ויראו אחי יוסף כי מת אביהם ויאמרו לו ישטמנו יוסף

"And when Joseph's brothers saw that their father was dead,
they said: It may be that Joseph will hate us
and will fully requite us for all the evil which we did to him"

This anxiety was natural and justified. As long as Jacob was alive, Joseph spared his brothers and suppressed all feelings of vengeance and retaliation from his soul. He gave no hint that he harbored the slightest feeling of bitterness in his heart about their unbrotherly behavior. But now, thought his brothers, when Joseph no longer needed to take his ill father into consideration; now, when they were facing each other 'eye to eye' in a foreign land, will he still be able to curb and subdue his natural urge for vengeance and retaliation? לו ישטמנו יוסף – now the hatred that had been suppressed and repressed for so long will explode ever so strongly. The old, barely scabbed-over wound will start bleeding again. The brothers feared Joseph's hostility.

Some commentators gave this verse a much deeper and, psychologically, a more satisfying meaning by understanding and translating the small word לו as a wish, an optative particle: "Oh, how we wish that Joseph would finally hate us!" The brothers suffered because of the extraordinary goodness and helpfulness of Joseph, whom they once sold into Egypt. The blessings, which they and their families derived from Joseph's position in Egypt, shamed and humiliated them. The magnanimity of their younger brother, whose youthful happiness they maliciously destroyed, weighed on them heavily. His patience, his generosity, his untiring solicitude were more painful to them than any act of vengeance could have been. It is written: "If your enemy be hungry, give him bread to eat and if he be thirsty, give him water to drink. For you will heap coals of fire on his head and the Lord will reward you" (Proverbs 25:21). Joseph gave his brothers bread and water. The brothers, however, wanted to be punished; they thirsted for atonement. A Russian

---

[141] UGGIK #23, January 1933, 4-5. Original in German.

author showed us the criminal's soul (Raskolnikow). His pangs of conscience drive him into the arms of the authorities. Punishment gives him relief, a moral rebirth, an inner renewal. For him, punishment is the only ever-so-narrow passage out of the dark prison of his soul. Therefore, Joseph's brothers' cry is: לו ישטמנו יוסף – "If only Joseph could at last hate us!"

To this, Joseph replies: "You have nothing to fear! Am I in God's place? You intended to do me evil but God planned it for good – in order to save the life of a great nation." Only God has the power to punish the guilty. He understands and weighs the magnitude of the crime, and knows the type of punishment that will allow you to be expiated. Man is a bad judge. The first requirement of atonement is that the severity of the punishment must be equal to the crime. "An eye for an eye! A tooth for a tooth!" This legal principle was never applied literally in Jewish jurisprudence. In this lex talionis, the Torah wanted merely to express, in a clear unambiguous way, the principle of מדה כנגד מדה – that the punishment must fit the crime. What was the brothers' crime? They sold their younger brother to strangers. This was unquestionably an evil deed. But the sold brother did save a great nation from destruction. Through his wise counsel, millions of people were saved from starvation. The brothers' sin resulted in a blessing. Their inhumane action was a crime at the beginning, but through a series of circumstances, it became a fountain of salvation in the end. If Joseph wanted to punish his brothers, he would have had to impose a punishment corresponding to the crime; a punishment whose initial phase would be cruel and harsh, but whose consequences would ultimately be beneficial and life saving. That, Joseph could not do. Man is completely incapable of devising such a punishment. Who could impose such a punishment? "Am I in God's place?" Joseph says to his brothers. "God alone will judge you!"

We too say to our enemies:

ואתם חשבתם עלי רעה אלקים חשבה לטובה

May God turn your evil intentions, your plans to destroy our existence and diminish our living space, into blessings!

?על¹⁴² מה אבדה הארץ

"My eye sheds tears and cries because God's flock has been imprisoned!"
God's eye shed three tears – one for the destruction of the first Temple,
the second for the destruction of the second Temple,
and the third for the dispersion of the Jewish people (Hagigah 5).

The three tears represent three separate and defined eras in Jewish history. The first was the bright era of our independence, which ended with the blow dealt us by Nebuhadnezzar in 586 BCE. The second ended when the Romans placed their suffocating iron fist on Palestine and transformed it into a province of its mighty Empire. And the third era, the era of *Galut*, of exile, of fire and blood, continues to this day, and will finally end with the coming of the Messiah.

Our Sages tried to understand the cause for the downfall of the Jewish state by searching the spiritual and moral spheres. It was clear to them that the destruction of the Jewish state could not have been due to socioeconomic forces, outside military might, diplomatic blunders, or poor political tactics. In the opinion of our teachers, these material and "real" factors play only a secondary role in the life of a nation, and are not in themselves determining factors for its existence or future. The main source of a nation's strength is hidden in its soul. As long as a nation's soul remains pure, untarnished by the venom of hatred, undimmed by the fog of prejudice and warped theories, unpolluted by the gloominess of pessimism and passive fatalism, its existence is assured. No storm will sway it. No calamity will destroy it. The nation will find a source of strength within itself in the midst of a whirlpool of turmoil and confusion. Material poverty will be countered by inner strength. The sun of its soul will shine through the clouds and darkness of life. In contrast to today's state leaders, who ascribe the blossoming or decline of the power of the state solely to "real" issues, thereby

¹⁴² UGGIK #36, July 1933, 2. Original in Polish.

focusing their entire attention and energy on political and organizational tactics, our teachers regarded the ethical awareness of the community, the level of morality, the transmission of sublime ideals and love to our youth, the establishment of peace and harmony among nations, as the only firm, unshakable foundations of a state.

II

Rabbi Abbahu said: "Jerusalem was destroyed because the Shema prayer was not recited within it every morning and evening" (Shabbat 119). We know that at the turn of the third century, R. Abbahu, in addition to being steeped in Jewish scholarship, was also fluent in Greek and was regarded as the official Jewish representative to the highest dignitaries of the Roman state. He was a frequent guest at Caesar's court, and would be greeted by a chorus singing: "Great one of your people, spokesman for your nation; lantern of light, may your coming be in peace." (Sanhedrin 14a) It is therefore difficult for us to understand how a scholar of his stature, a man responsible for such broad and far-reaching welfare work, a man held in such extraordinary regard by his generation, could consider the seemingly insignificant sin of not saying the Shema prayer enough cause for the destruction of Jerusalem.

We will understand Rabbi Abbahu's opinion about the causative relationship between not saying the daily Shema prayer and the destruction of Jerusalem better, if we remind ourselves of the mission to which this sage devoted himself throughout his life. During Rabbi Abbahu's life, faith in the indivisible nature of God was severely tested and shaken in certain Jewish quarters. There was a group called "Minim" whose understanding of the nature of God was influenced by Christianity and which imitated the new faith. Rabbi Abbahu opposed these advocates of the new philosophy with all his being, and fought in defense of the unity of God in the spirit of the Jewish tradition. The intellectual dispute that raged between various sects on the religious battleground can be illustrated by an interpretation of a Biblical verse by Rabbi Abbahu. In explaining the words of the prophet Isaiah (44:6), "I am the first, and I am the last, and beside Me there is no God," Rabbi Abbahu stated: "'I am the first,' means that I have no father; 'I am the last,' means that I have no brother, and 'beside Me there is no God,' means that I have no son." (Shemot Rabbah 29). The sharpness of this commentary is clearly aimed at the new understanding of the nature of God.

The Shema prayer must have taken on a special significance in that time of debate over the nature of God. Since time immemorial, this prayer has been a means for expressing our fundamental faith in the unity of God. "Hear, O Israel, the Eternal, our God, the Eternal, is one!" The Shema became our confessional, our motto! Another opinion of Rabbi Abbahu's now becomes clear. He decreed that after saying the Shema, one should recite the well-known phrase "ברוך שם כבד מלכותו לעולם ועד" – "May the name of His Majesty be blessed for ever and ever," aloud. This sentence served to emphasize the eternal truth encompassed by the Shema: The eternity and unchangeability of God (Pesahim 56).

We can now more fully understand the opinion of Rabbi Abbahu that the destruction of Jerusalem was caused by the lack of regular recitation of the Shema prayer. He thereby wanted to warn his contemporary Jews against beclouding faith in the unity of God by citing an example from our past. He wanted to emphasize the catastrophic consequences of tarnishing monotheism. He publicly declared the thesis that loss of the fatherland, the greatest misfortune that befell us, was caused precisely by ignoring and neglecting the very essence of the Shema, i.e., faith in the unity of God and the unity of the people. שמע ישראל – "Hear O Israel" indicates the unity and cohesion of the nation; ד' אחד – is a declaration of faith in the unity of God...

III

Rabbi Judah said: "It was possible to destroy Jerusalem only because scholars were treated within it with contempt" (Talmid Chacham). The authority of scholarship had declined; the luster of spirituality had been tarnished. Jerusalem succumbed to anarchy and licentiousness. The Holy City was lead by "Baryonim,"[143] enthusiasts of militarism, with an unsheathed sword. Judgment gave way to fanaticism. Leaders who longed for peace and harmony, and who advised submission before an inexorable enemy were terrorized and forced into silence. Blindly and armed with empty phraseology, the deaf ran full force ahead into – an abyss. Jerusalem's fate, a toy in the hands of revolutionaries, was sealed. A sword hung suspended over Zion. The clear sky of Palestine glowed with the conflagration of destruction.

Among the besieged, there lived a man who, in the last minute, would bring salvation and deliverance. He was Rabbi Yohanan ben Zakkai, a student of the mild mannered Hillel (Sukkah 28). Forty years before the catastrophe, he called out: "היכל היכל, – Holy Temple, you are doomed – succumb to destruction!" (Yoma 39). He allowed himself to be carried beyond the borders of his own city, perhaps for the first time, and to sympathize with the dissenters.

He was inspired with a spirit of peace, and he wanted to establish harmony and brotherhood among nations. In discussing the admonition in the Holy Scriptures against using hewed stones or iron tools in building altars, Rabbi Yohanan expressed a beautiful thought that reflects his pacifist world view: "The Torah commanded us not to use iron, a destructive instrument, in building altars, which are a means for bringing about peace between man and God. Altars neither hear, nor speak, nor see. It stands to reason, therefore, that man, who hears, speaks, and sees will be protected from destruction if he pursues peace between cities, nations, and countries." After the outbreak of the Roman-Jewish war, he conducted himself according to this interpretation and attempted to help the involved nations reach an understanding, and conclude peace. But the warning voice of Rabbi Yohanan was not heeded. *Inter arma silet pax!* His sensible words were lost amid the clash

---

[143] The term applied by the Rabbis to those who rebelled against mighty Rome. They called themselves "kanaim" (zealots), patterning themselves after Pinchas, but the Rabbis thought they were a disaster for the Jewish people, and called them "baryonim" (outlaws or thugs).

of arms and the shrieks of the clamorous camps....

The call of the Sage was not heeded in Jerusalem. The advice of the Talmid Chacham, Rabbi Yohanan ben Zakkai, was disregarded...

HERO AND MARTYR[144]

Text of an address given on Shabbat Chanukah.

Judaism is once again on trial. Our Holy Writings are being scrupulously examined; our sacred texts are being investigated; our old tomes are dissected in order to find in them some substantiation, a foothold, on which to base the frequently and openly repeated accusations against their ethics and worldview. It is therefore important for us to learn, to become enlightened, and look into the depth of our own soul so that we may understand the secret of our existence.

Who, however, would venture to assert that he understands the message of Judaism; that he understands the eternal and Divine Jewish genius, without first climbing to the summit of Jewish mental vigor; without first and foremost making an effort to penetrate the essence of the Jewish prophets and their immortal champions? For whatever we have become during the long dark *golus* night [night of exile], we have not become out of our own free will; because we wanted to; because of an unforced choice or personal preference. Far too often, outside forces and foreign powers have strangled the impulses of our hearts, the first faint impulses of our desire, with ruthless force even before they could unfold and ripen into visible actions. If we want to examine the Jewish character in its pure, unadulterated form, we must return to its origin, to that sublime time that, for Judaism, represents excellence. We must immerse ourselves in the lives and creations of the Prophets.

A twofold characteristic that in truth originates from the same root radiates from them, heroism, and a readiness for martyrdom. The prophet is both hero and martyr; fighter and patient sufferer.

He is a hero when he courageously confronts his powerful and respected contemporaries and fearlessly, without concern for his own welfare, accuses them of degradation and depravity in their moral conduct. It was heroic of the Jewish prophet Amos to

---

[144] UGGIK #46, December 1933, 9-11. Original in German.

suddenly appear in the Temple of Beth El, in the seceded Israelite state, in the midst of a National Assembly, and warn King Jeroboam and his flourishing house that they were facing destruction. Amos tried, in vain, to warn him about the danger threatening him from within his own camp. His well-meant advice went unheeded. חזה לך ברח לך – seer, flee to the land of Judea and prophesy there, for here you will not escape the tentacles of the King's officers (Amos 7:12). Indignantly, Amos refuses to follow this well-intentioned advice. He does not want to hear about personal safety, about danger, and punishment that threatens him. Completely devoted to his mission, he lives only for the idea, the prophetic ideal. And wasn't Elijah a hero when, alone armed only with the power of truth and faith, he confronted a host of false prophets on Mt. Carmel? A zealous, true prophet, against 450 enthusiastic followers of the Baal cult? What a heroic power of conviction must have dwelled in Elijah when he stood for his belief against 450 people with a different opinion. How easily we allow ourselves to be swayed by a majority! How easily can our point of view change when it is under assault from opposing viewpoints! An English thinker[145] entitled a section of his work, *"Hero Worship,"* Hero as Prophet. For the foremost signs of a prophet are uncompromising determination, conviction, and heroism.

But the prophet could also be a martyr when the fulfillment of his assignment requires it. At the decisive moment, he must be ready to sacrifice his life and tolerate the greatest of suffering. He could be a hero, like Abraham when he destroyed his father's idols. But, when duty demanded it, he could also be a martyr, like Isaac, who allowed himself to be brought as a sacrifice to God. Often, he had to confirm the truth of his words with the blood of his heart. Moses was a martyr when he died close to the border of the chosen land. The prophet of the disaster, Jeremiah, was a martyr. This prophet and witness to the destruction of the Jewish state paid the penalty of imprisonment for his warnings and exhortations. He was tormented, hated, and finally, according to tradition, stoned in exile

---

[145] Thomas Carlysle.

by the very nation he loved and wanted to save.

The Jewish prophet was both hero and martyr. When subsequently the Divine inspiration, the spirit of prophecy, left Israel, the entire Jewish people took the place of the individual prophets. From then on, the nation in its totality became the heirs to both heroism and martyrdom. From then on, the fate of the Jews was to become heroes or martyrs. Summit and depth, elevation and downfall, upswing and decline – these have marked the path of Jewish history. Hero or martyr! If a Jew is neither one nor the other, then surely his last hour has chimed; the peeling off of the Jewish essence – assimilation, has begun.

We will perhaps understand these better if we examine two of our forebears who play such an important role on Shabbat Chanukah: Judah Maccabee, the central personality of the festival of Chanukah, and Joseph, whose life story and suffering, from it's ascendancy to the blotting out of his name and achievements soon after his death, is told in the current weekly portion. They show us how deeply the tendency to heroism or martyrdom is imprinted on the Jewish personality. They could serve as symbols for these two forces, which penetrated Jewish existence from its beginnings, and continue, to this very day. Judah Maccabee, the warrior, and Joseph, the passive sufferer, represent two ways of expressing Jewish existence....

Judah Maccabee owed his existence to the benevolence of Providence, his heroic determination, his passionate energy, his fearless courage, and the Divine inspiration of his band of heroes. At the head of a small group of men, exhausted by poverty and hunger, he took a hostile world by storm. The more hopeless the battle and the more oppressive the superior power, the stronger his determination!!

In the frame of history, we see a picture of a pale and powerless Joseph. He doesn't strive, doesn't fight, and doesn't force his way into a position of authority. If in life there is such a thing as chance, then we must conclude that chance was the prevailing and motivating force in Joseph's life. His father sends him to visit his brothers who forge a plan of vengeance against him, by chance. It is by chance, that after his brothers threw him into a pit, a caravan passes by through whose intercession he reaches Egypt. It is by chance, that he shares a jail, into which Potiphar threw him, with the king's chief baker and cupbearer, whose dreams Joseph interprets. Fate, or according to Jewish interpretation Providence, favors him, supports him, leads him to the threshold of the throne. A long chain of interlocking incidents paves his way to power. He is led by Providence, as if carried on the wings of an eagle; he is lifted from the depths of despair to the pinnacle, and, almost in his last moments, as the shadow of death surrounds him, he realizes that his life has been misspent, and that he has remained a stranger in the land to which he devoted his life. On the throne, he remained the same martyr he was in his youth when he had to bear his brother's hatred. "When God one day sets you free, take my remains with you," was Joseph's instruction to his brothers. He spent his entire life as a refugee, homeless, without brotherly love. A martyr wrapped in a royal cloak.

Judah Maccabee fights, Joseph avoids the fight. Judah Maccabee is victorious, Joseph is led to victory. Judah Maccabee is great in his determination, Joseph, in his self-denial. Judah Maccabee's descendants are free people living in a free land; Joseph's are slaves in a foreign land. Judah Maccabee is, therefore, a symbol of a Jewish fighter and Jewish heroism; Joseph is a symbol of Jewish forbearance and Jewish martyrdom.

Judah Maccabee and Joseph reflect two elements of Jewish history. Sometimes we were fighters, at other times passive forbearers. During the Maccabeean times we were heroes; during the middle Ages, martyrs.

In the West, we stopped being martyrs about 150 years ago, but we also ceased being heroes. The era of the Emancipation made western Jews into a middle class, and cloaked it in a thin Jewish atmosphere that neither conformed to the pathos of *golus* suffering, nor to the passion of heroism. And when Jews are neither martyrs nor heroes, their Judaism slowly dies away.

It is noteworthy that the gifts given to us by other nations never brought us much joy. The place of refuge that the Egyptians once gave to our father Jacob soon became a place of enforced labor for his children. The emancipation that the nations presented to us as a voluntary gift, ended tragically; it proved to be deceptive, precisely because it was not won but fell into our laps as a gift. The moment of birth of the Balfour Declaration[146] was sublime and happy, but it has brought us disappointment and grief, perhaps because it bears a stamp of English mercy, and is not the product of battle.

חסד לעומים חטאת – the only path to a Jewish future is either through heroism or martyrdom. Our only durable possessions have been won either in battle, or as a result of suffering.

What of today? Is it a time of Jewish heroism or martyrdom? Are we heroes or martyrs? The answer to this question will determine our spiritual attitude to the world and our inner approach to the future.

The answer to this crucial question can only be that we are both heroes and martyrs. And from this, stems the extraordinary complexity of today's Jews.

In Eretz Israel and in areas of Jewish productivity connected with the restoration of the Jewish national home, we are heroes. The Maccabees at one time freed the Holy Land from enemies with weapons. Today, the weapons with which we are winning the old homestead are hoes and spades. Today, we look at Mathisias, the aged Priest, who started the battle for freedom with awe. With the same thankfulness and respect, we mention the name of Menachem Ussishkin[147] who, steadfastly and tirelessly, has worked for גאולת הארץ – the liberation of Palestine. This man, whose 70th birthday is currently being celebrated by the entire Jewish world, brought us the plains of Sharon and the Emek. Our sages say: המהלך ד' אמות בא"י מובטח לו שהוא בן עולם הבא – "whoever covers a distance of four ells in Palestine has a secure place in the world to come." Ussishkin's reward must then be huge,

---

[146] Arthur James Balfour who, as British Foreign Secretary, signed the declaration that bore his name on November 2, 1917. The declaration, addressed to Lord Rothschild, stated: "His Majesty's Government view with favour the establishment in Palestine of a national home for the Jewish people."

[147] Menachem Ussishkin (1863-1941) was a Russian-born Zionist leader and head of the Jewish national Fund.

since he developed hundreds of dunams of the Holy Land for the Jewish people, and has transformed stretches of wilderness into cultivable land! For thousands of years, Jews have neither bought land nor possessed soil. What a wonderful feeling for a stateless people to once again be landowners; to be able once again to call the land of its fathers its own. There, in Palestine, we are without a doubt experiencing today an era of Jewish heroism. There, we are heroes!

And here? Here, we have been and, unfortunately, continue for the time being to be, martyrs. Here, we must be prepared to suffer for our Judaism. Our surrounding world demands this sacrifice of us. Here, we must often pay for our Jewish existence with our happiness and that of our children.

Do you now understand that we are living in such violent times, that we must be martyrs and heroes simultaneously? That almost daily, we experience an expansion of our possessions in Eretz Israel, and, simultaneously, a decline in our living standard in the Galut. Do you then understand how difficult our emotional life is, and must be, when we are brought low here, and stand erect there? When in Europe we are despised, and in Eretz Israel, respected and proud? In the Galut we are embittered and gloomy, and in Palestine – free and joyful?! Do you understand the tragedy of the Jews today, of these martyr-heroes?

We had a brother who mastered this double life; who understood this duality; who could blend this conflict in our souls into a harmonic unity. Unfortunately, we lost him a short while ago. Leo Motzkin[148] presided over Zionist Congresses. He belonged to the family of heroes of the modern Maccabees. He was an advocate for Jewish rights at minority congresses where he sought to make our *Galut* load lighter, and more bearable. He worked assiduously for Eretz, but was equally great for his work on behalf of the Galut.

---

[148] Leo Motzkin (1867-1933) was a Zionist leader as well as a leader in the struggle for Jewish civil rights in the Diaspora. He became critical of the Hovvei Zion and joined Herzl at the First Zionist Congress. He became a leading activist for the Hebrew language. At the conclusion of WW I, he demanded that the Zionist movement concern itself also with the problems of Diaspora Jewry. When the Nazis came to power in Germany, he brought the oppression of German Jewry to the attention of the League of Nations.

Great as hero; great as martyr...

We will probably have to continue to lead this dual life for a long time. We will have to wear the crown of martyrdom on our heads, and brandish the hero's sword in our hands for a long time. But there will come a day, when Jewish heroism and Jewish martyrdom will be united into a higher, loftier rhythm of life, which the Jewish prophets once inspired.

In that day, Israel will once again become prophet to the nations. Then, the clouds and fog that dim the vision of our enemies will be dispersed and the light of our Holy Writings will once again shine forth brightly on the world...

והלכו גויים לאורך ומלכים לנגה זרחך

And the peoples shall walk in your light;
the nations in the light of your brilliance...

ויחי[149]

Jacob lived in Egypt for 17 years. This is a long enough period of time for him to have adapted to a foreign lifestyle, to become fond of the newly acquired homeland, and to strike roots in the foreign soil. And yet, ויקרבו ימי ישראל למות – when Jacob realized that the end of his life was approaching, he sent for his influential, very capable son Joseph and told him, "do not bury me in Egypt; carry me to my fathers in the land of Canaan, and lay me to rest in the family plot." In the last hours of his life, he was drawn irresistibly to his ancestors, to consecrated land.

He had not resisted going abroad, as long as this made it possible for him to search for new ways of sustaining life; as long as he could uncover new sources of life. After all, hadn't he spent 20 years far from his parents' home, in idolatrous surroundings in Laban's house? When hunger and yearning for his son, whom he thought lost, led him to Egypt, he knew and understood how to rebuild a life consistent with his worldview and philosophy. Inwardly, he was sufficiently secure and clear, so as not to succumb to foreign influences. For he could say about himself: עם לבן גרתי ותרי"ג מצוות שמרתי – I lived together with Laban and, despite that, I kept the 613 commandments." He could live anywhere, but when it came to dying, he wanted to go home to his fathers, to his own...

Was Jacob's request to be buried with his forefathers only an indescribable yearning or nostalgia that often overcomes us at critical moments of our lives? Doesn't Jacob's last wish, to be brought to the Holy Land, have a deeper meaning?

Jacob did not make his last request of any of his other sons; he entrusted only Joseph with transporting his mortal remains. He did not request it of his oldest son Reuben, nor of his bravest son Judah; he turned exclusively and not without specific reason, to Joseph. Jacob was afraid that Joseph's attachment to Egypt might seduce

[149] UGGIK #47, January 1934, 3. Original in German.

him to regard this land as his true homeland. After all, it was in Egypt that Joseph built his home, found a wife, and raised his two children, Ephraim and Menasseh. The Egyptians considered him one of their own and gave him an Egyptian name, Zofnat-Paaneakh. Wasn't Jacob's fear that Joseph would soon forget his heritage, his origins, and his true home, justified? The other children felt themselves to be immigrants, foreigners in Egypt. They lived in their ghetto, in Goshen; changed neither their names nor their language; and cherished the old traditions and practices. But it was different for Joseph. Joseph was a statesman; Pharaoh's favorite; the one whom the foreign culture threatened to swallow... It was therefore precisely Joseph to whom Jacob turned. He told him about the family plot in Canaan. "Egypt is not your homeland, Canaan is," the dying Jacob appears to have said to his son, "and I want you to be conscious of your origins whenever you remember your father. Through the public transport of my mortal remains to Canaan, I want to make not only you, but the entire Egyptian people aware that you are a foreigner, a Hebrew."

This was no trifling sacrifice that Jacob demanded from Joseph. He asked him to make a public announcement of his origins, in the face of the danger that the Egyptians might henceforth withdraw their trust and their sympathy from him.

And Joseph understood his father. He led the funeral procession that accompanied his father's coffin to Canaan. The Egyptians were astonished to see their First Minister in the bosom of his brothers. Oh, so when it comes down to loyalty, the famous Minister is not an Egyptian! Oh, he is a Hebrew! But he was too far away to hear their scorn, their reproach about his foreign origins. So instead, they turned respectfully to see the funeral procession consisting of "all the servants of Pharaoh, the elders of his house, and all the elders of the land of Egypt." His honest patriotism had made an impression. One could respect and esteem this public declaration. All the Kings tipped their crown before Jacob's coffin. This proud, brave declaration of his origins brought forth a powerful reaction...

When Joseph returned to Egypt from his father's funeral, he was completely reconciled with his brothers. From then on, they belonged together. They had found each other in their shared grief. They had clasped hands over their father's open grave.

Not far from Hebron and the site of the double vault of the forefathers, is the grave of Joseph's mother, Rachel. Joseph might very well have stood on this hillock at the grave of this lonely woman who, in life, fought for love and, in death, lies far away from her loved ones. Here, he must have discovered a way to his past, to his childhood. Here, he must have developed the wish to eventually also lie in consecrated ground. He had once again found his home...

THE BABYLONIAN EXILE[150]
586 – 537 BCE

The Babylonian king, Nebuchadnezzar, finally conquered Judea in 586 BCE. But in 597, 11 years before the destruction of Jerusalem, he had already deported many Jerusalem inhabitants, including King Jehoiahin, to Babylonia. These Judeans, deported by force from their homeland, continued to have a close relationship with their fatherland. The distance from their motherland intensified and deepened their yearning for their ancestral home. When an uprising against Nebuchadnezzar was organized in Judea, the exiles took an active part in the preparations from afar. Their hope for a rapid return to the national hearth had not been extinguished in their hearts. The exiles considered their status a misfortune that would pass shortly, and end in deliverance and salvation from the hands of the enemy. They therefore lived in a state of constant tension and inner anticipation. They awaited an end to their suffering, and to the disgrace of captivity. They made no effort to take root in foreign soil, or to settle in the Babylonian state. They lived together in a group, united by a shared misfortune and connected by a shared hope. They did not mingle with the indigenous population. In their hearts, they were still living in their beloved homeland, from which the king had torn them away with oppressive force. They anticipated that help and eventual liberation would come from their homeland...

Then the day of mourning came; the day of the destruction of Jerusalem in 586 BCE. New waves of captives were brought from Judea to Babylonia. New multitudes of Judeans. They brought with them gloomy reports about the destruction of the homeland. Their last shred of hope now lay scattered among the cinders of destroyed Jerusalem. Despair and disillusionment spread among the exiles, which included the Judean aristocracy and the ill-fated King Zedekia, whom the cruel Nebuhadnezzar had blinded. It seemed as

---

[150] UGGIK #67, November 1934, 8; #68, November 1934, 4-5. Original in Polish.

if the luster of the nation had been extinguished along with the king's eyesight. The king, shackled in chains, was thrown into the same prison in which King Jehoiahin had barely been able to hold onto life.

But, in addition to the sad news about the national tragedy, the new exiles also brought a new spirit and new strength. This rejuvenated and comforted the old colony of exiles. Their numbers grew and their spirits were raised. Misery brought them close together and created a harmonious and friendly atmosphere. As often happens in times of danger and threat, an impulse for self-preservation was awakened. The exiles united and formed their own settlements near the town of Nippur (on the Euphrates and Kebar rivers) where their partners in misfortune, including the prophet Ezekiel, had previously settled. In time, they came to terms with their fate. Gradually, they became accustomed to their new circumstances and to their foreign environment. They followed the advice of the prophet Jeremiah, who long ago prophesied that the Temple would be destroyed, and recommended that they build houses and till the soil of Babylonia, since the captivity would last a long time. At first, they resisted, but soon they became convinced that the prophet was right; that he did not exaggerate. His prediction had come to pass. They began to settle on the foreign soil, planted gardens, tilled the soil, conducted business, and practiced their professions. They founded towns and settlements, such as Tel Aviv (Ez 3:15) and Tel Harsha. In 1893, an American expedition discovered several hundred tablets with Babylonian cuneiform writing near the town of Nippur that are an important source for understanding this era.

The Babylonian authorities apparently treated the exiles well and caused them no difficulties. They were allowed to settle and work everywhere. It was easy for them to interact, and develop relationships with their surroundings since Aramaic, the language used by the Babylonians, was similar to Hebrew. The exiles formed separate communities and lived together. Families who came from the same Judean locality usually joined, and formed their own association. For example, there was a community of Bethlehemites, and a community from Jericho, etc. Every family kept their genealogy, usually entrusted to the elders or leaders. Families with a common ancestor generally stayed together.

The form and structure of later Jewish communities was crystallized in Babylonia, but a fundamental change had to come about in religious life. The Temple lay in ruins. Sacrifices had ceased, and prayer and devotion were substituted for them. On Saturdays, the exiles would gather and read their religious books. The books of the Prophets, which had predicted a national tragedy and eventual salvation, became a source of comfort and inspiration for them. During prayer, they would stand and face Jerusalem. The days of the siege and destruction of Jerusalem were declared as days of mourning. Ritual and religious proscription created a wall that protected the exiles from assimilation, and from drowning in a foreign sea. The regular religious gatherings were the foundation for the synagogue, while ritual filled a vacuum left by the destruction of the Temple.

Two prophets, Ezekiel and a second prophet usually referred to as Isaiah II, about whom little is known, lived during the Babylonian exile. The religious literature that the Judeans brought with them consisted mainly of the Holy Torah and the older prophets. In addition, the prophets and leaders remembered traditions, songs, doctrines, and stories from the old days. It is believed that the historical books, later included in the Bible, were written at that time. A historian, who presented the history of the nation for the first time in a pragmatic manner, composed the books of Judges, Samuel, and Kings. He not only gathered individual events, occurrences, and historical facts, but also probed the contents of the past searching for a hint of the future. In times of spiritual and material poverty, people generally seek comfort and strength from the past.

Religious books were not the only source of instruction and solace for the exiles. To the fixed writings of the old prophets, were added the sermons of contemporary prophets active in exile. In the meantime, their authority had grown immensely. For after all, people were now witnesses that the warnings voiced by them long before the national tragedy were not empty words, but became a bitter reality. Long before the first ominous clouds appeared on the Jewish horizon, the prophets had predicted the destruction of the State. No one believed them then. Now, it was evident to everyone that these predictions had to be inspired by God. The words of Micah, "you will come to Babylonia and there you will be saved" (4:10) had been fulfilled.

The prophet Ezekiel was one of the exiles. His priestly origin left an indelible stamp on his worldview. He arrived in Babylonia together with King Jehoiahin (597 BCE) and settled on the river Kebar. When he left his homeland, the Temple was still standing, undisturbed. In his sermons, pronounced over a ten-year period between the deportation of Jehoiahin and the destruction of Jerusalem (586 BCE), he argued against an attempt by the exiles to start a rebellion against Nebuchadnezzar in Judea. The prophet was absolutely convinced that God intended to destroy Jerusalem. No one was allowed to oppose this verdict. With this argument, the prophet weakened and smothered the exiles' hope that God would soon end their suffering and restore them to their homeland. Mercilessly, the prophet destroyed his brothers' illusion. He did not do this from a lack of empathy or understanding of their suffering, but because he was convinced that the sooner they came to terms with the magnitude of their tragedy and the gravity of their situation, the sooner they could become accustomed to the changed condition of their lives. The prophet predicted the destruction of the Temple and the captivity of the king and his court. An uprising by the Judeans would, in the prophet's opinion, be national suicide.

The prophet had announced the depressing and pessimistic message that the nation had deluded itself with a false and empty hope, for a long time, even while the Temple still stood. When all illusions burst and the tragedy became an inexorable reality, the prophet changed from a harbinger of tragedy into a prophet of consolation. He now tried to protect the soul of the nation from despair and defeatism. He showed the nation, lamenting over the destruction of the Temple, a new ideal, and a loftier religious symbol. It was their duty to perfect their personality religiously and morally. Every individual was to bear full responsibility for his own deeds. Every person was to atone for his own sins and would be rewarded for his own good deeds. Every individual represents a unique world and should aim to reach the peak of perfection through his own power. In those days, some held the view that "parents eat sour grapes and their children's teeth are blunted" (18:2). Namely, children suffer for the sins of their parents. The sins of past generations burden their descendants. The prophet is absolutely opposed to this point of view. Everyone is responsible only for himself. The prophet teaches that sin does not pursue man like an inevitable fate. Human beings can be absolved by repentance, atonement, and by abstaining from evil. Man can correct his past. He can liberate himself from the chains of transgression by returning to God...

In addition to acknowledging a world-view through the individual, the prophet also emphasizes a national momentum. He instills hope in his brothers, exhausted by oppression and cruel fate, by predicting that they would be freed from captivity. The prophet's beautiful vision of the dry bones (chapter 37) is well known, and is told in order to rekindle a spark of hope for a better tomorrow and a national revival. The prophet finds himself in a valley full of dry, dead bones. Suddenly, a question is raised, "can these dry, dead bones return to life?" And then a miracle happens. The bones approach each other, become covered with muscles and tendons and a revived soul enters them. The corpses come to life, and rise tumultuously. The prophet compares the entire house of Israel to these corpses brought back to life. Israel too will arise from the dead. A people, scattered and dispersed in captivity, will unite into one nation and God himself will be their King. The prophet outlines a plan for such a future state. Its heart will be the Temple. Its leaders will be priests. The king's authority will be restrained since religion will be the highest power in the state. The structure of Ezekiel's state is a theocracy. The prophet-priest predicts victory and hegemony for his generation.

The exiles' distress would soon yield to changes. Nebuchadnezzar's state was facing its own disaster. Babylonian power seemed invincible. Babylonian power, especially in Palestine and Syria, seemed boundless. Her old adversary and antagonist, Egypt, yielded to Babylonian might and was quiet. Nebuchadnezzar built himself two magnificent residences, one in Babylon and the other in Borsipp. He used Judean labor in construction and imported expensive cedar wood from Fencilia. Soon, however, his magnificent residence on the Euphrates would be destroyed.

After Nebuchadnezzar's death, the Babylonian state was shaken by internal battles for the throne. Disputes and party squabbles undermined the up-to-now cohesive and consolidated state. Nebuchadnezzar's son, Ewil Merdach, only ruled for two years. He proved to be kind and magnanimous towards the Judeans. After 37 years of imprisonment, he freed the Judean king, Jehoiahin. He took him out of his dark, underground prison and installed him in an honored position in his court. But Ewil Merdach did not remain on the throne long. His brother-in-law, Neriglissar, tore the scepter out of his hands. There seemed to be no end to disputes and internal battles. Danger approached from Iran; the Persians were knocking on the gates of the Babylonian state.

Kyros (Koresh, Cyrus), the young fighting King of Persia had been successful in throwing off the yoke of Media, and in establishing a united Media-Persian kingdom (550 BCE). By defeating Lydia and their king, Krezus, Cyrus was able to enlarge the borders of his state to include all of Asia Minor up to the borders of Greece (546 BCE). Babylonia was incapable of stopping him. The stories of the triumph of Cyrus quickly spread over the entire East. The Judeans heaved a sigh of relief. A new hope was revived within them. A redeemer had unexpectedly appeared. Cyrus was famous for his magnanimity and his generosity. He was especially renowned for his tolerance of foreign religions and practices. The Judeans, therefore, expected that Cyrus, after incorporating Babylonia into his vast empire, would grant them permission to return to their homeland. This hope proved to be well founded.

A description of the exiles' enthusiasm for Cyrus and an echo of the hope of deliverance, which the Judeans attached to him, come to us from the writings of a prophet who is otherwise unknown to us. Since his prophecies were attached to the book of Isaiah, scholars have named him Isaiah II. The prophet begins his sermons with the words, "rejoice, rejoice my people." It is a hymn of praise to Cyrus, which paints a beautiful picture of the soon-to-come freedom. Cyrus is the servant of God; a tool in the hands of Providence; an anointed one carrying out God's will. Haughty Babylonia must fall so that Judea may be rebuilt. God is master and leader of all nations. The universalism of the Jewish religion finds a beautiful expression in the addresses of this prophet. The Jewish nation is a martyr, who suffers torture and humiliation, but this suffering is not in vain since Israel is a teacher of the nations and paves the way to truth and light. Christianity later borrowed the idea that suffering can have a salutary effect. It became the foundation of the faith about deliverance for the martyr. Isaiah II makes a connection and an association between the national and the universal. Through its suffering, the Jewish people redeem all of mankind. Through the Babylonian captivity, the Jewish nation, inwardly absolved and purified, will return and establish a new state, not on the basis of military power and might, but on a foundation of justice and love.

In 539 BCE, the expected war between Persia and Babylonia finally took place. Cyrus easily defeated Babylonia, and treated the vanquished with charity and magnanimity.

Belzacar was one of the last Babylonian kings. The Bible tells us that he once organized a banquet at which he used the holy vessels stolen from the holy Temple in Jerusalem by Nebuchadnezzar. Under the influence of wine, the guests saw a mysterious hand appear and write a puzzling inscription on the palace wall, "mene, mene, tekel ufarsin." The Babylonian magicians were not able to interpret the meaning of these words. The Jewish wise man, Daniel, finally uncovered their meaning. "God counted the days of your reign, placed them on a scale, and found you deficient. Your kingdom will be divided, between the Medians and the Persians." That very night, Belzacar was murdered. According to this story, the defeat of Babylonia was punishment for the destruction of Jerusalem.

By becoming the ruler of Babylonia, Cyrus also became the leader of Judea. He was kind to the Judeans, and gave them permission to return to their homeland and rebuild the Temple (538 BCE). The King gave an order that no one was allowed to place any obstacles in the way of the Judeans' return to their homeland. Cyrus, in accordance with his tolerance for all religions and practices, looked favorably on the Temple and the Jewish religion.

Not all exiles could take advantage of Cyrus' permission and return to Judea. Some had in the meantime, taken root in the foreign land. They acquired fields and farmed the soil. Many had an assured source of income, and were anxious about finding a source of livelihood in deserted Palestine. The wealthier members of the community, therefore, remained in Babylonia. Zerubabel, grandson of king Jehoiahin who died in Babylonia, and the priest, Joshuah ben Zadok grandson of the high priest Zerai whom Nebuchadnezzar condemned to death in Jerusalem, led those who decided to return to Judea. Cyrus provided these leaders with full authority, including letters of recommendation, and returned the holy vessels, which they took. The King also gave them money from the state treasury to cover the first expenses needed for the rebuilding of the Temple. Those returning to Judea received money, pack animals, and provisions for the journey from their brothers remaining in Babylonia. In 537, they left Babylonia for their homeland in Palestine. Their sudden deliverance form captivity appeared to them to be a beautiful, but unreal, dream.

After the Return from the Babylonian Exile[151]

The sight of a ruined and destroyed homeland made a gloomy impression on the Judeans returning from captivity. The beautiful country of their forefathers had changed almost beyond recognition, partly because it was deserted and devastated, and partly because it was settled by neighboring people. Judea's neighbors had eagerly taken advantage of the Judean's forced exile, and appropriated some districts, especially those bordering their own countries. While the main body of the Jewish nation was in captivity, and only a small number of the lower classes, deprived of any means of defense, remained in Judea, the Edomites had taken the Negev (South), and the Amonites took possession of the East. However, it was the Samaritans who gave the returning captives the most trouble.

The Samaritans lived in the North, in an area of the previous Israelite state. They were a diverse, not ethnically uniform, people. After the destruction of the Northern kingdom of the Israelites (720 BCE), Assyrians, Babylonians, and Arameans, who came from other areas of the vast Assyrian empire, settled in the deserted Israelite towns. These pagan settlers incorporated many of the customs and habits of the Israelites, but in a distorted and inexact way. In time, they mixed with the remaining population and began to consider themselves Hebrews. Their religion was a conglomeration of several philosophical elements. In addition to some old Israelite ideas, it also had some pure Assyrian pagan elements. The Judeans feared that this religion would have a negative influence on Jewish life, which was still in its formative stage. This fear was well founded, since the Judeans had incorporated some beliefs and practices from their surroundings during the Babylonian captivity. These penetrated so deeply into the Jewish soul that it proved impossible eliminate them. Therefore, the Judeans now had to protect the purity of their ideas, and shield

---

[151] UGGIK #69, December 1934, 6; #70, December 1934, 4. Original in Polish.

themselves against the danger of spiritual assimilation in their own land. It became very difficult to protect the Judean's environment from harmful pagan and foreign influences, since mixed marriages were a daily occurrence, and social ties between the Jewish and surrounding populations could not easily be broken.

Their need to separate themselves from their pagan environment was an act of self-defense for their religion and national identity, before an oncoming flood of idolatry and superstition. But, as timely and necessary as it was, the Jewish soul could not be satisfied only with self-defense. It thirsted for a positive religious expression. It yearned, above all, for the rebuilding of God's Temple on Mt. Moriah, and a renewal of the service to God. The Temple was the personification of national freedom. As long as the service to God was not performed as in the old happy days, the feeling of freedom remained dimmed and stifled. In Tishri, the month in which the Jewish holidays fall, the people therefore gathered in Jerusalem and built a new altar on the cinders of the Temple. The practice of sacrifices was renewed and prepared them for the rebuilding of the Temple. In exchange for appropriate compensation, the inhabitants of Tyre provided the building materials, cedar wood from Lebanon, and skilled workers. A year after the return from captivity, a foundation was laid for the new Temple. The laying of the cornerstone was cause for great celebration. Levites sang hymns of praise. Priests put on holy vestments. The people celebrated. Only the old ones, who had witnessed with their own eyes the magnificence of the old Temple, wept. How modest the new Temple (circa 536 BCE) looked in comparison to the old!

This was barely a first step in the rebuilding. The neighboring pagan people interfered with the work. They watched the development of the revived Jewish land with envy and ill will and tried to block the rebuilding of the Jewish national settlement by every means. The Samaritans gave them the most difficulty. Partly related to the Judeans, they requested Zerubbabel and the elders of the nation to allow them to participate in the rebuilding of the Temple. They justified their request by stating that they acknowledged the same religious principles and worshipped the same God as the Judeans. By participating in the rebuilding, they wanted to declare themselves part of the Jewish nation. The Jewish leaders, led by Zerubbabel, could not accept this proposal. The Judean nation was still shaky and weak in its faith and philosophy. It was not yet sufficiently secure to be able to absorb a still partly pagan nation, without doing damage to its own religion. The rejection of the proposal to work together evoked indignation and anger in the Samaritans. They decided to fight, and destroy the Judean plans. But they did not fight directly. Instead, they used intrigue and slander. Shamefully, they incited Persian officials against the Judeans. Whenever Judeans complained to the central authorities, the Samaritans bribed even those higher civil servants, thus frustrating all Judean intentions. They finally achieved their goal, and work on the Temple had to be interrupted for several years.

It was a difficult time for Judea. Cyrus' death and the Persian-Egyptian war caused chaos and unrest in the entire empire. Kambyzes, Cyrus' son and successor, led the Persian army against Egypt. The Persian army had to cross Judea. The threat of war on the Judean border brought about a decline in the material well being of the country. The neighboring peoples did not hesitate to take advantage of the problems of the Persian authorities who, occupied with their own affairs, did not pay much attention to maintaining peace and order inside the empire. They crossed into Judea and plundered and destroyed the property of its inhabitants. When Kambyzes died after humiliating Egypt, uprisings broke out all over the Persian Empire. A great storm broke loose. Judea was defenseless and without protectors. To make matters worse, economic difficulties were added to the lack of security. The land, which during the years of captivity lay fallow, lost its old fertility and refused to yield. Traffic stopped because roads were unsafe as a result of the war. Only slowly, and with much suffering, did Judea raise itself from ruin.

The reign of Darius 1 (521-485 BCE) brought better times to Judea. He was not driven by unfulfilled ambitions or a desire to enlarge the borders of his powerful empire. Famine and greed to annex new lands, which had previously driven Persian rulers to wars with their neighbors, were no longer factors. Darius saw his role differently. He realized that territorial annexation can damage the state because the newly acquired territories are often only loosely attached to the mother country. He decided to concentrate all his energies and attention on reorganizing and consolidating the state. Order and harmony reigned in the land. The days of anarchy and chaos were over. The unruliness and independence of lower officials and self-appointed despots came to an end. The consolidation of authority by the rulers, and the resulting increased safety, benefited the entire population including the Jews. Together with the rest of the population of the vast empire Jews took advantage of the administration of law and justice, which became *fundamentum regnorum*. It is also possible that the general cleanliness of the Judeans and their religious concepts, which, in contrast to other eastern religions did not demand human sacrifices, prompted Darius to be well disposed and friendly towards them. Darius was, after all, a fervent opponent of human sacrifices. Somewhat freed from persecution, the Jews once again started to work on rebuilding the Temple.

Haggai and Zechariah, the prophets living at that time, strongly advocated the rebuilding of the Temple. They accused the wealthy and the leaders of the nation of tardiness, and of not showing a sufficient degree of ardor in rebuilding the Temple. The widespread material poverty of the people, in their opinion, resulted from neglecting to rebuild the Temple. Is there a people who dwells in well constructed homes, while God's house stands in ruins? The Prophets' words of reproach did not go unheeded. Zerubbabel, whom the central authorities appointed as Governor of Judea, together with the High Priest, Joshua, started the work immediately. The construction took four years and many obstacles had to be overcome. But the industriousness of Zerubbabel and the High Priest, Joshua, prevailed. In the 70th year after the destruction of the first Temple, the rebuilding of the new Temple was finally completed. The dedication of the new house of God took place in the month of Adar. Even though it was not comparable to the first in splendor or beauty, the Prophet predicted that this new Temple would become a source of peace and harmony. Zerubbabel announced, in God's name, that the secular ruler of the day would gain victory "not by power nor by might, but by the spirit of God." A "day of small beginnings" would be followed by full success. A modest start would be crowned by complete victory. Days of fasting and mourning for the fall of Jerusalem would be turned into days of rejoicing and holiness. A sensitive ear can, however, detect a note of pessimism and sadness in the prophet's proclamations. Reality was disillusioning the people. Reality was not in harmony with their desires and wishes, their dreams and hopes about the future. We are familiar with such a mood. It prevails whenever a sublime ideal descends from the heights of heaven into the narrow, arrogant reality. Hopes and expectations are often more beautiful than their realization.

Jerusalem once again became the religious center of the nation, but Judea did not regain its old luster. It remained, as before, a Persian province, subjugated by a foreign state and deprived of freedom. Zerubbabel, a descendant of the House of David, was not crowned with the ancient royal crown. Suddenly, the thread of his activities is broken. Suddenly, he descends from center stage and disappears. A haze of mystery shades the remainder of his life. Tradition tells us that he returned to Babylonia where he remained for the rest of his life. But it is also possible that he was sacrificed on the altar of party warfare and thereby shared the fate of other Jewish leaders before and after him, who fell, betrayed, at their post. For some time, the history of the Jews in the vast Persian Empire becomes a puzzle. Historical sources and artifacts are silent. The continuing plot of the story is lost. The situation changes only in the days of Ezra and Nehemiah.

The first restoration and rebuilding of Judea after the return from Babylonia was only the beginning of the rebuilding of the Jewish center. There was still no order or clear direction in the political and social spheres. Zerubbabel had disappeared from the horizon. Persian officials filled the position of Governor, since Judea did not yet have an authoritative autonomy. The ruling group was composed of a small number of aristocrats, headed by the High Priest. The wealthy, a financial aristocracy, also played a large role. Economically, the nation was divided into a scant stratum of the wealthy, and a large mass condemned to abject poverty. The rich exploited the poor without compassion or mercy. In years of poor harvests, impoverished farmers sold or pledged their land, vineyards, homestead, and often even their children to the rich in order to be able to pay taxes and bribes to the Persian *satraps*. The burden of taxes crushed the nation. Everyone was forced to pay a double tax, one to the state and another to maintain their own government. In addition, Jews had to maintain the Temple by tithing, and other charges.

In addition to the economic crisis, there was also a moral crisis. Foreign pagan elements penetrated into Jewish society. Mixed marriages became a common phenomenon, and no longer aroused opposition or even a reaction from friends or neighbors. Some men divorced their Jewish wives and married pagan women. Pagans had entered Jewish life primarily during the period of the Babylonian exile when the inhabitants of Judea resided in exile and towns were abandoned. Pagans settled in the towns deserted by Jews. Mixed marriages led to the danger of assimilation since pagan women brought their foreign practices with them and brought up their children in paganism. Jewish culture was too weak to overcome and neutralize these foreign influences, and was threatened with a loss of its own characteristics and uniqueness. If this danger had not been stopped in time, paganism would have undermined Judaism, and relegated it to the ranks of one of the many splinter cults of the east.

The last Prophet, Malachi, portrays the conditions of the time, and condemns those who leave Jewish wives to marry women from foreign tribes. The Prophet castigates the Priests and Levites for neglecting their duties. He anticipates the arrival of a great person, who will rejuvenate and awaken the nation. Before long, the rescuer of Judaism revealed himself. He came from the Jewish settlement of Babylonia, and his name was Ezra.

EZRA[152]

At sad and decisive times, when the nation loses its way and spiritual equilibrium, God sends a determined redeemer with a pure, uncomplicated soul who illuminates the way with a "pillar of fire," and shows it the true reason for its existence. The nation recognizes and welcomes him immediately, without argument, and without requiring proof from its long awaited leader. It submits to his orders voluntarily, without hesitation, and instinctively feels that a new era in its history has begun. In the time of Ezra, the Jewish people, despite being internally weak, spiritually broken, and completely removed from the sources of their own culture, were still sober and sensible enough not to thoughtlessly turn away the salutary hand extended it by Ezra. They made his difficult mission easier by not behaving passively and stubbornly. That does not mean that from time to time they did not revert back to their old mistakes and, in moments of weakness, did not sink into their old, abysmal habits from the spiritual heights to which Ezra had brought them. These were understandable relapses and were the almost inevitable result of being accustomed to another way of life for many years. These were expected moral defeats of a nation striving to break the chains of a foreign culture to which it had been forcefully, but closely, attached for many years. From that pain, a new Jewish spirit was born, and the bright figure of Ezra stood watch over its cradle.

Ezra came from a priestly family and initially lived in Babylonia. Because of his deep erudition, his constant preoccupation with the Holy Writ, and his pedagogic activity, he was nicknamed the "sofer." Ezra's interest in religious works was not only theoretical. He was not satisfied with the mere academic study of the holy books. His major aim was to make Moses' law the foundation and basis for future Jewish life. The Torah would, henceforth, become the only binding constitution of the Jewish

---

[152] UGGIK #72, January 1935, 3. Original in Polish.

people. To achieve this end, he worked in Babylonian and Persian communities when he was informed about the spiritual decline of the Jewish community in Judea. He therefore decided to re-settle in the old Jewish homeland in order to take an active part in its rebuilding. He was drawn to Judea. It was there, that he would fulfill his life's mission. In order to be able to carry out his plan without outside interference, he sought letters of recommendation from the Persian government. King Artaxerxes I Longimanus gave him the power to appoint officials and judges, to organize a fund drive for Judea in the Babylonian colonies, and to take those Judeans who wanted to join him in returning to the homeland. Artaxerxes ordered his officials to support Ezra in his efforts.

Around 1500 families joined Ezra, and traveled with him to the homeland. Before embarking on their journey, they fasted and begged God for a blessing and a successful conclusion to their undertaking. The group of re-immigrants arrived in Jerusalem on the first of Av. The conditions he found there filled Ezra with a deep foreboding about the nation's future. Spiritual decline. Mixed marriages. Foreign forms of practice, and idolatrous religious ideas. Widespread signs of assimilation, and moral decay. Licentiousness and anarchy. Deeply moved by the demoralization and cultural decline that reigned throughout the nation, Ezra gave voice to his feelings in prayers that he led in the Temple. The service spontaneously changed into a beautiful public demonstration. The admonishing words and warnings of the great master, found a favorable response in the hearts of those present. They solemnly obligated themselves to annul their mixed marriages, and to start living according to the laws of the Torah.

Soon after this joyful declaration, a mass public meeting took place in the square in front of the Temple. Ezra called on the nation to learn and remember the historical mission it inherited from our ancestors, to foster spiritual goodness and ethical behavior, and to return to the tradition. Under Ezra's leadership, a religious council was established whose major task was the rapid dissolution of mixed marriages. This was a most difficult task, made more difficult by the fact that it touched the most private of matters. But carrying it out was a matter of life or death and, as it later became apparent, an indispensable way of maintaining and developing the nation.

The women who returned to their parents' home full of indignation, sought vengeance for their humiliation, and ignited a fire of hatred against the Judeans in the hearts of the neighboring people. The exasperated neighbors attacked the Judeans, destroyed the still remaining parts of the walls, and burned the gate of the city. A new danger threatened the still weak Jewish settlement. The Judeans became convinced that their most pressing task was to fortify Jerusalem, and to secure the new national home from attack and assault. They therefore concentrated their efforts on repairing the walls of the city.

In order to accomplish his goal, a religious-national revival and a renaissance of the tradition, Ezra now needed a secular, practical, and energetic leader with organizational skills who could consolidate and organize the demoralized nation. God sent the nation such a secular leader in the person of Nehemiah.

NEHEMIAH[153]

Nehemiah held the position of cupbearer in the court of King Artaxerxes.[154] Reports about the deplorable conditions of the Judeans in the fatherland, the lack of safety for their lives and property, and the uncertainty about their immediate future, filled him with sadness. Could he continue to lead the carefree life of a courtier, and be comfortable with the King's favors when his brothers were consumed by anxiety and helplessness? The deep hurt that touched Nehemiah's heart left its mark on his face, which the shrewd King's eye recognized as a sign of spiritual depression. When the King asked for the cause of his bad disposition, Nehemiah explained that the anarchy prevalent in his homeland was having a profound and depressing effect on him. King Artaxerxes gave him a leave of absence, and provided him with the appropriate documentation that would enable him to bring order to Judea. The central authority also asked the satraps to give him their full support.

Arrival of Nehemiah in Jerusalem
Nehemiah arrived in the Holy City in 445 BCE. He did not inform anyone of his arrival. No one knew him. He didn't have much confidence in the elders of the nation, and he wanted to check the magnitude of his future work for himself. The gates of the city were burned. Its walls were damaged. After determining the extent of the problem, he decided to repair the city fortifications, and called on the nation to help him in the task. The people enthusiastically supported Nehemiah's appeal.

The Samaritans Interfere
Judea's enemies did not approve this eagerness to rebuild. Nehemiah frustrated their plans, whose intent was to smother the new national flame at the very moment of its birth. They therefore decided to join forces. Sanbalat, leader of the Samaritans, joined

---

[153] UGGIK #73, February 1935, 4-5. Original in Polish.
[154] Artaxerxes I - King of Persia (464-424 BCE); son of Xerxes I.

with Tobias, leader of the Edomites, and Geshem, leader of the Arabs, to make Nehemiah's work impossible. The hatred and ill will of their enemies grew concomitantly with the energy and activity of the Judeans. The non-Jewish aristocracy, which until then had been on good terms with their Jewish counterparts, watched the development of Judean power and their strengthening feelings of independence and separateness with fear and alarm. The outward manifestation of these feelings was the repair of the walls. The walls, whose primary function was defensive, also acted as a barrier between the Judeans in the city and their foreign surroundings. Their repair was a symbol that, henceforth, the Judean nation intended to devote its energy to broadening its own culture, and to distance itself from foreign influences. The Samaritans, and the other peoples linked with them, apparently did not possess a culture of their own and wanted spiritually to lean on Judea. Judea's negative attitude embittered them because it deprived them of a deeper meaning to existence...

Judea's enemies, too weak to oppose Nehemiah on their own, decided to utilize the old and well trod road used by Israel's enemies throughout the ages – denunciation...They informed the state authorities that the Judeans were plotting high treason. Not waiting for intervention by the authorities, they readied themselves for an armed attack against Jerusalem. Nehemiah armed the workers, and placed guards around the city walls. With one hand they built, and with the other, they bore arms. They frustrated their enemies' intentions. Unable to stop the work, the enemies decided to secretly murder Nehemiah, its developer. They tried every means of sabotage. After a while, the work was finished. Jerusalem was no longer defenseless. Surrounded by strong walls, it could now easily repulse the attacks of its enemies.

Populating Jerusalem

The capital city had an insufficient number of inhabitants. Nehemiah tried to convince the villagers to move into the city. Until now, people had avoided the city because they did not feel safe in it, but now the capital city was the best protected sanctuary in the country, and thus became an attraction. Despite this, the population grew at a snail's pace, forcing Nehemiah to order 10% of the villagers to move to the city. Nehemiah's goal was to make the inhabitants of Jerusalem the nation's elite, and he wanted to make sure that, as demanded by tradition, they were of pure origin. The new inhabitants of the metropolis therefore had to prove their identity and demonstrate their Jewish genealogy.

Social Issues
Internal Jewish social life was weakened by conflicts and disputes arising from class differences. The rich exploited the poor, taking away their vineyards, fields, and even their children, as security in return for small loans. The selfishness of the wealthy knew no bounds. Everyone was concerned only for their own welfare, and wanted to accumulate as much wealth and material goods as possible without considering the welfare of society as a whole. The end justified the means. And the main end, achieved by any means, was to satisfy their egotistical lust. There was no feeling of solidarity and no sense of responsibility for the future of the nation. Only concern for the welfare of the entire nation can create a bridge between individual factions, and protect us from class excesses. But such a shared concern about the whole, flowing out of a deep consciousness about the unity of the nation, was lacking. Nehemiah, therefore, appealed to the rich to sacrifice their private and personal interests, and subordinate them to the interests of the society as a whole. He served as a good example by renouncing all levies and gifts to which he, as governor, was entitled. The wealthy followed his beautiful example, and committed themselves solemnly to return the houses, vineyards, and fields to their indentured brothers and forgive their debts.

The precepts of the Torah that Ezra taught and interpreted paved a path to the hearts and minds of the nation, and were put into action by Nehemiah. Both leaders complemented each other. The teacher and the organizer; the spiritual regenerator and the secular leader.

A Peoples' Assembly
On the first day of Tishri 444 BCE, a general assembly of the people took place near the "water gate" (Shaar Hamayim) at which Ezra

publicly read the Torah. The nation was then sunk in ignorance and was uneducated. Their assimilation and low moral standing were not due to ill will or a predilection for foreign forms of practice, but rather a complete lack of knowledge about the treasures of their own nation. People yearned to correct their mistakes and return from sin, but they did not have the strength to draw out of themselves a new ideal of life, and did not know the old Jewish ideals. By reading some of the most important passages from the Holy Writ, Ezra wanted to awaken the soul of the people out of its lethargic sleep. The Levites explained and interpreted the less clear ideas. The text and its interpretation by the Levites made a deep impression on the listeners. All were deeply moved. Only then did they realize all the sins they had committed against God, and how deeply they had offended and profaned the majesty of their holy religion. Some burst into tears. Ezra comforted them by relieving their consciences from the overwhelming, depressing burden of guilt over their past. Their self-flagellation gave way to well-developed resolutions for the future. Their gloomy dispositions, brought about by becoming aware of their sins, changed into a sublime, holy mood. Joy, caused by the rediscovery of the right path in life and the thread of history, lost during turbulent times, prevailed everywhere. The following day, Ezra explained to the people the significance of the festivals, especially the upcoming festival of Sukkoth, which, this time, all celebrated with great joy. Other assemblies, whose main aim was educational and pedagogic, followed. Finally, the representatives of the community in Jerusalem signed a document in which, in the name of the entire nation, they obligated themselves henceforth to keep the precepts and laws of the Torah. According to tradition, 120 representatives of the nation signed and sanctioned this new covenant with God with a solemn vow. This decisive assembly, known as the "Great Assembly" (Anshei Knesset Hagdolah), was later transformed into a permanent deliberating body, which was responsible for many important decisions in ritual and liturgy

Nehemiah Leaves
Nehemiah was the supporting pillar of the new organization built with so much hard work. He was the instigator and, together with

his co-worker Ezra, the soul of the renaissance of the Jewish nation. As long as he stood watch and supervised, everything remained in order. But as soon as his leave of absence expired and he was called back to the king's palace (433 BCE), a serious crisis erupted. Foreign influences once again became stronger. Saturday became a market day. The neighboring villagers publicly sold their produce in Jerusalem on Saturday. Mixed marriages once again took place. An offspring of the High Priest, Elisheb, married the daughter of Sanbalat, Nehemiah's passionate enemy. Wealthy proprietors stopped paying the tax or tithe to the priests and levites. Religious people were overcome by deep despair.

Nehemiah Returns

Armed with new orders and authorizations from King Artaxerxes, Nehemiah appeared on the horizon for the second time, having decided to react decisively, severely, and ruthlessly to the inexcusable weakness of the nation. He became convinced that one couldn't nurture confidence in a people that allowed itself to be so easily ravished and carried off by every demagogic catchword. Nehemiah therefore used radical means. He exiled the offspring of the High Priest who married the pagan. He ordered the gates of the city closed from the eve of the Sabbath until its end. All activity in Jerusalem stopped on Saturdays. The Samaritans were convinced that all their efforts and hopes to unify with the Judeans were aimless and would always remain unfulfilled. Therefore, instead of constantly throwing themselves on a foreign tribe with different characteristics and philosophy, they decided to organize themselves independently and develop their own community. Sanbalat, the Samaritan leader built a temple on Mt. Grizim (near Shehem) which was supposed to rival the one in Jerusalem. The exiled offspring of the High Priest was appointed High Priest of the new temple. The Samaritans believe in the contents of the Books of Moses. In later years, they incorporated a changed and distorted book of Joshua into their Bible. They changed some passages of this book in a tendentious manner in order to present the historical past of the Samaritans in a better light. The Samaritans consider themselves descendants of the old Ephraimites, and especially idolize Joshua, who came from that tribe. Since those days, they have developed a bitter hatred of Jews. In their view, they are the genuine descendants of the 10 tribes taken into captivity. To this day, a small community of Samaritans persists in Nablus (Shehem). Because of their insignificant and continuously diminishing number, their complete disappearance is only a matter of time.

Rabbi Moshe ben Maimon on His 800th Birthday[155]

The bustle, tumult, and somewhat excessive enthusiasm that has recently been generated around the figure of Maimonides, in connection with the official and unofficial celebrations of the 800th anniversary of his birth, fills those who always live within the orbit of his thoughts and ideas, who, even on non- celebratory days, draw knowledge about Judaism and inspiration about the highest human ideals from the never exhausted, rich fountain of his writings, with trepidation and reflection. The modern era takes delight in boisterous demonstrations and loud empty manifestations; in glaring advertisements and shrill fanfare. But Maimonides was, after all, not some politician chasing a cheap proclamation; nor a party leader bandying empty slogans; nor was he even a national hero, in the common meaning of the phrase, to whom a grateful posterity burns incense on its knees. He was a king of the spirit; a mighty leader in the land of scholarship; a deep thinker who penetratingly confronted the various problems of his day; a philosopher who lit the path and carried a faith for those who strayed; a theologian who wrestled with the eternal secrets and puzzles of existence; a Jewish genius who, with his constructive and clear mind, enriched and organized all the scholarly material that had accumulated over the centuries. His immortal spirit is master of the borderless state of the mind where reverent silence, concentration, unadulterated dignity, spiritual intensity, and a holy and solemn atmosphere, reign supreme. If we want to enter this land, we must first remove our shoes, shake off the dust of triviality, remove any accretion of materialism and temporal matters, and gradually accustom our eyes to flashes of genius.

Let us first examine the life of Maimonides during the turbulent years of his youth, his first internal and external experiences, and the beginning stages of his scholarly endeavors.

[155] UGGIK #77, April 1935, 3-4. Original in Polish.

Years of Youth

Moses, son of Maimon (Maimonides – רמב"ם) was born at 1:00 PM on Saturday, the 14th day of Nissan, 4895, corresponding to March 30, 1135, in the city of Cordoba. His father, Maimon, was a descendant of an aristocratic family of sages and Rabbis who traced their ancestry to the famous teacher of the Mishna, R. Yehudah Hanasi. Maimon held the office of Dayan (member of the city's rabbinate) in the Cordoba community. The breadth and depth of his education, made Maimon a worthy son of his generation, one of whose goals was to unify and harmonize general world knowledge with Jewish wisdom and opinions. Many of his scholarly treatises, written in Arabic, give evidence of his interest in the general literature of his time.

There are many legends about the early years and intellectual development of Maimonides. Tradition has it that in his very early years, Maimonides, much to the distress of his learned father, had a great dislike for study. On one occasion, his father punished him for this and Maimonides ran away from home, and sought shelter in one of the community synagogues. A combination of fear and fatigue soon caused him to fall into a deep sleep. While in this deep sleep, a spirit visited him, and filled him with a love and a desire to learn. Henceforth, Maimonides was overcome with a great yearning for study. Maimonides gives his father credit for teaching him the basic principles of scholarship. He often quotes his father, and thus pays tribute to his first teacher and spiritual mentor.

Great changes were taking place in the political arena. In 1148, the Almohades, fanatic followers of the Mohammedan religion, crossed into Spain, destroyed and ravaged everything in their way, and forced its inhabitants to accept Islam. Abdulmumen was the leader of this raging group of apostles of the new faith. Having conquered Cordoba, he gave the public a choice, convert to the faith of Mohammed, or emigrate. In their blind religious infatuation, the Almohades could not tolerate a different religion. They destroyed synagogues and closed educational institutes and schools. Many Jewish families picked up the wanderer's staff, and left the country. But there were also those, who could not part from their homes and their beautiful land. To save their lives and avoid persecution, they accepted the Mohammedan faith on the surface. Externally, they resembled their conquerors by seemingly observing their faith, but secretly they prayed emotionally to the God of their ancestors. Like the later Marranos (during Christian times), these Jews went to the sanctuary of a foreign religion, but, in their hearts, they remained true to their own faith. For the human conscience does not allow itself to be defeated by power and force.

Because of these events, Maimon and his family decided to leave Cordoba. Years of exile and privation followed. Wild hordes of Almohades advanced and captured more towns, leaving behind them a trail of material and moral devastation. In order to flee the danger, the Maimon family was constantly forced to change their place of residence.

Paying no heed to the danger and misery around him, the young Maimonides studied assiduously. He had an especially unquenchable thirst for Biblical and Talmudic studies and, as a result of his growing knowledge, received ever-greater recognition and accolades. In addition to Jewish scholarship, he immersed himself in philosophy, astronomy, logic, and mathematics. An unrestrainable force, undeterred by the wretched conditions in his parents' home or by the political storms raging around him, seemed to drive him to drink from the fountain of knowledge. His learned father unveiled a world of beautiful Jewish scholarship, while Arabic scholars taught him philosophy and medicine. When it came to scholarship, Maimonides acknowledged every authentic authority, even from a people who were behaving like enemies to Jews. He learned from everyone, paying no heed to the origin or faith of the teacher. He did not confine himself to Jewish scholarship because, in his opinion, acquaintance with general knowledge leads to a clearer, deeper, and more thorough understanding of Judaism.

When he was barely 23 years old, Maimonides published two scholarly works – "Cheshbon Haibur," about the Jewish calendar, and "Milot Hahigayon," about the terminology of logic. Maimonides emphasizes that his goal was to tackle problems in a simple manner so that they would become clear and accessible to everyone, and that he would strive to give pleasure to his readers by the physical appearance, systematic presentation, and organization of his work. He wrote the treatise on the Jewish calendar in Hebrew.

Logic, the subject of his second work, is the soul of all scholarship for Maimonides; the "lifting jack" and regulator of all knowledge. Just as grammar draws the boundaries of language; stands guard over correct construction; and restrains language's lawlessness and licentiousness, so the principles of logic restrain human thought and direct it along the proper track. Grammar teaches us the exact use of language; logic teaches us the rules and methods for correct thinking. Maimonides then proceeds, in general terms, to present the laws of logic, and to classify some technical terms. In this work it is easy to see the influence of Aristotelian philosophy. This book was written in Arabic, and later translated into Hebrew, Latin, and German.

In 1160, Maimon and his family were forced to leave Spain, where his ancestors had lived their lives, but which, as a result of a foreign invasion, had become a hell for their descendants. They traveled to North Africa, and settled in the city of Fez. But here too, the wanderers did not find peace. For here too, religious uprisings soon broke out, fanaticism was triumphant, and Jews could no longer practice their faith openly. Continuous persecutions and increasing religious oppression caused a decline in the cultural level of African Jews. They were overwhelmed by ignorant and warped views about Judaism. Maimon, the father of Maimonides, wrote a letter in Arabic to his brothers, the Jews of North Africa, urging them not to despair or be spiritually depressed.

Soon, a situation arose that tore the young Maimonides from the quiet of the study hall into the din of public arena. This afforded him his first opportunity to show his erudition. A certain Jewish scholar gave an opinion that Jews who accepted the Mohammedan religion, even though only outwardly and in secret continued to practice the religion of their ancestors, were traitors to their people and should be considered as heretics and apostates. For Judaism demands that, if necessary, its adherents give up their lives for their faith, and suffer martyrdom. Whoever publicly renounces the God of his ancestors, goes to a mosque, and hides his Judaism, is an apostate.

This opinion, which marked many families with the stamp of apostasy, caused deep consternation among African Jews. What were they supposed to do? Which path were they to follow? The thorny path of the religious martyr leading to the grave or an outward Islamic mask hiding their true belief in Judaism?

Maimonides freed his brothers from this spiritual dilemma by publicly defending those who, in the face of death, took on Mohammedanism on the surface. He annulled the mistaken and radical view of the scholar who so mercilessly attacked his unfortunate brothers. In his treatise, "Iggeret Hashmad," Maimonides differentiates those who voluntarily, of their own impulse and without outside force give up their faith, from the countless Jews who cling to the Jewish faith with their entire soul, and only drop out of Judaism for appearance, out of fear, and a threat of death. It is indeed true, he states, that a Jew should suffer martyrdom for his faith and whoever fulfills this deserves to be called a saint. However, one who does not reach this heroic level should not automatically be excluded from the nation. Those who, during times of religious persecution, sin against the religion to mislead and lull the vigilance of their persecutors and survive the period of fanaticism are not sinners or apostates, since it is impossible to demand from an ordinary human being, such extraordinary heroism and sacrifice. Moreover, it is important to note that whereas the Mohammedan fanatics demanded that Jews make a declaration accepting Islam, they did not force them to perform any actions in conflict with Judaism, and did not demand control over their private lives. So this oral expression of a formula accepting the Mohammedan religion cannot be equated with a denial of Judaism. Towards the end of this treatise, Maimonides nevertheless recommends that all who have the means should leave the country in which their human conscience is violated, in which the most elementary rights of people are trodden under foot, and that, regardless of the sacrifice, they should move to a country where one is allowed to live according to the precepts of the Torah. The world is surely wide enough!

That literary polemic had unpleasant consequences for Maimon's family. The authorities began to keep track of Maimon's activities, and especially those of his son, which were intended to comfort and strengthen Jews in their religious practice and to fight defeatism. The fanaticism of the authorities increased, especially when some among the pious Jews, no longer able to tolerate the humiliation and their double life, no longer able to suppress and conceal their Jewish feelings in their hearts while parading as adherents of Islam, threw off the shackles of their foreign religion, demonstratively declared their adherence to Judaism, and joyfully accepted a martyr's death. The Talmudic scholar, Rabbi Yehudah Hacohen, was condemned to death in Fez, where Maimon's family then lived. As a result, Maimon decided to flee the country and seek asylum in Palestine.

Maimon's family boarded a boat for the Holy Land on the 4th day of Iyar, 4925 (28th of April 1165) and left Fez. On the sixth day of the journey there was a huge storm. The boat heaved on the raging waves, and was threatened by catastrophe of sinking into the abyss of the raging elements. Maimonides turned to God for help and vowed that if God would save them, he would commemorate the day of their departure and the day of the storm with fasting and repentance for the rest of his life. His prayer was answered. The storm blew over and the ocean quieted. After 28 days, the boat arrived in Acco. The family declared the landing day as a holiday, a day of celebration. Maimonides met Rabbi Yefetem ben Elia in Acco, and they stayed there for six months. They then decided to move on to Jerusalem accompanied by the Rabbi of Acco. The journey was difficult and presented many challenges. They had to cross forests and deserts. They spent only three days in Jerusalem, and moved on to Hebron. After enduring so many hardships and long periods of wandering, they would gladly have settled in the Holy Land, but Palestine was devastated, deserted, and its inhabitants pauperized and fearful as a result of the Crusaders. Maimon therefore decided to take his family back to Egypt.

In those days, the Caliphate of Fatimid ruled Egypt. Approximately 3,000 Jewish families lived in Alexandria and Maimon settled his family in nearby Fostad. Maimon died there and his sons, Moshe and David, became closer to each other and combined forces to support themselves. They began dealing in precious stones. The younger brother, David, directed the enterprise and this required him to spend much time on sea voyages. Moshe devoted himself to study and took care of the family. Soon, physical and financial misfortunes visited Maimonides' house. The saddest blow was news of a catastrophe at sea, and the loss of his only brother. With the loss of his brother, Maimonides lost his bearings and his personal happiness. For a long time he could find no solace. "We have been left alone," he wrote to his friend, the Rabbi of Acco. "A number of misfortunes have visited me. My father, צ"ל, died...illness undermined my own health...financial losses markedly undermined my material well being...evil slanderers have defamed me, thus threatening my life...but my greatest tragedy came recently. It is the death of that saintly human being who, together with many goods, ...drowned in the sea leaving behind a widow and young daughter...today, I still mourn his death and cannot be pacified...he was, after all, my brother, my student, the director of my business, my guardian while I sat peacefully at home. Whenever I come across a letter from him or some book of his, my pain returns and the old grief reawakens within me."

In time, however, Maimonides shook off his despair and anxiety. Scholarship would at long last bring him real consolation.

ויקח קרח
AND KORAH TOOK[156]

"And Korah took" and strode before Moses. The expression, "ויקח – and he took" reveals the true souls of the fickle masses who did not possess their own convictions or firm resolve, and allowed themselves to be easily "taken" and seduced by others. Korah took his mob, like one usually takes an object, from one place to another.

People rarely live and act according to their very own insights and opinions. Only rarely do people mold their lives according to basic principles, which they deduce through independent thought and their own empirical knowledge. The majority is happy to be led. Blindly, they adopt slogans and programs manufactured and developed by others. They repeat these strange and pre-digested ideas so often, and for so long, that they finally believe that they are their creators, and forget that they are only followers and ruminators. Korah took his people. They did not resist. They followed him willingly because they had no inner inhibitions or opinions of their own to overcome.

"And when Moses heard the accusations made by Korah and his mob, he fell on his face." He saw all hearts turning towards Korah. He saw demagoguery being triumphantly celebrated, and truth defeated. Instinctively, he must have thought of the time he first came to Egypt and, in the name of God, told the people the news of their deliverance. How he had to fight and struggle then before he was able to make himself heard. How long he had to court the people before winning their sympathy and confidence, and capturing their souls for a short period of time. Korah, on the other hand, had an easy job.

And that is the way it is to this very day. Truthful ideas grow slowly; demagogic slogans are accepted as quickly as lightning. Truthful ideas have a hard time plowing a road into the world; slogans charm their way in easily, gliding on their smooth brilliance

---

[156] UGGIK #82, June 1935, 7. Original in German.

and deceitful magic.

Moses' defense is moving: "I have not taken one ass from them; neither have I hurt one of them." I was unselfish and self sacrificing. I have served this nation without expecting thanks or rewards. And what I received in return is disappointment.

The plea of another Jewish leader, who lived much later, sounds so similar. Samuel too had to defend himself: "Here I am...whose ox have I taken, or whose ass have I taken? Whom have I defrauded or whom have I robbed? From whom have I taken a bribe?" (I Samuel 12:3). He too emphasizes his unselfishness. Rumors, which raised questions about his honesty, must also have been spread about Samuel.

The parallelism between Moses and Samuel would not have been so striking, were it not for a Midrash that states that Samuel was a descendant of Korah. Samuel, Korah's descendant was forced to defend himself against the same accusations once brought against Moses. Years had passed since Korah's conspiracy against Moses. A member of the Korah family had finally reached the pinnacle of his people. Samuel, in whose veins flows the blood of Korah, is the leader of the people. The opposition has finally come to the helm. What happens? The opposition has to endure the same battle; it is forced to defend itself exactly as Moses once had to defend himself from them.

Moses, the hero of our *sidra*, and Samuel, the hero of our *haftara*, shake hands over the chasm of years that separate them. They were fellow sufferers. Both were victims of malicious criticism, the typical fate of Jewish leaders. Both experienced a decline in truthfulness, and the ascendancy of the demagogic cliché. In Moses' day, the demagogic cliché was: "All of us want to be leaders! The whole nation is holy!" In Samuel's day, the aroused nation screamed: "We want a King! We want to be just like the other nations!" In both situations, there was a leadership crisis. In both situations, there was dissatisfaction with the existing form of government. Then, as today, it is a difficult, an almost insoluble problem...

ON THE MARGINS OF THE DAY:[157]
RABBI KOOK'S DEATH[158]

News from Palestine has enveloped the entire Jewish people in mourning. We stand in inconsolable grief over the coffin of Chief Rabbi Kook. With his death, we have lost one of the greatest Jewish authorities and leaders. We must search in the ancient Hebrew dictionary in order to find words with which to describe the magnitude of our loss, and define this unusual personality. He was truly a מרה דארעא דישראל – the spiritual leader of Palestine. But his influence went well beyond the borders of Palestine. He was also the master of the *golus*. His words and pronouncements, full of substance and deep wisdom, were received with loud affirmations in all Jewish communities.

The most unique stamp of his character was his love for every Jew, regardless of party or group affiliation. Even people who stood on the opposite religious pole, and professed different ideas than he, were embraced by his love and his boundless, subtle goodness. Intolerance and fanaticism were foreign to him. His brothers' misery was his misery. Their pain and affliction were his pain and affliction. Patiently, he taught, scolded, and showed the way. He never surrendered or lost hope that those who had strayed from Judaism would return, would reconsider, would renounce their recklessness, and would in the end, join in the work of rebuilding the holy land in a holy spirit.

It was this that he longed for. For a holy Palestine, which he saw in his messianic vision. He therefore stood steadfast, and guarded the purity of the ethics and justice in the *Yishuv*. He was a champion of truth, and did not hesitate to stand up against anyone who abused it. His feeling and defense of righteousness won him

---

[157] UGGIK #87, September 1935, 3. Original in Polish.
[158] Rabbi Abraham Isaac Kook (1865-1935) was the first Ashkenazi Chief Rabbi in Palestine. He immigrated to Palestine from his native Lithuania in 1904, and was elected as Chief Rabbi in 1921.

the respect and esteem of all segments of society. Even those who opposed him, humbly paid tribute before his majesty.

He was an illuminating example for his students; a modern Orthodox Rabbi who does not seclude himself in the narrow sphere of theological studies, but uses his intellect to deal with all actual Jewish problems, and is a genuine spokesman for the people.

A star has been extinguished on the Jewish firmament. A great spiritual *halutz* (pioneer), in the most profound meaning of this word, has died. תנצ"ה.

FOUR COINS[159]

The *Midrash* tells about four coins, which were struck by four different Jewish personalities (Rabba Breshit 39:16). These coins had a constant and lasting value, and their worth was independent of devaluations or economic fluctuations. The images that appeared on both sides of these coins continued to have a symbolic meaning and significance despite the passage of centuries since their creation. This highly valued currency has been hidden in the Jewish treasury and, despite economic crises and social revolutions, has somehow managed to survive to this very day without losing its value or power.

I

Our forefather, Abraham, created the first of these coins. There was an image of an old man and an old woman on one side, and that of a young boy and a young girl the other. Youth and old age are bound together. A generation barely marching out to conquer the world is holding hands with the generation leaving it. No discord or dissension has come between them. A bridge of understanding binds them together despite the chasm of age that divides them. The son continues the work of his father, and walks in his path. He does not ruin or destroy what he has inherited in order to offer sacrifices to new gods, and pursue a new way of life. An unbroken thread joins the past to the future. Abraham symbolizes this unity of the generations, whose spiritual purity is revealed in the moment when he and his son, Isaac, walk together in complete harmony towards Mt. Moriah in order to offer him as a sacrifice to God. Father and son are nourished by the same wish; march to the same rhythm; are inspired by the same spirituality. That is one idea behind the images on the coin.

The images on Abraham's coin proclaim an additional message

[159] UGGIK #90, October 1935, 3. Original in Polish.

– that we can overcome and be victorious over the decrepitude of old age. To get old does not have to mean to wither, to submit to progressive fossilization. Old age does not have to bring an end to creative work. We know of examples of spiritual rejuvenation in the twilight of life; of an intensification of creative work with the last spark of the soul on earth. With his coin, Abraham tried to teach us to preserve the glow of youth in old age. He himself was the embodiment of this, for the Holy Writ states that when he became old and "approached an advanced age," the Eternal blessed him with everything (Genesis 24). His soul's strength overcame the decline of his body. The words of the Psalmist about the righteous, עוד ינובו בשיבה – they will yet blossom in their old age, were fulfilled for him. He lived as Koheleth enjoined us: "In the morning sow your seeds and in the evening do not allow your hands to rest"!

II

Joshua, Moses' pupil and his successor, struck the second coin. One side showed an image of an ox and the other, an antelope. In our literature, the ox represents strength; the antelope represents beauty. It was certainly not by accident that Joshua found these symbols appealing. They were a reflection of the situation in which he found himself. Providence charged him with conquering Palestine, and establishing a unified Jewish state on the ruble of former small states. For this great leader, strength and beauty were the guiding ideals for which the future Jewish community should strive. A state that is not unified and strong, becomes, in time, prey for predators and war-disposed neighbors, or is condemned to disappear as a result of inner conflicts and upheavals. But primitive unbridled strength alone would make the state into a military camp, and would drive the nation to embrace materialism. Did God free us from Egyptian bondage in order to become advocates of brute force and oppressors of other peoples? Joshua, therefore, showed an emblem of beauty on the other side of the coin, indicating a second ideal for which Jews should strive. Naturally, this was not to be a spiritless, corporal beauty that would intoxicate and bewilder the eye of the beholder, titillate his gaze and his senses, and act as an opiate for his brain. Instead, it was to be a beauty that expresses itself as harmony between body and soul, a combination of outward beauty and inner purity, virtues of the heart and body blended into one. אל תבט אל מראהו – "do not look on his countenance, or on the height of his stature, for I have rejected him! For not as a human being sees (do I see). Indeed a human being sees what is before his eyes, but God sees the heart" (1 Sam 16:7). Outward beauty alone, which does not radiate an inner glow, is not beauty, and is not considered our ideal. That was the pagan god of the ancient Greeks.

III

We owe a debt to King David for the third coin. On one side of this coin there was an image of a shepherd's crook and bag, while the other side showed a picture of a tower. In his youth, David had been a shepherd of his father's flock, and later in life Providence picked him to become the shepherd-king of the nation. Instead of the shepherd's crook, he now held the royal scepter. From the royal tower, he now extended his care and protection over his people. How changeable were the vicissitudes of his life! His own son rose against him, and forced him into exile. In order to escape from his oppressor, he had to abdicate the throne, and, once again, he was accompanied by the shepherd's crook and bag on his wonderings. The pendulum of his life swung between good fortune and misfortune. But in times of good fortune, the King did not forget the times of adversity. He was not ashamed of his past. He did not deny his origins nor hide the occupation of his youth. He always realized his good fortune, and always expressed gratitude to God for his elevation in status and the many privileges it granted him. With genuine humility he said: "Who am I, my Lord, and who is my household that You have brought me this far?" (2 Samuel. 7:18) That is the symbolism on the coin, which depicts both a royal tower and shepherd's tools. It is an artistic representation of the words, "though your beginning be modest, your future will be very great" (Job).

IV

The fourth coin, which also illustrates the changeability of human fate, is one made by Mordehai during Haman's times, and shows a sack and ashes on one side, and a gold crown on the other. On one side – mourning; on the other – power and happiness. In those days, the Jewish people were on the brink of disaster. An implacable enemy was lying in wait to destroy it. All hope seemed lost, and, as a sign of despair, the people covered their heads with a sack and ashes. Suddenly and unexpectedly, the situation reversed. Sadness changed into joy, ceremonial garments took the place of the attire of mourning, and a golden crown took the place of the sack and ashes.

We have come to know the outward appearance as well as the moral significance of these four Jewish coins. Centuries of suffering and sad experiences have not succeeded in diminishing their symbolic strength. They continue to teach us today, as they have since their creation, that we should not bend under the weight of old age; that strength must be connected with beauty; that at the peak of success, we must not forget our former misfortunes; and that in times of mourning, we must not lose hope.

THE FESTIVAL OF REJOICING[160]

The days, which our tradition has aptly named ימים נוראים – days of awe and dread, days of religious inspiration and spiritual concentration, have now passed. The holiday of *Sukkoth* was endowed by Jewish genius with other qualities and features. Whereas *Rosh Hashanah* and *Yom Kippur* show us a serious and solemn face, *Sukkoth* smiles to us, and displays a joyous and sunny disposition.

Joy is the emblem and hallmark of this holiday, which we call זמן שמחתנו – a time of our rejoicing. We must immediately stress that there is a characteristic Jewish joy, just as there exists a characteristic Jewish sorrow. הביטו וראו אם יש מכאב כמכאבי – look and reflect whether there is a pain like my pain. No! Jewish tragedy has no equal in the annals of human history. The sorrow that has accumulated and filled the depths of our souls over the centuries is unique and singular. But our joy, to which we sometimes submit, also has its own melody. אל תשמח ישראל אל גיל כעמים – "do not be joyful, O Israel, in the same manner as other nations are joyful." This injunction by the Prophet was entirely superfluous. Even if we wanted and yearned, we would be incapable of being as joyful, of smiling in as carefree a manner, of being as happy and delighted with life, as other nations. We have lived through too much. We have suffered too much. We have known too much anxiety and sadness for uproarious joy, for cheerful play, for ostentatious gaiety. The festival of *Sukkoth* is indeed a time of *our* joy, שמחתנו, our quiet and subdued joy. An inspired joy, full of the solemnity of an old and experienced nation. A nation that has preserved the radiance of ancient wisdom in its soul, marked of the horror of the middle ages on its body, and whose eyes, enchanted with a vision of the prophets, are fixed on a bright and blissful future. The joy of the festival of *Sukkoth* is in essence, a spiritual joy.

For we differentiate the joy emanating of corporal pleasures and

---

[160] UGGIK #90, October 1935, 4. Original in Polish.

physical feelings, from spiritual joy emanating from intellectual experiences. Physical joy has boundaries that are impossible to cross. If hunger gnaws and you satisfy it, you feel relief and a certain amount of joy. Do you still yearn for food? No! The goal has been achieved. You have driven the curse of hunger away. You are satiated and no longer think about food. You have reached the finish line, the predetermined border. But the situation is entirely different with spiritual happiness. The deeper you penetrate the mysteries of knowledge, the greater will be your thirst; a desire to uncover and understand further areas of knowledge will overwhelm you. And you will never be able to satisfy that yearning. You will never be able to say "eureka"! I have finally found the last truth. I now possess the ultimate secrets of the cosmos. This joy, which reaches into infinity, is encompassed in the word שמחתנו – our joy; the joy of the people of the book whose soul dwells in the heavenly spheres.

But there is a further difference between physical and intellectual joy. Physical joy is often associated with harm and detriment to others! How often does one person rejoice at another's expense! What is fortunate for you may be a misfortune for someone else. You have acquired wealth, bought houses, accumulated goods, and are climbing up the rungs of the ladder of society. But didn't someone have to come down from the summit before you could take his place? Didn't someone have to fall in order for you to be able to rise? Didn't someone lose the goods that you have acquired? Your joy is therefore a direct cause for the tears and affliction of others. ולשמחה מה זה עשה – what a flimsy joy that is! In contrast, a spiritual joy causes no pain to anyone; causes no tears to be shed. That is an exquisite joy, an ideal joy without blemish, without flaw, and without a dark side.

Clouds of sorrow are obscuring the world's horizon. Joy is diminishing while sorrow flows in a wide stream, its current overwhelming ever-wider areas. The fountains of material joy are drying up. So it is with great gratitude that we accept God's gift in the form of the festival of *Sukkoth*, which opens for us the gates of a land of higher joy, of spiritual joy.

THE FLAMING MESSAGE OF THE HANUKKAH LIGHTS[161]

A Midrash tells us that four Kings, David, Asa, Yehoshofat, and Hiskiyah, prayed to God in their hour of need, and each framed his wish in a different form.

David prayed: Grant, O God, that I may follow my enemies, pursue them, and overtake them. His wish was granted. He followed his enemies, pursued them, and won a victory.

Asa said: I have no power to beat my enemies. I can only pursue them and You, O God, destroy them. His wish was granted. He pursued the enemy, but God destroyed them.

Yehoshofat beseeched: I have no power to beat my enemies. Neither do I have the strength to pursue them. I will, therefore, sing Your praises O God, and You will punish my enemies. And it was so. The King sang religious hymns. God annihilated his enemies.

Hiskiyah said: I have neither the strength to defeat my enemies, nor the strength to pursue them, nor even the power to sing hymns of praise to You, God. I will rest in my encampment, and you can do everything for me. And it came to pass just as the King wished. While Hiskiyah and his men slept, God sent an angel, who slaughtered the entire Assyrian army in one night.

In David's time, we still possessed an offensive power. We were still able and permitted to attack our enemies, to pursue them and do battle with them. Occasionally, we even went out to conquer new territories in order to annex them to the Jewish state. But there followed a time when we lost our offensive power and could no longer act aggressively. We could still defend ourselves when we were suddenly attacked and invaded. That was the case with King Asa who no longer felt himself in a position to beat his enemies. His modest wish was that he be allowed at least to follow and pursue his enemies. Then came the Middle Ages with their funeral

---

[161] UGGIK #94, December 1935, 6. Original in German. This essay is signed with the initials Ch rather than with the entire name.

pyres. Jewish communities went up in smoke. Jewish blood flowed in torrents. We didn't have the strength to beat our persecutors. We didn't even have strength to resist them. We could, however, still sing. Ardent songs. Fervent hymns. Prayers carried to Providence by a boundless faith. Wrapped in *talis* and *tephillin*, in rapture and ecstasy, with the Shema prayer on their pale lips – that is how the Jewish martyrs awaited their death. They mounted the funeral pyres with singing and jubilation. Now is a time reminiscent of the times of Hiskiyah. Sleep with folded arms reigns. We cannot fight. We don't want to fight. We have unlearned this skill. We can't even defend ourselves. After all, they have superior strength. We are a small handful. But even the song and music is gone from us. The songs are silenced. Here and there, someone still mutters a prayer in time of danger. The word dies on the lips. Like Hiskiyah, we sink in our encampment. You, O God, fight for us. Our strength is depleted. Alone, we sit in the night staring out into the darkness to see whether a savior is coming...

Aren't we just like the *shamash* of the Hanukkah lights? He lights up all the other candles; he gives them a gift of his warmth and fire. Alone, the *shamash* light remains standing in the corner. He remains disregarded. We have been the *shamash* for the other nations. We have lit the light of knowledge and culture in all lands where we have lived, and where we have been able to gain a foothold. We have shared the light of our laws with others. Our Psalms are heard in their houses of God. The wisdom preached from the pulpits of the world religions is drawn from our sources. The *shamash* remains unnoticed. The Hanukkah lights want to overcome this pessimism that emanates from the *shamash*. For Hanukkah reminds us that a people never sinks to the lowest rung of the pariah ladder, as long as it still possesses a spark of self-confidence. Napoleon was supposed to have said to his soldiers in front of the Egyptian pyramids: "Four thousand years are looking down on you." A thousand years of Jewish history speak to us from the flames of the Hanukkah lights. They speak about the power of the spirit over the material; about the triumph of a minority over a much larger majority...

Our sages have been criticized for devoting relatively little space in our old literature to the Hanukkah miracle. While entire tractates are dedicated to other festivals, the Hanukkah story is disposed of with a few words. But this accusation is not justified. It is important to keep in mind the uniqueness of the Hanukkah events. We were silent witnesses to the miracles of Pesah. We played no active role in the miraculous events swirling around us. The miracle came to us. This same passivity on our part is also true of the miracle of Purim. We were, therefore, in a position to describe and exhaustively portray the reality that took place without our assistance. But how can we capture in words the rapture that stirred the Maccabees; how can we illustrate the emotions and sentiments in mere words; how can we reproduce experiences that affected us so deeply? Experiences that penetrate deeply into the soul usually remain our own personal secrets. National exaltations, like the Maccabean revolution, stir the heartstrings of the entire people, overwhelm the imagination of the nation, stimulate poetic expression, and ignite our most sublime emotions. The news of the experienced miracles is spread by word of mouth. Every mother transmits it to her children on festive occasions. Instead of dry words, the passionate glance and expressive face of the narrator are necessary as a medium of proper transmission to future generations. The miracle of Hanukkah must not be hidden away in books. It must live on as a living blessing.

Neither the dead written word, nor the rigid letters tell us each year about the Maccabees. The bright flames of the Hanukkah candles tell the story.

VIII

'A NEW LIGHT SHALL ILLUMINATE ZION'

Rabbi Chameides was a Zionist and never tired of singing the praises of the rebirth of the Jewish people on their native soil. He saw this as the only ray of sunshine and hope for the Jewish people on an otherwise gloomy horizon. In "The Broken Tablets," he writes: "And indeed have we not ourselves survived to see the miracle of the splinters coming together and becoming whole again? Have we not witnessed parts, torn asunder come together into a new community? Haven't we defied all satanic powers and, in spite of universal derision, haven't we accomplished, or more correctly haven't we begun, something that should fill us with a feeling of pride and satisfaction?" But he also expresses concern about party factionalism and unwillingness to compromise, as well as concern about a split between religious and secular communities. As he expressed it: "Only when Jerusalem and Tel Aviv no longer vie with each other; only when the heart of Jerusalem and the head of Tel Aviv have both found a home within the Jewish people will the broken Jewish tablets once again become whole, and only then will Israel once again become the messenger bearing God's tidings at Sinai." These divisions cause him to have grave concerns about the future of the Jewish people.

In addition to his strong religious Zionist outlook, he also felt that knowledge of the Hebrew language was essential in transmitting the Jewish heritage. On the occasion of the 50th anniversary of the founding conference of Chovvei Zion, he wrote:[162] "A knowledge of Hebrew vocabulary derived directly from the original ancient literary sources is necessary for another reason. Just as personal relationships are influenced by the circumstances of the first meeting, every Hebrew word maintains the color and character of the literary creation from which it stems and where it was first encountered. For a Jew whose first encounter with the word 'heaven' is in a dictionary rather than in the first sentence of the Bible where it is placed in the context of creation of the world, the word will never have a deeper meaning than its Polish equivalent, 'niebo'; or the German, 'himmel.' In contrast, a

---

[162] Kalman Chameides quoted in Yosef Chrust and Yosef Frankel; 20, 22.

Jew who receives a traditional education will subconsciously have a different reaction to this word. Emotional and conceptual associations surround the word 'hashamaim' in the poetic words of the author of the book of Psalms, 'the heavens relate the glory of God,' or in the majesty of the sentence, 'in the beginning God created the heavens and the earth.' A prosaic word like 'ladder' conceals within it some of the enchantment of the dream of Jacob if it is engraved into our memory for the first time as a component of the beautiful picture of this dream in the Bible ('and he dreamed, and behold a ladder is standing on the ground and its top reaches heaven and behold angels of the Lord are ascending and descending, etc.') It is clear from this, that studious reading of the Bible and our ancient religious texts in general, leads to a deeper understanding and appreciation of the Hebrew language, not only in terms of its linguistic and etymological richness, but above all the artistic and emotional side of each word."

Chaim Nachman Bialik, the Jewish national poet, died on July 4, 1934. He was considered the Jewish national poet because his voice gave expression to the despair, the hopes, and the dreams of the Jewish masses in Eastern Europe in language not heard since the days of the prophets. His death was deeply mourned and two essays are devoted to him. As one reads Rabbi Chameides' synopsis of Bialik's description of the conflicts within the soul of the traditional yeshiva bochur, one wonders whether it was, for him, also a personal description of a shared experience. For Rabbi Chameides too, grew up in the culturally rich, but closed, atmosphere of the shtetl, and then went out into the world to absorb what it had to offer. He too, spent his brief life trying to bridge the two worlds. He too, must have felt that he now stood, "on the threshold of the Beit Hamidrash," rather than inside it.

It is difficult for us, living in the 65th year of Israel's independence, and in the "post Zionist" era, to appreciate the impact that Theodore Herzl had on the masses of Jews in Eastern Europe. This extended across the spectrum of Jewry. Rabbi Chameides was a religious Zionist. His sympathies were with the Mizrahi movement, but this did not prevent him from recognizing the debt owed by the entire people to dreamers, like Herzl, who were not religious. His hope for a Jewish future is expressed in many articles, as is his conviction that the exile had imposed on the Jews characteristics of "galut" which were not Jewish and that, with independence, the people would return to their pure roots of prophetic times.

In "Small Vessels," Rabbi Chameides deals with the threats to Jewish survival – assimilation, conversion, ignorance, poverty, and persecution, all of which were present in his community. He takes solace from Jewish history that somehow the Jewish people, as a whole, will survive even though his particular community may not. He is convinced that salvation for Jewish survival will come from the newly created community in Eretz Yisrael.

In "Broken Tablets," Rabbi Chameides once again returns to the dilemma that obviously troubled him, since he dealt with it in other essays: Has the world benefited in any way from the giving of the Torah? Has mankind improved as a result of it? He comes to the sad conclusion that it has not. He consoles his community, and uses Zionism as an example of a recent accomplishment of the Jewish people.

פכים קטנים
SMALL VESSELS[163]

Talmudic scholars paid relatively little attention to the festival of Hanukah. In the Talmud, they described the historical essence and background of the holiday in a few sentences. The conquerors of the Temple in Jerusalem profaned the holy oil. After the Maccabees' decisive victory, there was nothing with which to kindle the eternal light in the Temple until a small, untouched vial of oil was found. The foe remembered everything. They destroyed the altar, smashed the holy vessels, plundered the Holy of Holies, banished the services of the priests, and silenced the singing of the Levites. The magnitude of their hatred knew no bounds. Their lust to destroy and plunder overpowered and suppressed any feelings of humanity they may have had. However, their acts of destruction, carried out in the flush of victory, were far from complete. For in their haste, they forgot a minor detail – an insignificant vial of holy oil bearing the seal of the High Priest. Who could blame them for this oversight? Is it appropriate, in a moment of triumph to concern oneself with a tiny crucible? But what a miracle! For it was precisely that disdained, overlooked, and unnoticed immaculate vial of pure oil that was destined to become the symbol of the rebirth of Judaism, and a luminous symbol of the renewal of its spirit. A similar phenomenon can be seen several times in Jewish history. Vengeful and greedy to plunder, the foe breaks into God's sanctuary, turns it into cinders and ashes and leaves its devastated threshold, convinced that with the blow he has dealt us, he has finally cut the thread of our vitality, and that we will never again rise to a normal existence. But somehow, in time, reality gives a lie to these proposals and plans. עם ישראל חי – the seemingly dead body of the nation gradually regains consciousness. Death yields; out of the ruin, new life blossoms. The foe has not achieved his goal. The fault

---

[163] UGGIK #22, December 1932, 1. Original in Polish.

was his alone. Occupied with plundering the external jewels and decorations of the temple, he forgot about the hidden vial of oil. This miraculously-saved, frail remnant is the beginning and cradle of new life for us.

I

According to the Talmud (Bava Batra 4a), King Herod, son of the Iudumean Antypatra, having exterminated the last remnant of the Hasmonean line, and having acquired, with Rome's help, the throne of Judea, killed all Jewish scholars. He thereby wanted to end the principle declared by tradition that a Jewish king must have Jewish origins. By destroying the flower of the nation and the pillars of scholarship, he hoped that he would succeed in deluding and beguiling the common people, conceal his foreign origins, and give his reign an appearance of legitimacy. Herod's dishonorable intentions might have become a reality. The chain of tradition was almost interrupted in his era, if it had not been for that "small vial" which our enemies always somehow seem to forget. Herod didn't destroy all the scholars. He kept one of them, Babi ben Butri, alive in order to be able to use his counsel and wisdom. And it was this same scholar, saved by a miracle, who managed after a while to awaken this monstrous king's conscience, to convince him to rebuild the destroyed Temple, and to repair, at least partly, the evil that he had created. "The surviving remnant" was victorious.

II

Hardly a few decades had passed since these events and another danger threatens Judaism. A mighty enemy is knocking at the gates of Jerusalem. Roman legions, led by Vespasian, are laying siege to the town. Despair overwhelms the Jewish population. It is well known that the Roman legions have no pity. Extermination seems to be inevitable. At this time, a small gate opens secretly in the walls of Jerusalem. In the darkness, there appear silhouettes of human figures carrying a coffin. A short distance from the city, the famous Rabbi Yohanan ben Zakkai steps out of the coffin. Received in a friendly manner by the haughty leader, the Jewish scholar begs the Roman representative to give him the insignificant locality of Yavne. Vespasian scornfully acquiesces to his request. Later, colleagues reproached Yohanan for not rising to the occasion at the critical moment. His request was too modest, too small. He should have asked for something more important. But it became a reality. Yavne was saved. Here, Rabbi Yohanan established a school and educated a large number of students who strengthened and consolidated the nation. Henceforth, study would become the protection and defense of Judaism. The walls of Jerusalem did indeed fall. Rome was victorious. But despite that, Judea was not vanquished. The foe forgot about the "small vial." The vial was Yavne, which became the flame of scholarship and the heart of a scattered and divided nation. The mighty Roman Empire has disappeared from the face of the earth. But the Torah taught so long ago in Yavne is eternal. The small vial has won.

III

Some of the homes of our brothers are like temples deserted by God. The old God of our ancestors has been chased away. He has been replaced by sterile rationalism. The deep thoughts and maxims of our teachers have become mute. Nowadays, shallow, trite platitudes and hazy formulas about the poorly understood modernity and reality are parroted there. Day after day passes without a religious atmosphere, without Sabbath worship. For a religious person, every day has its own unique hue, its own melody, its own characteristic trait. In contrast, for those brothers who are being led astray by rationalism, a special day has to be marked in the calendar rather than written in the heart. After the monotony of work, they search for rest and renewal outside their homes. They run away from their own hearth because their homes are empty. When clouds of anxiety and sorrow darken the luminescence of their sky, no sun of comfort or relief, stemming from a sense of national community, from faith and confidence in a higher being, shines for them. A child is growing up in these orphaned surroundings. A bright child, already acquainted with inanimate technology at a tender age; already initiated into all the secrets and problems of life; an aware child, honest, hard working. But a child without God; without a yearning for the beyond. A child who is, in fact, poor, and is to be pitied because it does not know the bliss that can flow from ideals, from the heights of generosity and love. Once a year, the home takes on a festive though somber appearance. A small light twinkles in the corner battling with the ever-present shadows. A light lit in memory of a father or a grandfather, whose anniversary of death the family is commemorating today. From a portrait on the wall, the deceased watches the lives of his descendants with a sharp eye. Does an ironic smile play on his lips? That light, he seems to be saying, is a symbol of my descendants' attachment to Judaism. That, a twinkling light on the anniversary of my death, is the entire treasury of their religious feeling. A small vial of oil. Nothing more. Will the small vial be victorious? Will this single, modest little light be capable of dispersing the darkness, and igniting a spark of love in the hearts of future generations towards their nation, towards their parents?...

IIII

The Jewish nation is pressed by boundless burdens of suffering. Hatred from the outside, and poverty from the inside. Our youth is wasting away. Hope for a better future is melting away. Our only joy is blooming in the East. A silent, deep joy. A new Jewish reality is being established in the Holy Land. A new generation is growing up on the old land. The eyes of millions of believers are turned towards it. A land of eternal longing. The cradle and source of religion. The fire of faith. Our only harbor for the future! Our small vial. Will the miracle of Hanukkah repeat itself? Will there be enough oil? Let us believe and work for it! Let us work and believe!

THE BROKEN TABLETS[164]
A Resonance of Bygone Festivals of Revelation

The question poised on our lips is whether the aristocratic, ennobling Divine Torah has in any way influenced humanity, nations, or world events. Have the Ten Commandments, proclaimed at Sinai, been imprinted on human memory? Have they become blazing deeds, or have they merely remained blazing words?

The Talmud tells the following story: When Moses left heaven after receiving the Torah, Satan came before God and said: "Master of the Universe, Torah *heichan hi* – where is the Torah – the Divine wisdom?" "I gave it to the earth," replied God. Satan then turned to the earth, which answered: "God alone knows the whereabouts of the Torah. I do not have it." Satan inquired of the sea. *"Ein imadi* – the Torah is not in my possession," the sea thundered in reply. Finally, Satan descended to the netherworld, into the abyss, in order to search for the Torah there. Out of the depth of the abyss, the reply rang out, *"ein bi* – the Torah is not with me." "I have searched over the entire world, and I have been unable to find the Torah, the divine wisdom, anywhere," complained Satan. "Go to Moses," said the Eternal One, "perhaps he will be able to tell to you where the Torah may be found" (Shabbat 89a).

Satan shudders and with him all satanic powers shudder and tremble, when they learn that a new Torah, a new wisdom, may be coming into the world. They fear every new ideal that could terminate their dark dominion. Mankind, they fear, might be influenced by it, and possibly seek a new direction. The Torah was given in Satan's absence and without his knowledge (Sanhedrin 26). Soon, Satan discovers the birth of a new ideal, the beginning of a new era. Since he was unable to prevent the revelation of the Torah to mankind, it appears that Satan has taken on a new assignment. He occupies himself incessantly in bringing proof that the Torah has had no effect on human nature; that it does not have the power

---

[164] UGGIK #56, May 1934, 5-6. Original in German.

to re-forge and change it. His Mephistophelian laugh resounds mockingly in heaven. "Where is the Torah? Where is its influence? Where is the evidence of its much publicized power?" He struts down to earth in order to discover how extensively the Torah has transformed it. He sees for himself that the earth knows nothing of the Torah. *Ki mal'ah haaretz hamas.* As in former times, before the revelation, deception and subjugation, enslavement and oppression rule the earth. "Where is the Torah"? It is not the Torah itself that Satan is looking for. He is searching for its influence on human character; for the revolution it was supposed to bring to mankind, to his worldview, to his ethical sensitivity. He cannot find evidence of that transformation on earth. Robbery and indecent assault cast their dark shadows here (Hosea 4:2). The earth is wrapped in a shroud of mourning. Satan turns to the sea. The sea, which was created to connect the continents, and unseal vast horizons for humanity, have long ago ceased being in a state of peace. Here too, there is war and conflict. Here too, hatred rages. Men pursue each other even on the ocean floor. Alone, under the ocean's surface, they rage at each other. "Where is the Torah"? "Go to man, to Moses. Perhaps a spark of the Torah still glows in his heart."

Today, we too must ask, not sarcastically or satanically, not spitefully or maliciously, but rather sadly and ground down with pain, where is the Torah? Where is the beneficial influence of the Torah on humanity, whose revelation we are celebrating? Are we supposed to examine man's heart to see whether the light of the Torah still burns there? But *akov halev mikol* – the heart is deceitful above all things, and desperately wicked; who can know it? (Jeremiah 17:9) Have we not placed our trust in the human heart? And didn't this heart of man, this much-heralded humanitarianism, disillusion and deceive us? Where then is the Torah?

During the shaping of the golden calf, Satan wanted to confuse the Jewish people and their ideal, so he created a mirage of Moses' coffin in the air, in order to convince the people that Moses, their leader, had died, and that it was therefore permissible to worship idols.

In these terrible times, we too believe that sometimes we see a coffin floating in the air in which lie, lifeless, the Mosaic ideals and the ashes of Jewish wisdom. Moses' ideals appear to be dead. Satan has triumphed...

II

Is this pessimistic mood justified? Let us next examine the historical foundation of our Festival of Shevuot, of Revelation!

The two stone tablets, which God gave to Moses, were to serve as an everlasting reminder and an eternal monument to the Mosaic revelation (Exodus 31:18). But Moses broke these first stone tablets when the people created the Golden Calf and betrayed God. Only fragments of these stone tablets remained. After reconciliation with God, Moses received a second set of stone tablets. Moses brought these second stone tablets to the people on the Day of Atonement. Why then, isn't there the slightest reminder attached to the Day of Atonement about the receipt of the second tablets which, contrary to the first, remained whole and undamaged? Why is our entire attention focused solely on the first, which were, after all, smashed?

Because for us ideals do not lose their meaning and brilliance when they become desecrated, smashed into pieces, or demolished. Mere crushed chips of stone remained from the first tablets. Only splinters of our ideas and ideals shine to us from the chaos of the world. We, however, venerate even broken tablets. We keep hoping and believing that the shattered pieces will, one day, come together to form a whole; that the fragments will once again be joined together into whole stone tablets. The intact and the broken first tablets lay next to each other in the holy Tabernacle (Berahot 8b). We have never been reduced to desecrating and destroying the remnants of our holy objects. We have never undermined our ideals when, abandoned and alone, they have been smashed against the cliffs of life. On the contrary, we have collected the remnants and carried them with us...

And indeed, have we not survived to see the miracle of the splinters come together and become whole again? Have we not witnessed parts, torn asunder come together into a new community? Haven't we defied all satanic powers and, despite derision from all forms of devils, haven't we accomplished, or more correctly haven't we begun, something that should fill us with a feeling of pride and satisfaction? Didn't they openly deride and scoff at Theodore Herzl just a short time ago in Vienna and call him "king of Zion"? And didn't a united world Jewry recently celebrate the 25th anniversary of the founding of Tel Aviv, the first stage in the fulfillment of Herzl's dream? "Do not scorn," says the Talmud "an old man who, because of loss of memory, has forgotten his knowledge," since these broken tablets were also stored in the holy Tabernacle. And this old man, who may no longer be able to follow your supple intellect, your lofty thoughts, is like those broken tablets from which we may not withhold reverence and respect. The nations of the world despise the Jewish people, that old man who has forgotten his knowledge, and have labeled us as unproductive and uncreative. We have destroyed this lie. Tel Aviv is a symbol of the awakened Jewish people, and a sign of the resurrection of Eretz Yisrael. It is an expression of the untiring and inexhaustible Jewish creative power; an expression of our desire to rebuild and reconstruct. It is proof that as long as splinters of our ideals still exist, and as long as a spark of hope still shines in a nation, Satan has not yet won, Satan must not yet rejoice...

In these days of joy and celebration over the Jewish town of so much promise, my gaze wonders longingly to our broken tablets, to Jerusalem. For just as Tel Aviv represents our whole tablets with which we confront the world and on which is written, "Judea lives and will continue to live," so Jerusalem, which hides the wreckage of our Jewish holiness, remains the city of our yearning, the city of our Jewish dreams. "Your air is life for our Jewish soul" (Yehudah Halevi). Whoever has experienced you once will carry your landscape, your sun, your sky, eternally in his heart. But who can describe the thousand years of sorrow that rest on your peaks? Who can explain the meaning of the quiet, serene wisdom of your valleys? When mother Rachel arises from her tomb near Jerusalem each night to watch over her children, she sees before her a curious picture. On the one hand there are the somewhat too noisy, boisterous children of Tel Aviv, and on the other, the white-bearded solemn men of Jerusalem whose faces radiate the brilliance of Kabalistic secrets; the worldly tumult of the new city, and the majestic stillness of the old town. Confused, she turns her glance heavenward to God, who in the Holy Land is so close to man, and her lips bring forth a fervent prayer: "Let, Oh God, the spirit of Tel Aviv and the soul of Jerusalem become one. Let there be a union between the cleverness of Tel Aviv, and the radiant wisdom of Jerusalem; the zest for life with the solemnity, the thirst for enterprise with the dream, the worldly with the holy. Build O God, an arc of fire from the old to the new." And together with her, we too pledge אם אשכחך ירושלים – if I forget thee O Jerusalem, let my right hand wither." Only when Jerusalem and Tel Aviv no longer vie with each other; only when the heart of Jerusalem and the head of Tel Aviv have both found a home within the Jewish people, will the broken Jewish tablets once again become whole, and only then will Israel once again become the messenger bearing God's tidings at Sinai.

Then Satan's accusations and mockery will also be silenced for

יגער ה' בך השטן ויגער ה' בך הבחר בירושלים

God will chase you away, O Satan

He, who chose Jerusalem

THEODORE HERZL[165]
1860 – 1904

Barely thirty years have passed since the death of Theodore Herzl, and his dream has already partly come true, and continues to come ever closer to reality. The road from vision to action, from dream to reality, is long and remote, thorny and rough. Sometimes, 200 years pass before an idea, pronounced by a prophet or visionary, leaves the heights of fantasy and the loftiness of the imagination, and comes to life. Many of our prophets paint a picture of a blissful future and then add the words והיה באחרית הימים – and it shall come to pass in the end of days, to indicate that their prophesies will only be fulfilled in the distant future; that their pronouncements and ideas were far removed from becoming a reality. Their contemporaries considered their beautiful proclamations to be nothing more than dreams and illusions, and the prophets became a public laughing stock. People would jeer them, point their fingers at them and cry out: "There is that crazy prophet, that mad thinker" (Hosea 9:7). Providence spared Herzl that unpleasant fate. Though at the beginning he was misunderstood and mocked, he was nevertheless able to find a group of friends and followers who embraced his ideas, interpreted them, and disseminated them widely. The people, reacting instinctively and intuitively, felt that a new era in the history of this persecuted and scattered Jewish people was dawning; an era of action, heroism, and freedom.

But there can be no physical liberation without prior spiritual liberation. We have always prayed על גאולתנו ועל פחת נפשנו – for liberation of the body, and freedom for the soul. For hundreds of years, the Jewish soul filled every corner of the Beit Hamidrash with prayer, yearning, mysticism, and poetry. It avoided the secular activities of a crowded and noisy world. It withdrew from the political battles and physical struggles of the medieval world. It

---

[165] UGGIK #56, May 1934, 4. Original in Polish.

confined itself to a land of visions. It slept through the era of the awakening of nations; of the renaissance of art and knowledge, and did not notice the birth of a new world and a new human being. It passively survived uprisings and revolutions in its own surroundings; uninvolved, sunk deep in thought and pious divine reflection. From time to time, the quiet of the Jewish street was interrupted by savage mobs demanding blood and booty. The voices of the tormentors would then tear through the air, and grown young men, in the strength of their years, hid fearfully and trembling in cellars. They did not rise in opposition. Instead, they stared in terror and awaited the enemy, and then gave up their souls with the prayer, "shema," on their lips...We were paralyzed. We were burdened by an eternal dream. It overwhelmed us into boundless indifference. We became accustomed not to act; we renounced self-defense. We became a people without a will of our own, without aspirations. In the midst of this desperate situation, Theodore Herzl appeared with a call to action, to self-sufficient, creative work. He awoke the nation from a lethargic sleep. He breathed a new desire to live into it. He revived it with a new burst of energy. Once again, the Jewish nation became a subject instead of an object, of history...

Jewish energy, slumbering unused and restrained for years, accomplished miracles. Hands that had never worked, magically created out of the desert land of their fathers, long left deserted and empty, beautiful orchards, forested areas, and built modern cities and settlements out of sand dunes. Palestine, rejuvenated and settled by Jewish pioneers, is blooming and gradually changing into Eretz Yisrael. Jewish children, whom Mendele called, "small Jews," rather than children because they had never experienced the blissful, carefree, freedom of youth and a profound sadness already lurked in their eyes, are developing in an atmosphere of freedom and national consciousness. In the cultural sphere, many treasures have been developed with the hard labor of love. These include schools and institutions of higher learning, scholarly projects on Mt. Tzofim,[166] a large number of publishing houses, an exuberant and

---

[166] The Hebrew University opened in 1923.

multi-opinionated press, and most important, the revival of the Hebrew language. And above all these blessed accomplishments, developed with blood and sweat and wrapped in the yearnings and pain of millions of our suffering brothers; above this prayed-for dream-come-true, which for thousands represents their last hope and harbor, hovers the spirit of Theodore Herzl, that most beautiful personality of the last era; that genial visionary who was not allowed to live to see the fulfillment and development of his creation. He came to us from estranged regions, from assimilated surroundings, and from people who had no national identity, to present us with a gift of his idea; to share his fire, his enthusiasm, and his splendid appearance with us. He completed his assigned task, and left us, for ever...

His mortal remains rest in the Moedling cemetery.[167] His spirit lives on in each of us who has become familiar with him, who grew to love him, and who has felt the tragedy of his life. Today, on the 30th anniversary of his death, his pleading voice resounds, calling us to unity and harmony; to the continuation and fruitful completion of his work. We live at a pivotal point in our history, when the fate of the Jewish people hangs in the balance ואם לא עכשיו אימתי – and if, at this moment, we don't mobilize and concentrate our efforts, who knows whether we will be granted another opportunity for the rebirth and revival of our nation? May the memory of our leader be a strong knot that joins us all for harmonious work in the development of our national hearth in Eretz Israel! May the memory of Theodore Herzl, henceforth, be a source of courage and faith in our victory; a source of hope and confidence in our future work.

[167] In accordance with his last will, his remains were re-interred on Mount Herzl in Jerusalem in August 1949.

HERZL'S DREAM[168]

Thirty years have passed since Theodore Herzl breathed his last. News of his death spread through the Jewish world like wildfire and the Jewish soul was overcome with grief and mourning. A royal leader had died. His bright spirit lit the cloudy sky of the Jewish people like a meteor; tore through the darkness; drove away the mist, and pointed to a new way in the remote distance.

Herzl was consumed by an idea. When he left the arena of mortal activity, he was barely 44 years old. His dazzling good looks, radiating elegance, a buoyant personality, and exuberant health gradually changed until we saw, in the last years of his life, a wrinkled and bent figure, the majestic frame leaning on a walking stick and bent towards the floor, the shine of his bright eyes dimmed, and his kind face reflecting evidence of his sick heart. That heart, which could no longer bear the burden of Jewish suffering and Jewish humiliation. That heart, which was often the target for venomous arrows, shot at him by various Jewish factions. Herzl's pure heart, full of love, was suddenly stilled. Multitudes cried at his bier. The mouths of thousands of his brothers in the East, languishing and hoping for salvation, recited the last prayer for the dead – "Yitkadal, veyitkadash, shemei rabah." Those children of poverty in the East; those eternal dreamers of the Messiah's deliverance; they, who at midnight on the 9th of Av cry over the destruction of Zion; they, who place ashes on their bodies and take the holy soil of Eretz Yisrael with them into the grave – they immediately understood Herzl. And after his death, it is they who felt orphaned.

In one of his philosophical discussions, Herzl described four young men, who had just finished their University studies and sat in a tavern saying good-bye to each other. Each had his diploma. Now, their roads would part. Each had different expectations from life.

---

[168] UGGIK #58, June 1934, 5-6. Original in German.

The first said, "I want wealth. Wealth is the way to satisfy all human wishes. Wealth can make one independent and happy."

The second said, "I want honor. To be honored by one's fellow man is surely the greatest of joys. Every mark of esteem, every acknowledgement of superiority, is also an expression of submission."

The third student spoke, "wealth and honor do not always bring happiness and are not always attainable. My wish is a modest one. I would like a middle class income and a happy home."

The last student now spoke, "I am still not clear about what I want. I am still not finished with myself. The best I can do is to say that I wish for something that will be fulfilling."

The students decided to come together again in 20 years to see how they had fared. The years passed by quickly, and finally, the day approached when the four friends – the one who wished for wealth, the one who wanted honor, the one whose life's dream was to find family happiness, and the one who was searching for something that was fulfilling, came together again in the same tavern.

"I achieved it!" started the millionaire. "I am rich. I worked hard. I sank many times, but I was always able to climb out again."

"And what is it like on top?" asked his friends.

"Not especially pleasant. If I were to stop struggling, I would die of boredom. So I don't stop. I push on. Will I remain rich or will I die from overwork? That is the question that perpetually haunts me, and this uncertainty is in fact the only thing that excites me, and keeps me going."

The second, who had longed for honor, now spoke: "I am much respected. I am a high official and possess a high sounding title. In my early years, I searched for patrons; now I am one. But I am not happy. I can never act freely lest I damage my position and my image. My honor imprisons me. It is as if I lived in a room whose walls are completely covered with mirrors. One careless move and a mirror will shatter. People no longer greet *me* – they only greet my position..."

Then the family man spoke: "I established the middle class life I had hoped for. I have healthy children and adequate material comforts. And yet, deep down, I have a feeling of emptiness...

Loneliness overwhelms me. Why am I here? This will last another 20 or 30 years. I will win or lose a certain number of cases in my legal practice. I will continue to pay my taxes on schedule. My house budget will come out exactly even. But to what end? What is the purpose of it all? Can anyone tell me – what is it all about?."...

Then the last one spoke: "We have heard about the privation of wealth, the humiliation of honor, and the lack of content in middle class family life. Let me tell you about my life. I have neither wealth, nor honor, nor even a middle class home. Nevertheless, I am happy for I have found something that fulfills me. I established a poor-house, and I live together with the poor. I have trained a professional staff of good-natured young people, and, together, we provide a much needed education for the poor. I try to show the poor how generous, large, and beautiful the world is. I teach them to hope and to continue the struggle. I console them and give them courage. I strengthen the despairing and help straighten those who are bowed down. I am happy that I am with the poor; that I suffer with them. I feel that I am a citizen of the future because I am working for the future. I feel immortal, eternal and not ephemeral since my work is immortal, eternal, and imperishable..."

That tale that Theodore Herzl tells is a mirror of Jewish fate in the last era. We too are standing on the threshold of emancipation holding a diploma of equal rights and civil equality, and we too ask "whereto?" We are closing our academies, leaving the ghetto walls behind us, storming out of the darkness of the narrow Jewish street into the brightness of the foreign world, which was inaccessible to us for so long. Many strove for wealth because they thought that gold would achieve equality and recognition from the Christian world. They acquired wealth, but their Jewishness was not forgiven by that world. Others thirsted for honor. They were delighted if they could acquire a title and they did not shirk from the baptismal font, if that would assure them a State position. But all these ranks, positions, titles, and honors turned out to be false coins and defective life preservers in times of trouble. The vast Jewish masses wanted only to lead a comfortable, narrow existence, and did not want to be reminded of their Jewish origins and responsibilities. As a result, there arose those smug Jewish types who outwardly appeared cultivated and satisfied, but who, inwardly, were decaying, broken, and hollow. Who were no longer capable of receiving support and comfort from anything that was inherited and handed down. Who no longer had roots; who had lost their connection with Jewish society, and who were objects of derision and pity in the foreign world. One man stood up from among their midst, rejected wealth, threw away honors, divested himself of the veneer of lies that were spun around the correspondent of the "Neue Freie Presse," the Parisian's "lady's man."[169] Agitated, he was looking for something that would completely fulfill him. He no longer wanted, could no longer tolerate the mercies of others. No more groveling, serving, flattering, feigning affect, and denying his own identity. He no longer wanted to be merely tolerated by others. His self-confidence, his Jewishness was forcefully stifled within him. But suddenly, through his degradation, his violated self-confidence reared itself up within him. Then, this uncrowned Jewish king straightened to his full stature and strode proudly and majestically before the heads of state of Europe, and spoke to them in a voice not used by Jews since the last uprising of Bar Kochba. "In the name of millions who have been deprived of rights; in the name of those innumerable innocent people, who at various times and in various lands, were killed by bloody, murdering hands; in the name of those whom the fanatic Church enthusiasts caused to be burned on the pyres of Spain; in the name of those on whose blood inhumane hordes of Cossacks became drunk in Russia; in the name of those sad, decaying, slowly dying masses in the East, I, Theodore Herzl, in whose veins flows pure, noble Jewish blood, demand from you, who have made us an object of contempt and persecution, a place in the sun; a corner where my hunted brothers may rest. For we will no longer tolerate our children being strangled, our wives violated, and our old people abused. We, young Jewish men, will no longer bleed on your battlefields, only to be branded by you afterwards as traitors. We don't want our youth

---

[169] Before he founded the Zionist movement, Herzl was an assimilated bon vivant, a popular correspondent of the Viennese newspaper, "Neue Freie Presse," and a playwright.

to grow up in an environment of hate, contempt, and humiliation any more." Thus spoke Theodore Herzl, the voice of a thousand years of Jewish suffering and martyrdom. And when his sick heart stopped forever thirty years ago, there died with him one of the greatest interpreters of the Jewish tragedy; one of the greatest visionaries of Jewish freedom...

What prompted Herzl to take a stand on the Jewish question? What suddenly diverted him from an artistic path, and catapulted him to become a leader of his people? Perhaps it was the very artist in him, for, above all else, he was an artist. The ugly face of Jewish poverty wounded him precisely in the same way as a flat note hurts a musician. The caricature of Jewish existence in *golus* evoked his disgust. The artist in him struggled against the distortions, dislocations, and shriveling of the Jewish *golus* psyche. The artist within him bristled at saying "yes" and "amen" to a world in which it is possible to condemn one of its oldest cultures to a physical and psychological nomadic state. And since it was as an artist that Herzl first experienced and became conscious of the problems of the Jews, he utilized those devices that artists primarily rely on – intuition and fantasy.

Without knowing much about earlier attempts to solve Jewish problems; without delving into the history of Zionism which had its origins, in the form of Messianism, as early as the first Jewish exile; without knowing the emotion, peculiar nature, and mentality of his brothers, Herzl approached the problems of the Jews with his fiery heart, with his rich, energetic fantasy, and with his creative storehouse of intuition. Whereas, during the profound deliberations of Chovvei Zion, Ahad Haam wrote his phlegmatic essays on the condition of the Jewish people, Herzl's fantasy wove a richly colored tapestry of the future in the form of "Judenstaat."

We must never forget that a poet stood at the cradle of the modern Jewish renaissance movement. But our patriotic feelings must never be expressed in forms that would deeply offend those true Zionists who drew their Zionist inspiration from the Prophets and the songs of Yehudah Halevi. Long is the road over which each one of us must travel back in order to find our own pure Jewish soul. It will take a long time for the crust of the *galut*, formed around our hearts over a period of a thousand years of exile, to peel off. We no longer have to use Herzl's words, "if you will it, it is no dream," for even if we don't want it, it is no longer only a dream. A generation is growing up in Eretz Yisrael that no longer knows the *galut*. The rivulet started by Herzl has long ago left its banks of narrowness of a party, and, today, flows powerfully around the entire people. Herzl's dream has become a reality. Herzl's dream has become a deed.

CHAIM NACHMAN BIALIK[170]

When Rabbi Zeira, one of the most distinguished sages of the Talmud died, it was said of him: "Babylon gave birth to him; Eretz Yisrael matured him and made him great; the town of Tiberias has lost its jewel." (Mo'ed Katan 25)

Chaim Nachman Bialik's cradle stood in the *Galuth*; the breezes of Eretz Yisrael, once breathed by Prophets and Sages, blew over him in the evening of his life; Tel Aviv, where he last lived and worked, has, through his premature departure, lost its jewel and crown.

The entire nation is plunged into deep mourning. In exile, Jewry is crying. The Yishuv is grieving. Tel Aviv is orphaned.

I

Bialik's personality and poetry can only be understood in light of his life experiences. The man and his work constitute one entity. Like body and soul. Like a melody and the instrument that gives it voice. His birthplace was a Volhynian village. His childhood blossomed in the richness of nature. Woods and meadows; babbling brooks; and radiant sun... But soon his father died, and poverty and privation moved into the widow's home. His grandfather, a stern and pious man who meted out punishment fondly, took over raising the boy. The poet has only sad recollections of his childhood: "My father was the bitter *golus*; poverty, my gloomy mother." And do you know where his songs came from? In his father's house, concealed in a crevice, there was one solitary songbird – a cricket, the songbird of poverty. When night caused all sounds in the house to cease, it would begin to chirp its monotonous melody. On Friday evenings, when the children soothed their pangs of hunger with dry bread and herring, and sang the Sabbath songs in hoarse voices, its voice was also part of the choir. In the wee hours of the morning, his mother would get up and, with her last bit of strength she would knead bread for her little ones. A tear flowed from her eyes into the dough, and

---

[170] UGGIK #60, July 1934, 6-8. Original in German.

became part of the bread eaten by her children. The reflection of this tear shines forth in all its hues and colors from Bialik's poetry. Even when he laughs, it does not completely disappear…

Bialik comes to the *Bet Hamidrash*. Here, the entire range of Jewish literature becomes accessible to him. He travels its breadth and width. One day, he would become the poet of the Jewish house of study; a witness of its tragedy, its longing, and of the inner conflicts of its youths. Until then, who knew anything about the *yeshiva bochur?* About the *Beit Hamidrash* youth? Who knew about his burning soul, his unquenchable thirst for knowledge, his iron will, his self-destructive energy, and the languishing zest for life that he suppresses with all the force at his command? He sits with his pale face to the wall for six years. Outside, nature unfolds all its charms to try to entice him away from his post. But he resists its seduction. Spring and summer leave him cold and indifferent. The tree in front of the academy becomes green, and finally bare. The *bachur* does not notice. The half darkened room resounds with the melancholy sing-song of the students. This mesmerizing, yet fiery, melody will accompany the *beit hamidrash* student everywhere, throughout his life. Its echo follows him into the hubbub of daily life. Early each morning, before the sun has gently lifted the curtain of darkness of the night, he hurries past the garden and meadow into the schoolhouse. Stars are still twinkling in the sky; the grass is whispering mysteriously; a cool breeze rustles his locks of hair; and his tired, strained eyes are begging for a little more sleep. He is almost ready to surrender to nature's temptation. But his sense of duty awakens. He remembers the lectern that is awaiting him in the study hall, and in a few minutes he is bent over a folio of the Talmud. His drowsy eyes, overcome by sleep, pass over the letters, yellowed by the light of the tallow…

Bialik is the bard of the Jewish house of study. He is its enthusiastic, devoted admirer; but also its critic. Instinctively, he questions the utility of this heroism, and the purpose for this martyrdom. He was influenced by the philosophy of the Enlightenment. He stands "on the threshold of the Beit Hamidrash" – he no longer belongs inside…

Bialik carried great treasures out of the Beit Hamidrash. Here, and later at the Yeshiva of Volozin, he acquired a thorough grounding in Jewish literature. Here, he found the spring that fed his national and romantic poetry. Here, the Shechina unveiled its countenance to him...

The waves of the Enlightenment dash themselves ever more powerfully against the walls of this Jewish bastion. The youth runs away into the world, where the springs of European culture babble. "The wind has carried everything away. The light has scattered everything. Only I alone am left." Then the Shechina wraps its broken wing around the poet. She is afraid that he, too, might be swept away...

In 1903, Bialik revealed himself for the first time to his people as their National Poet. The dreadful pogroms in Kishinev found their Jeremiah in him. He paints the cruel scenes of murder with shuddering, graphic power. Pale faces of men stare at us; violated women; strangled children. In his "City of Slaughter," he castigates the cowardice of the murdered and their lack of resistance in the face of death with a poetic power of expression.

The Jewish people heaved a sigh of relief. At last, here was someone who could scream their pain to the world. The afflictions of our time weigh us down so heavily because we don't have a Bialik, who can capture the hell of our existence in words. And so, we stutter and stammer, and speak of our suffering – in faded, used up words...

II

Every attempt to translate and interpret Bialik's poetry into a foreign language is frustrated at its outset. Every translation remains, in the end, only a weak reflection of the original. That is, perhaps, the best evidence of his uniqueness and originality. His spirit is at home only in Judaism and only there does it shine in all its splendor. His language is so deeply rooted in Hebrew sources, is so anchored to the entire strata and spheres of our literature, that they are organically bound to the essence of his poetry. Separate the form and you wound and mute the content.

Bialik's memory should admonish us to provide our children with a Jewish education so that they will be able to experience Bialik and have a feeling for his creations. The hymns of praise ringing out everywhere now, shortly after his death, brings to mind the words of Lessing: "Who will not praise a Klopstock creation?[171] But does anyone read him? No! We would rather have less praise and more assiduous readers!" All the tributes, titles, hymns of praise, and epithets have little in common with true appreciation. Once, when a prayer leader extolled God's greatness by listing a profusion of attributes, "oh You great, heroic, terrifying, mighty, etc.," Rabbi Hanina called out ironically, "have you finally exhausted the praise of your God?" (Megillah 25). That is what we do with anything or any phenomenon that transcends the bounds of the usual and the routine. But a description of a flower, even an exact portrayal of its size, color, and fragrance, can never replace the experience of actually seeing it. One, who has never seen it, will never be able to correctly visualize it. It is impossible to experience a musical composition from a written description. Similarly, all who become familiar with Bialik in a foreign garb will find only a weak echo of his true genius.

The magic of his poems is at least partly due to the fact that he allows us only a premonition of whatever moves him. He skirts us along the edge of an abyss into which we can only gaze through the thin, transparent mist of his words. He complains that he still has a rift in his heart; a song that never found expression in words. He took it with him to the grave. "Whence came the rays," ask the elders "that surrounded Moses' body? When Moses wrote down the Torah, a drop of ink remained adhering to his pen. He rubbed the pen over his body and a crown of rays was formed." Moses' greatness is contained in the drop of ink with which he never wrote; the last secret of the Torah, which he never revealed to man. How beautiful would Bialik's last song have been, if he had only shared it with us...

The significance and value of Bialik's poems also lies in the pictures they paint of a rapidly vanishing era of our history. Just as

<hr>

[171] German lyric poet, Friedrich Gottlieb Klopstock (1724-1803).

Mendele,[172] in his stories, froze pictures of the "*shtetls*" for future ethnic historians, so it was Bialik's destiny to perpetuate the romance with the Beit Hamidrash and the religious experience of his time. When the "Jewish street" was slowly disappearing and the rhythm of the old, traditional way of life was disintegrating, it was time to capture this collapsing world in a literary form in order to preserve its images for posterity. Where once a candle flickered, electric lights now burn brightly; where once Mendele's wagon was pulled by a horse, automobiles now speed by. Like his external living conditions, the inner life of the Jew has also changed. Many of the images for which we search in vain in our surroundings, we will find eternally fresh in Bialik's poetry.... But it is exteremely difficult for us to reconstruct the inner spiritual world of the erstwhile Babylonian or Spanish Jews. Dry historical dates and descriptions are insufficient. Even authentically transmitted discussions seldom fit together to form a complete picture. The poet is still the best historian. He writes the history of the soul of his people...

III

Bialik was not only a poet with the sublime pathos and ethos of a prophet. He was, above all else, the people's teacher, his contemporaries' instructor. He opened the world of Aggada and the treasures of the poetry of the middle ages, and made it accessible for the common man. Bialik collected the jewels of Jewish thought scattered in the tractates of the Talmud and Midrashim, shaped them linguistically, combined them, and formed a crown. The splinters came together in his masterful hands into perfect forms, which, for the first time, allowed us to understand the true development of the Jewish worldview. His scholarly work has one purpose: to present the old in an attractive form, and thereby enable ancient wisdom to become the possession of the entire people. He has reverence for all products of Jewish genius. He affirms the totality of Judaism and

---

[172] Mendele Moher Seforim (Mendele, the bookseller), is the pen name of Shalom Jacob Abramovitch (1835-1917) who is known as the grandfather of Yiddish literature. He was especially celebrated for his ability to depict the plight of the poor Jews living in the shtetls of the Russian Pale settlement.

all phases of its historical development. He derives linguistic and philosophic building blocks from all strata of Jewish literature for his brilliant creation. He breathes new life into old expressions, long considered to be dead. He marries a concept from the esoteric doctrine of the *Kabala* with a prophetic figure of speech; a word from the Babylonian Talmud with a definition from Spanish Jewish philosophy, and thus builds bridges between cultural eras.

It is no wonder that even the *Halacha*, that often misunderstood, disdained, and by many considered not to be in keeping with the times, casuistic, and life-denying religious-legal part of Jewish scholarship, found an intelligent and warm champion in Bialik. The *Aggada*, which contains spiritually rich explanations, clarifications, legends, sayings, and instructive ethical statements, was the product of fantasy. The *Halacha*, was the embodiment of the will of the people. It consists of the innumerable laws and rules that frame the life of a religious Jew, and, if viewed superficially, discipline, burden, and harden his determination. The religious Jew must always be prepared to be as "strong as a lion and as agile as a deer" in order to carry out the wish of the Creator. The *Shulchan Aruch*,[173] with its many complex regulations, does not allow our energy to slumber, and keeps our determination strong, alert, and prepared to act. It is precisely this *halacha*, containing jurisprudence, social ethical ideals, and pronouncements regarding the administration of justice and the social order, that continues to be a model, and is unsurpassed to this very day. The awakened Eretz Yisrael especially needed Bialik to lift this treasure out of obscurity and show the world its full beauty. Imagine, for example, how many conflicts could be avoided if the relationship between employer and employee were based on the principles of Jewish ethics. How many of the aberrations and unhealthy manifestations of assimilation would have disappeared from the life of the new *Yishuv*, if tradition were the foundation and theme of the rebuilding. For this reason, Bialik always endeavored to revive the tradition; to clean off the crust of *golus*; to shell out the genuine kernel, and to blend it with

[173] A compendium of Jewish Law by Joseph Caro (1488-1575).

the new into a rejuvenated form. "Back to the sources!" was his solution. For only dependence on a shared past will abolish strife from our midst and ensure a unified, shared, future.

IV

With a heavy heart, Bialik had to witness the ghosts of fragmentation and party squabbles disrupt the work of reconstruction in the new Eretz Yisrael. "I am sick and the *Yishuv* is sick," he said before his departure for Vienna. It was the *Yishuv's* illness and not his own, that left him pessimistic about the future. He never missed an opportunity to reproach the nation bitterly. He was honored, praised, beloved, and truly respected. But he spurned all homage and used the ceremonies and meetings, often organized to honor him, as opportunities to reprimand his brothers for their ignorance and assimilation and to harshly castigate the parties for their fanaticism. "At the wedding reception of one of the sons of Rabina, the Sages said to Rav Hanina, 'Sing a song!' So he sang, 'woe, we shall die; woe, we shall die' (Berahot 31)." All around him was the joyful jubilation of the wedding guests, and Rav Hanina thought about death. Similarly, into the happy rhythm of the rebuilding of Eretz Yisrael, Bialik interjects his warning and his disturbing cry: "Woe, we are going to perish! Woe, we are going to perish," if we don't correct our faults in time.

All the parties and factions joined around Bialik's coffin. The anger, though, is still great; the animosity is still inflexible and obstinate. But, at least for the duration of the period of mourning, the din in the opposing camps has indeed become quieter and more subdued. All pause out of respect for the poet and teacher who, for the first time speaks to us not in words, but in the silence of death...

Jewish tradition believes that at midnight on *Hoshana Rabah* the heavens open, and all wishes and prayers made in this brief moment will be fulfilled. The gates of heaven have opened wide for this short period of time, to allow Chaim Nachman Bialik's soul to enter. In this solemn moment, we want to express a wish, his wish: Shalom! Peace! The death of one of our Jewish leaders tore us apart. May the death of a great poet bring us together!

The Jewish people have woven mysterious stories around the death of its poets.

Yehudah Halevi, driven by an overpowering yearning, traveled to Eretz Yisrael. He left his beautiful home in Spain so that he could kiss the ground of Zion. He had hardly arrived in the Holy Land, when his tracks are lost. His end is unknown. There is a story that an Arab killed him. Mystery surrounds his last hour...

The death of the divine poet, Solomon ibn Gabirol, is also shrouded in darkness. The story is that a Moorish poet, envious of his poetry, locked him in his garden and treacherously murdered him. He buried his coffin under a tree. The tree produced miraculous blossoms and its fruit drew the attention of the King. As a result, the tree was dug up and the coffin of the murdered poet was found. The Moor paid for his wicked deed with his life.

What story might someday be woven around the death of Bialik? Perhaps our children's children will, one day, tell the following tale: It happened on the 20th day of Tammuz in the year 5694 as the entire Jewish world began to commemorate the 30th anniversary of Herzl's death. Herzl looked down from heaven at his life's work and saw that it was blossoming and becoming ever more beautiful. But he also saw that the serpent of brotherly hatred was gnawing at its roots. Sorrowfully, he came before God and said: "Master of the universe! Why did you allow my work to blossom, only to destroy it? Have I and innumerable of my followers sacrificed ourselves, only to have it all sink into chaos?" Then God answered him: "Hold on! I will warn them and shake them up! I will take away one of their greatest to make them listen carefully and quake!" So spoke the Almighty on the 20th of Tammuz, 5694.

And on Tammuz 21, 5694, Chaim Nachman Bialik died. Silence descended on the Jewish world. The leaders bowed their heads in shame. All pondered the simple obituary that the poet wrote for himself:

> *"After my death — bewail me thus:*
> *There was a man and see; he is no more..."*

HERZL AND BIALIK[174]

I

United in Death

An impenetrable, dreadful mystery surrounds the moment of death of even the most ordinary of human beings. A unique destiny rushes him towards his end. A circle of life is closing. Before us lies creation and passing; the act of being and of drifting away of a human being. At this point, you can describe and interpret what that person has experienced, suffered, and created. You can sanction it or condemn it; admire it or deride it; preserve it or destroy it. But you can no longer add anything to this vanished life, nor take anything away from it. No line can be removed or altered from this painting. It is finished and irrevocable. The master has departed and taken his paints with him. Henceforth, you can only examine and contemplate...

And as we contemplate Herzl's and Bialik's painting, we find that the coincidence of their dates of death[175] possesses an immeasurably symbolic power for us. Thirty years separate their deaths. A considerable length of time. But the space that separated the spheres of their lives is larger. Where is the road that connects Budapest, Herzl's birthplace, and the village of Radi in Volhynia, in which Bialik's cradle rocked? What connection is there between the man of belle lettres and witty correspondent of the "Neue Freie Presse," who writes fine, artistic pieces and stage plays with his light and quick pen, and the yeshiva *bochur* in Volozin, who searches for solutions to the riddles of the universe in the yellowing folios of the Talmud? What links the aesthete, and the melancholy dreamer? The poet and the author? The ghetto Jew and the European? The diplomat and the – Prophet?

They are linked by their dreams and their pure, holy, fervor; their love for their people, and their noble desire to free them from

---

[174] UGGIK #84, July 1935, 6-7. Original in German.
[175] Herzl died on the 20th of Tammuz (1904) and Bialik, on the 21st of Tammuz (1934).

wretchedness and restore them to life. They shared an impulse and a hope to remove from us the curse of *golus*, the ugliness of the dispersion. They both despised our deformed and distorted *golus* spirit, and our servile inclination. They loathed our dissension, and despised our cowardice; scourged our weakness, and shook us out of our sleep. In differing ways, they both strove for the same goal, the liberation of the people from humiliation and shame! Both were driven by the same ardent desire, to restore the nation to a normal physical and spiritual life.

"When Rabbi Akiba died, Rabbi Yehudah Hanasi was born. When he died, Rabbi Yehudah came into the world. After Rabbi Yehudah's death, Raba was born. When Raba died, Rabbi Ashi was born" (Kiddushin 72). The death of one was immediately followed by the birth of another. In this manner, life and death are interconnected. This chronological coincidence of death and birth is neither an accident nor a caprice of fate. For the coming and going of great spiritual leaders was, and is, Providential. Their days are counted and strictly measured out by God because one of their days often outweighs an eternity.

Similarly, Providence deemed that Bialik's day of death should follow the day of Herzl's death. For, as long as there are Jews in the world who are alert to Jewish history; whose hearts beat with love and reverence for the heroes and leaders of our people, the names of the restorer of political Zionism, Herzl, and that of our greatest poet of modern times, Bialik, will forever be uttered in the same breath. Herzl represents political maturity and disciplined action, while Bialik represents a brilliant grasp, experience, and profound understanding for Jewish spiritual wealth of all periods and regions. But the same ardent longing, Eretz Israel, moves both of them...

II

Eretz Israel: Two Words – One Concept

ארץ means both land and earth; Herzl served this ideal. ישראל means both Jew and Judaism; Bialik served that ideal.

What did Herzl want, but a piece of earth for his uprooted, scattered people? After his visit to Russia where, for the first time, he came into direct contact with the Jewish masses and their destitution, he recognized only one magic solution for Jewish needs – land, earth, space, and air for the bent backs and pallid faces of the ghetto dwellers! His voracious appetite for fresh, life-giving earth even allowed him momentarily to become unfaithful to the land of his ancestors. Was he allowed to, could he, decline the Uganda proposal? Wouldn't this be a betrayal of those desperate, filthy, and infirm Jews who just moments ago had hailed him as their leader? Suddenly, he saw himself confronted by a great dilemma with grave consequences. To refuse the Uganda offer from the English government and with it, perhaps, the last hope of rescuing his poverty stricken brothers, or to accept the offer, and thereby indefinitely delay the fulfillment of the Zionist dream! Herzl chose and he chose correctly. His concern for the physical preservation of the Jewish people, which would only be possible by acquiring a new, even if temporary, milieu on foreign soil momentarily overcame his yearning and love for his own land. The bearers of the Messianic ideal of salvation must be rescued at all costs. But they themselves expressed a preference to perish with the hope for Palestine alive in their hearts than to live on without the Zionist dream. The Jewish masses rejected Uganda. They were allowed to; he was not. Only they, witnesses and victims of the pogroms in Kishinev and Mohiler. Only they were allowed to decide about their lives and their future. According to Herzl, Uganda was to have been a night sanctuary, a provisional shelter, a refuge, a lean-to against wind and storm, an Archimedean point from which the reuniting with Palestine would follow. The people, however, wanted nothing to do with intermediate way stations and Herzl was sincerely happy about this enthusiasm for Eretz Israel. With the help of pressure from the people's demand, his yearning for land was transformed into a yearning for the land, *the* Holy Land.

A holy land required holy people. A Jewish land required Jewish people. The gradual loosening of religious bonds, which earlier held the people together, gave rise to a great danger for the continued spiritual existence of the Jewish people. No one saw this danger more sharply, more clearly, and more explicitly than Bialik. Nothing was as offensive to him as *"am-haarzuth"* – ignorance of Jewish values and Jewish spiritual sources, which was growing at an alarming rate. Even the Zionist jargon, the superficial Jewish knowledge drawn from watered down newspaper articles and translations disturbed him. For him, the Hebrew language was the only instrument of genuine Jewish culture. The key to the Jewish soul. Not merely as a means of communication, as verbal fluency and facility, but as a manifestation of the Jewish genius expressed in our 1000-year-old literature; as an emanation of Divine power, manifested by our writers and thinkers. In addition, what won him sympathy in religious circles was his love for tradition. He cloaked the old, well rooted Jewish customs and life styles passed down from generation to generation, with genuine piety. He collected ancient Jewish legends and presented them to Jewish children in a new and perfect form. He made the beauty of Shabbos accessible to adults through the "Oneg Shabbat," which he initiated. He is a teacher, educator, and sculptor of Jewish society on their old-new soil. He wants to cleanse the Jewish people of their golus dross and once again restore to them the nobility contained in the name – ישראל.

So Herzl and Bialik worked independently, but were linked by their shared ideal of making ארץ ישראל a reality.

III

Back to Herzl!

On the 20th of Tammuz, we remember Herzl and his work. His name is inextricably linked with his creation. In recent years, his personality has faded into the background. He has become a mystical figure. To some extent, that is a natural phenomenon. Myth and history oppose each other like legend and reality; youth and mature old age; dream and awakening. Herzl was myth, legend, youth, dream. Today, we are experiencing the Zionist reality – hard, raw, facts. The triumphal progression of the Zionist idea in the last decade and its transition from wishful thinking and vision into a concrete form had to force the past into a hazy distance.

Today, let us return to Herzl. We discover him for ourselves. He is resurrected! Lately, we find ourselves politically, after all these years of hard work, almost back at the beginning! Misunderstandings, intrigues, behind-the-scenes politics, and a failure to appreciate our ideal were the monsters that Herzl had to battle in his day. These are the very ghosts that threaten us today. A new Herzl era has arisen...

The Jewish spirit, which sometimes sparkles in the light conversational tones of the journalist, and at other times turns and comes to light as an idea in the mind of Herzl, the thinker, hovers over Herzl's creation. This fusion of laughter and seriousness; of effortlessness and harshness; of merriment and melancholia, is the underlying tenor of our entire Jewish life.

During the summer, we read the serious exhortations in the "Ethics of the Fathers," and in winter we refresh ourselves with the richly colored portrayal of nature in the 104th Psalm, *"Borchi Nafshi."* On the day of joy, *Simchat Torah,* we remember the death of our teacher, Moses. On *Pesach*, the holiday of national liberation, we begin the first week of sefira. The weeks of national mourning, culminating with *Tishah b'Av,* fall in the middle of the most beautiful part of the year. Sadness and joy are mixed together. Light, optimistic philosophy of life alternates with serious reflection. While the Jewish mouth contracts in joyful laughter, the Jewish brow is furrowed with serious thoughts...

Cheerfulness and seriousness also follow each other in Herzl life's work. While still entertaining his readers with light literary fare, a metamorphosis, which will have a decisive significance for the entire Jewish people, is already taking place inside him.

In a story, "The Controllable Dirigible," which he wrote in 1896, Herzl introduces us into a society that is attentively listening to the stories of a painter about the inventor of "the controllable dirigible."

Joseph Mueller, son of a simple shoemaker, discovers, through tenacious work, the principle of the controllable dirigible. For 14 long years, he pondered, studied, calculated, and researched. He was already 35 years old when he finally made his discovery. He stumbled on it fortuitously. He believed that, strictly speaking, he did not deserve credit for the discovery. Fate had guided his hand.

Was Herzl different from the discoverer of the controllable dirigible? He wished to steer the ship of his people who lived on air, into a new harbor. People derided and mocked him, just as they had taunted Joseph Mueller, the discoverer of the controllable dirigible. How often must he have been tempted, under the whip of ridicule of his compatriots, to destroy that dirigible? Let them continue to crawl if they don't want to fly!

Herzl possessed what every great person must possess – forgiveness. He gradually became used to treating his brothers like children who don't know their own needs.

And so he bequeathed the controllable dirigible to us. And it is up to us to steer it successfully.

It is becoming ever darker in the Jewish street. Previously, we had to deal with individual enemies of the Jews. Today, states and nations have conspired against us. For many, Jew-hating has become a philosophy of life, the essence of life, a creed and, yes, even a religion. It is proclaimed and preached like a holy sermon from the highest lecterns. It is fomented, disseminated, and incited by false apostles and prophets. It penetrates like poison into the souls of the deluded masses, and disturbs the harmony of human society. In such a difficult time, we turn our gaze into the past. We remember our holy ones, our heroes and martyrs, and we remember both great heralds of the Jewish renaissance, Herzl and Bialik.

Let their lives be a model for us! May their greatness strengthen us! May their enthusiasm arouse us! May their determination animate us! Today and evermore!